ALL I WANT FOR CHRISTMAS...

To Mam and Dad for always being there for me, Ben, Eva and Chase, my three gorgeous kids and Julie, my wonderful wife, for always being there for me and for being a wonderful mother to our children

ALL I WANT FOR CHRISTMAS....

IWAN ROBERTS

with Karen Buchanan

VSP

Vision Sports Publishing
2 Coombe Gardens,
London, SW20 0QU

www.visionsp.co.uk

First published in 2004
This edition published by Vision Sports Publishing in 2005

Design: David Hicks
Editorial: Ian Cranna

Typeset by Palimpsest Book Production Limited, Polmont, Stirlingshire

Printed and bound in Denmark by
Nørhaven Paperback A/S

A CIP catalogue record for this book is available from the British Library

ISBN 0-9546428-4-8

CONTENTS

ACKNOWLEDGEMENTS

Iwan Roberts

I'd like to thank a million people, but I have to start with my co-author, Karen Buchanan, for proving that having a crazed fan as a stalker need not be a scary thing and can actually be quite enjoyable. I'd like to thank her husband, Gordon, for putting up with her for the last nine months of her writing this book at the expense of doing the washing-up. I'd like to thank my publishers for giving me the opportunity to tell my story, everyone at Norwich City Football Club who has contributed to making my seven years at this club such a happy period of my life, and all those mentioned in the following pages – friends and colleagues – for allowing me to talk about them in far too much detail! My final thank you must go to the gaffer and the lads – you've been superb.

Karen Buchanan

What a year! I'd like to say a massive thank you to the Big Man for just being an all-round top bloke and legend. And a very funny, modest, articulate one at that who made writing this book a dream. A huge thanks to Julie for all her help, support and proving that behind every great man stands a great woman. Thanks to Jim for having the brilliant foresight to realise that this year would be Norwich's year and suggesting we write a book about our Championship-winning season. Thanks also to Jim, Delia, Michael and Mick for their help, encourage-ment, inspiration and friendship. Thanks to everyone who works at the football club for being genius at what they do and helping make the dream a reality. Thanks to the gaffer and all the players for being genius at what they do and giving me some blinding hangovers throughout the season. Thanks to all Norwich City fans for being the best fans in the world. And thanks to my gorgeous husband, Gordon, without whom nothing would be possible or nearly as much fun.

FOREWORD
By Delia Smith

We supporters share a passion. We pay our money, travel the roads, hang on every word in the press or TV and scour the websites to catch any crumbs of information we can about the heroes we worship. Yet in a way we are also isolated from the reality of who and what they are. We feel the pressure, the pain, the joy, but never really know precisely how it feels from their side. That is, until now.

If you're a Norwich City supporter, you will know how very special Iwan is. If you're not, you will know after you have read this book. I've never read an account of a professional footballer's life where his thoughts have been so sensitively and openly revealed, for which I would like to pay tribute to Iwan's co-author Karen Buchanan. In an age when a tiny minority of footballers get a bad press, here we have an insight into another face of football – a warm, loyal player, a devoted husband and father with a quite ironic sense of humour, a lover of football and a lover of life.

Fortune has smiled on the project since its inception in August 2003, as it has been probably the most exciting season in the club's history, culminating in promotion to the Premiership, then winning the First Division Championship in what was sadly Iwan's final game for the club. As we drove in an open-top bus to present the First Division trophy to the people of Norfolk – who lined the streets in their tens of thousands in a sea of green and yellow, climbing lamp-posts and telephone boxes and hanging out of windows – there was one word that could be heard above all others: Iwan. 'Where is Iwan?' 'Can you see Iwan?' How fitting it is, therefore, that the journey that has brought us all to that particular amazing moment is chronicled in the following pages.

Read, laugh, cry, enjoy!

Delia

INTRODUCTION

I lost my first tooth when I was 10, and it hurt. It really hurt . . .

In 18 years as a professional footballer I've been elbowed, butted and kicked in the head by some of football's toughest defenders, but that first time was down to one of the hardest nuts I've ever come across – my best mate Dylan Hughes. We were mucking about playing football in the park back home in Dyffryn Ardudwy, near Bangor in north Wales, when Dylan did me – well, ok, when I did myself. Chasing after him and seeing him streak away – anyone who's seen me play football will recognise this image – I tripped him up on purpose. Cynical, yes, but as Dylan fell and I stumbled forward, his heel caught me and whacked me right in the face, chipping off half my top front tooth. God it was painful, but I carried on playing. Well, what do you take me for? I must have swallowed that half a tooth, because I couldn't find it anywhere (well, I wasn't going to show out to my mates by actually looking for it, was I?). Anyway, it stayed like that for about four years – a kind of half tooth stump – until one day I got an abscess in it and the dentist took the whole thing out. 1–0.

For two years after that I had a plate with a false tooth and I had a beautiful white smile when I joined Watford in June 1986, my first professional football club. That's where I lost the other one. We were playing a pre-season friendly at Exeter and I went back to defend a corner. Darren Rowbotham, who I used to room with in the

Welsh under 18s, caught me with his elbow, smack, right in the gob. I went down and there was blood everywhere. The physio came rushing over and asked me what was the matter. I told him I'd done my teeth, they'd been knocked right back and across and into my lip, but he insisted I'd just cut myself and I was all right. I knew I wasn't because I couldn't get my tongue in the gap where my plate usually went, but as usual I played on.

When I woke up the next morning my pillow was drenched in blood. I legged it straight over to the dentist whose sympathy and compassion were overwhelming. 'Well, I could save them,' he said, 'but it will be months of hard work and you're going to be playing football for the next 15–20 years. So I think we should just take them out.' Just like that. I shuddered, but with the way I play I was bound to get knocked in the mouth again, so I let him take them out.

It was the most painful experience of my life. I had eight injections and, as he took out the crooked tooth and the last of the old stump, they splintered, so he had to cut my gums open to get them out. I was on the ceiling. I can still feel every agonising detail now, him digging in and pulling out all those bits of tooth. I still can't bring myself to watch the Steve Martin psychotic dentist scene in *Little Shop of Horrors*. I must have been in the chair for an hour and a half. The toughest 90 minutes of my career – and probably the one in which I sweated the most. 2–0.

Does not having my two front teeth make me look older? It must do, because ever since I hit 31 or 32, people have referred to me as a veteran. 'Veteran striker Iwan Roberts'. Every time my name was ever mentioned. God knows what that makes me now, at the ripe old age of 35. 'OAP'? 'Legend' would sound so much better . . .

But those of you not keenly acquainted with the fortunes

of Norwich City or any of my previous clubs – Watford, Huddersfield, Leicester and Wolves – probably, if you know me at all, will only know of me as 'that gap-toothed ginger lunk'. Used to play up-front for Wales. Sometimes. Well, yes, that's me. Born in Bangor, 26 June 1968, 6ft 3 inches tall, married with three kids. Footballer.

But not for much longer. This will probably be my last season as a professional. After 18 years, five clubs and nearly 600 League games (it is just 600, despite what my body says), I'll be forced, kicking and screaming, into retirement.

So as I prepare for the 2003/2004 season, I've got some weighty issues on my mind. Does my body still have what it takes to see me through a punishing 46 League games in Division One? Have I still got the sharpness of touch and mind needed to get the 12 goals I need to become only the third player in history to score 100 goals for Norwich City? Will I get enough games to achieve that dream? Why is everybody – the press, the fans, the gaffer – talking about the need for a 20-goal a season striker when, in my humble opinion, they have one right here already? Am I on the football scrapheap already?

And then what? I'd hate to have to drop down a division (or two) to keep playing. But I'd love to carry on, it's all I've ever known. Turning 35 a couple of months ago didn't suddenly turn me into a crap player. Well, I hope not. I believe I've still got what it takes. I've been at Norwich City for six years now and I'd love to finish the job – achieve what I came here for – and that's fire the club back into the Premiership.

Since the gaffer came in just over a season ago, we've finished in the play-offs and, last season, just outside them in eighth. Third time lucky? I don't know. The play-offs are certainly a possibility, but we're most bookies' outside bets. We're not media darlings like West Ham, we don't have the ex-Prem players of an Ipswich, we haven't spent the summer signing anyone that moves, unlike West Brom and Cardiff, and we don't have a high-profile manager like Mick McCarthy at Sunderland. The pundits are also tipping Sheffield United and they had a great season last year, getting to the play-off final and two cup semi-finals. So it's going to be a hard slog. Realistically? I guess most of our fans are thinking play-offs or just outside them.

We've lost two key players: right-back Darren Kenton was snapped up by Southampton and right-back Steen Nedergaard went back to Denmark. But we've signed Canadian international Jim Brennan and the club's building a new South Stand, which will boost Carrow Road's capacity to around 25,000. There's a real buzz about the place. We've been selling out our home games for the last two or three seasons and there's a definite feeling around the place that this is a club on the up. We've got a good board, including major shareholders Delia Smith and her husband, Michael Wynn-Jones, who have backed this club to the hilt. If we don't do it this year, will we be able to hang on to the manager? Or Robert Green – possibly the best goalkeeper outside the Premiership? Like everything in football outside the Premiership, it could go either way . . .

A bit like my personal future. Some people seem to have written me off already. But in the back of my mind there's the fact that I'm just 12 goals away from becoming only the third player in history to hit that magic 100-goal mark for Norwich. If I am to bow out at the end of the season, that would be some way to go. Then maybe I could swap my pension book for the keys to the city!

And it's a city I love. More than any other place, I've felt settled here. When I do finally hang up my boots I'd like to stay at the club in some kind of coaching role, but there's the possibility of playing in the States. So I'm in two minds. I'll have to talk to the gaffer and see what he thinks. More importantly, I'll have to talk to my wife, Julie, and see what she thinks.

But if this is my last season as a pro-footballer, it's probably as good a time as any to tell my story. It's not a tale of untold riches, flash sports cars, frolicking with pop stars and frenzied drug-taking. Sorry. I'm just a middle-aged man who's worried about doing his job right and making enough money to look after his beloved family.

I've got no need for posturing. Come on, a big ginger thug without his two front teeth getting all pretentious? I just want to put on record the unbelievable happiness and misery that football has brought me. Tell it like it is. The mad fans, the kickings, the dressing-room jokes, the fights, the banter, the bad hair days, the *Miami Vice* clothes, the muggings and the robbings – the ups and downs of a game I'll miss like hell when I finally hang up my boots.

It might be more gory than glory, but this is football. And, hey, who's to say you can't have both? Touch wood . . .

WHO'S WHO . . .

THE REDCOATS
The Gaffer – Nigel Worthington
Assistant Gaffer – Doug Livermore
First Team Coach – Steve Foley
Reserve Team Coach – Webby, Keith Webb
Goalkeeping Coach – James Hollman
Chief Scout – Alan Wood
Football Academy Manager – Sammy Morgan
Assistant Academy Manager – Ricky Martin
Physiotherapists – Neal 'The Fridge' Reynolds, Peter Shaw
Sports Scientist – Dave Carolan
Club Doctor – Dr Peter Harvey

THE LADS
Robert Green (goalkeeper)
Greeno's fantastic. He's only 23 but is already one of the best keepers outside the Premiership. He was runner-up in the fans' Player of the Season vote last year. Very quiet, looks like a scarecrow but dates a former supermodel.

Paul Crichton (goalkeeper)
Crichts is the practical joker of the squad. Not had a look-in as Greeno's been in such fantastic form, but a really nice lad, although he does prove the rule that you have to be mad to be a goalkeeper.

Malky Mackay (central defender)
As tight as arseholes, on the pitch and off. Vain, busy (if there's ever any press to do, Malky will be there),

6

outspoken, honest, good mate, great to go for a beer with. Former Celtic player.

Craig Fleming (central defender)

Flem's been one of our most consistent players over the last seven years, a real unsung hero. He's desperate to hear the fans sing a song for him, but you ask him what and he doesn't know. I mean, what rhymes with Fleming? Lemming? We had a great laugh doing our coaching badges together and I really like him. Craig's a bit of a gentleman, a bit of a fine wine and food connoisseur, which is probably why we don't socialise together much. (I can't stand wine: I prefer lager with a shot of lime in it to give it a nice taste. You could give me a £1000 bottle of wine and it would taste like vinegar to me.) Craig might be into his wines but he's still got terrible dress sense and he's almost as tight as Malky.

Marc Edworthy (right-back)

Eddy has fitted in brilliantly since he signed from Wolves in the summer. A really nice bloke, clever, fairly quiet, but I really enjoy his company and feel I could tell him anything. Has done a great job for us so far, looks dead classy going forward. He's an absolute gent who will give anyone the time of day.

Adam Drury (left-back and team captain)

Adam is just simply the best left-back outside the Premiership. Lovely lad, dead quiet and unassuming, dead professional, especially when the club court is in session.

Mark Rivers (right-winger)

Rivvo's dead laid-back – loves his fishing. He's not the world's best trainer or the fittest lad at the club, but he's quick as. He was brought up at Crewe, a good passing side. He could definitely play at a higher level but he's so laid-back he's almost Australian. He hasn't got a bad word to say about anyone: he gets hammered about his barnet, but what I like about him is he doesn't care – it's water off a duck's back.

Ian Henderson (right-winger)

Hendo's a lovely lad, another one of those whose confidence can be misinterpreted for cockiness. He's only 19 and hasn't really played much for us, but he's played for England's youth team and he's definitely one to watch.

Paul McVeigh (midfielder)

I have no idea why we call him Squiz. The fans call him Pocket Rocket because he's little and fast. When he's on form, we're on form. He wears his sunnies constantly – in fact I think they're superglued on. Either that or he can't bear to look at the disastrous clothes he wears. He looks like a tramp most of the time – he can't have any mirrors in his house. But he still thinks he's the best-looking thing since Brad Pitt! He is a cute one, though. He drives the lads mad: at the end of our team meetings, the gaffer will say 'Any questions?' and you can guarantee Squiz will have one. The lads are all moaning 'Shut up, Squiz – we want to get out training!'

Phil Mulryne (midfielder)

Mullers came to us from Manchester United and is, I think, the best passer of a ball at the club. Sharp dresser, into his flashy gadgets. He's quite a looker, although not as much as he thinks he is – and he's got this cheeky Belfast accent.

Clint Easton (midfielder)

Easty is well known throughout football for being the tightest tightwad of them all, believe me. He organised our Christmas party last year in London, booked a meal for us at TGI Fridays and got us each to pay a fiver deposit. A few months later I found out that TGI don't take deposits. He's a great bloke, though. He's the life and soul, even when he's getting a barracking from the fans or not getting games. He's very stylish: really into his dancing and clothes. I'm sure he'd like to think he could carry off a sarong – though even he would probably draw the line at blue nail polish.

Gary Holt (midfielder)
Tough-tackling Scot whose style is summed up by the chant the fans sing: 'He's here, he's there, he's every fucking where, Gary Holt, Gary Holt.' Holty just gets on with his job: he's dead professional, quite quiet and a real family man. Sits at the back of the bus with the other laptop boys: Jimmy B, Damo, Adam and Greeno.

Damien Francis (midfielder)
Damo's really friendly – a smashing lad – but quiet, quite shy even. He's a lovely lad who's fitted in well since we signed him from Wimbledon. He's cool and stylish, the one all the wives fancy.

Jim Brennan (midfielder)
Jimmy B's a good-looking lad, but in a more rough-and-ready kind of way than Damo. Rugged and down-to-earth like his home country, Canada. Really outgoing, likes a drink and a laugh, so I'm quite close to him.

Iwan Roberts (striker and club captain)
Social secretary and free-scoring, pacy forward renowned for his overhead bicycle kicks, model looks and honesty.

AUGUST

August 9th

Nationwide League Division One
Bradford City 2   **Norwich City 2**
Muirhead 84   *Rivers (pen) 44*
Branch 90   *Easton 47*
Valley Parade   Att: 13,159

It's the first day of the new season and I feel like a wreck. When I wake up in the morning the whole of my lower back is seized up, every slight movement feels like someone's twisting a dagger into me. When I step out of bed I get a searing pain through my hamstring as I stretch out my leg, then I wince as I ease my ankles onto the floor and my reluctant, ageing and very, very tender achilles tendons take up the strain. Julie says it's like she's got a 70-year-old man in the bedroom the way I hobble down in the mornings.

My back problems first flared up about four or five years ago. I'm pretty sure it stems from all the travelling I used to do as part of the Welsh team. Five hours' drive to Cardiff straight after a game at Carrow Road, then six hours on a plane to the Ukraine, Belarus, Georgia or God knows where. That doesn't do you any good, especially if you're big like me.

Now I get pains in my lower back and bum and terrible sciatica. Last year I was going into games with glutes and hamstrings so tight I couldn't take a full stride and it would take me ages to warm up. I'd be throwing painkillers and anti-inflammatory pills down me before a game. But they'd give me a terrible upset stomach, and the one thing you don't want to have to do on the coach on an away trip is need the toilet – the lads tend to lock you in. So I've stopped taking them.

Touch wood, I've never had knee problems. A few hernia ops, the odd cracked rib, punctured lung – but nothing like cartilage or cruciates. I've got off lightly. Thank God. The biggest thing for me is to still be able to play with my kids when I'm 40 or 45. If someone told me today, 'Listen, if you want to have a decent quality of life afterwards you must stop playing now,' then I would pack it in there and then.

But today the new season kicks off and I'm still playing . . . with the kids at least. My creaking back and increasingly tight hamstrings have taken a hammering from a punishing pre-season on rock solid ground and I've been ordered to rest. So I kick off the new campaign on the banks of my old mate Joe Sylvester's lake, sitting with my 12-year-old son Ben and seven-year-old twin daughters, Eva and Chase. Fishing.

Yesterday I waved the lads off on the coach to Bradford, absolutely gutted. I've never, ever, scored on the opening day of the season and I probably just watched my last chance to put that right disappear up the A47. So, at the exact moment I should be running out with the lads at Valley Parade I'm catching tiddlers that would look more at home in a goldfish bowl. Pretending I'm having a good time. Pretending to believe Joe when he says that this lake is only stocked with small fish, that his other lakes are full of whoppers. But really both ears are on the radio, listening to BBC Norfolk's commentary team of Roy Waller and my old Norwich team-mate Neil Adams, both of whom I consider good friends – despite Roy having made the odd disparaging comment or three about me.

And they're relaying good news. It's midway through the second half and the lads are 2–0 up and cruising. I'm not a great fisherman, all fingers and thumbs, but I am having fun. Kind of. Then, on 84 minutes, Bradford score. I figure we are in for a hairy last few minutes and sure enough, with only a minute to go, they get an undeserved equaliser. Bollocks!

It gets worse. During Neil's post-match phone-in, some bloke comes on and starts spouting off about how he saw me and Phil Mulryne out drinking on Thursday night. I nearly fall in Joe's lake! This sort of thing really winds me up. I'm the first to admit I like a pint or two, but I wouldn't even dream of having a wine gum 48 hours before a game. Yes, we were out for a couple of beers, but it was the previous Saturday, we were both injured and I knew I definitely had no chance of playing at Bradford. As Neil told him, we do have a life outside of football.

This season can only get better.

Sunday 10th

After a grumpy flick through the *News of the World* and the local sports paper, the *Pink'Un*, I go for my daily hour of sauna and jacuzzi at Greens health club.

I've always had a problem with my weight, as fans from opposing clubs have often delighted in reminding me. I don't know about eating all the pies, but give me a Mars bar and I'm anyone's. Yep, I confess, I'm a complete sweetie addict. We buy Coke and Mars bars for the kids, but if they're in the fridge I just can't resist them. I'm getting better, though. I used to wake up at 3am every morning, as if a silent alarm had gone off inside my head, and sneak down to the kitchen for a can of Coke and a Mars bar. I was like the 'secret lemonade drinker' from those old TV ads, creeping downstairs for a midnight snack. It took me 12 years to finally break the habit. I still miss it.

I finally managed to kick it when Bruce Rioch took over as manager of Norwich in 1998, a year after I'd joined. That first season had been a nightmare for me. I was overweight. I've never exactly been lightning quick, but that season I was really sluggish and slow. I only scored seven goals and I got loads of stick from the fans. I'd been signed from Wolves for £850,000 so they were expecting big things, not a big thing. When I did the pre-season weigh-in when Bruce arrived I was 15 stone 3lbs and my body fat ratio was about 16–17 per cent. My fighting weight should be just under 14 stone with around 13 per cent body fat.

Bruce was very clever: he didn't issue me with an ultimatum, he didn't rant and rave or threaten me. He just said, 'Tom Walley would be proud of you.' Tom was my youth team manager at Watford and absolutely hated people being out of shape. I knew Tom would be furious if he saw the state of me. It was a gentle hint, but I realised if I didn't take it I'd be out. I had to sort myself out. So I did a lot of weights, which really is the only way to lose weight (running does burn off the calories, but weights tone your muscles so you burn fat more efficiently even when you're doing nothing – which is nice!) and got down to 13 stone 10lbs. That season I scored 23 goals.

If I hadn't taken the hint I would have been finished a long time ago, and I'm terrified of that fat lump return-ing, so these days I eat like a sparrow. Mostly. Okay, in the summer we went on holiday to America and I ate for Wales, but I was up at 7am every morning in the hotel gym before anyone else was awake burning off all those steaks and burgers. During the season I rarely eat anything during the day, I just have a big meal at night.

It works for me. We had a nutritionist here a few years ago who said I should be eating six small meals a day, but I'd be 18 stone if I did that.

It was my 18th pre-season this year, but I was still dead nervous on the first day. I always am. You don't want to be the one at the back of the pack gasping for air, with everyone thinking, 'Ooh, he had a good holiday.' But I was fine. Body fat around 10.5–11 per cent. Last year I was out injured for two months and did too many weights, trying to stay in shape, and my body fat went down to just 8 per cent which was way too low for me. I looked so scrawny. You could see my ribs and I caught cold after cold which my immune system couldn't shake off. That's how scared I am of lardy boy returning. I'm also a bit of a tightwad, and there's a £50 fine for being overweight.

Anyway, I get back from Greens and pack the kids and Molly, our mad, nine-year-old black labrador, into Julie's car and head up to one of our favourite places, Blakeney, an hour away up on the windswept North Norfolk coast. It's beautiful up there: all flint houses and wide open marshes. Molly goes swimming, we all get an ice-cream and enjoy some quality time as a family. Then it's back home for the usual Sunday roast and a quiet night in. Mmm, might need a bit longer in the sauna tomorrow.

Monday 11th

I'm a bit apprehensive about this morning. Our physio, Neal Reynolds, is giving me a fitness test to see if my back and hamstring have recovered enough for me to start training again. Will the old back stand up to Neal's famous fitness tests, which basically involve him running the bollocks off you? He's got lots of different torture methods: 10-second, 30-second and two-minute sprints, which you keep repeating over and over for more than an hour to see how your injury stands up. If you feel the slightest twinge you stop and stretch the offending body part again. Then he gets you striking balls. He works you harder than you would ever work in training, so I'm dreading it – both the test and the result. Neal doesn't disappoint, and by the end I feel like I've lost about 5lbs. The good news? Everything feels great and I'll be able to join the lads for training tomorrow.

A good morning, then, but a very, very sad afternoon as Julie and I attend the funeral of a very lovely lady called Brenda who last week lost her battle against cancer. Her son, Justin, and his wife, Nicky, are very close friends of ours and it's a lovely family. The church in Reepham is packed and Nicky gives a reading, which she does amazingly well to get through. I know I could never have done it.

Tuesday 12th

Carling Cup, Round One
Northampton Town 1 Norwich City 0
Low 8
Sixfields   Att: 5,476

I can't wait to get in for training – but when I do I discover there's no-one for me to train with. Everyone who's fit is travelling to Northampton for tonight's Carling Cup game. We really need a good cup run and Northampton are in the Second Division so we should beat them no problem, but it doesn't seem to work like that with Norwich. We've gone out in the opening round for the last two years I've been here, although the club has won it twice . . . a while ago.

So with no-one around I find myself hooking up with Ricky Martin (the assistant manager of the Football Academy, not the world-renowned singer) for a half-hour run and an hour-long shooting session. It's great, but at the end I have something I've never, ever had in my career before – blisters – thanks to having to wear a brand new pair of studs on rock hard summer ground. Would you believe it, my usual boots have travelled all the way to Northampton on the team bus!

After training I limp home to find Julie entertaining Gemma, the girlfriend of our muscular new midfielder Damien Francis, signed from Wimbledon. Julie's really good at making new players' wives feel welcome, because it can be a bit intimidating for them not knowing anyone, so she takes them out and shows them around. Tonight Gemma would probably just be sitting in a hotel waiting for Damien to get back from Northampton in the middle of the night, but instead we end up going out for a meal and then to the cinema to watch *Pirates of the Caribbean*. We have a great time until we leave the cinema and some bloke in the street tells me the lads have lost 1–0 to Northampton. We get home and even before the others are out of the car I'm checking the results on Teletext to make sure it isn't a load of Cobblers. It's not. I can't believe it. The gaffer is not going to be pleased . . .

Wednesday 13th

Say goodbye to Julie and the kids as they are off to my Mum and Dad's in north Wales for a week. I know I'm going to have a miserable time. I really miss them already, I feel lost without them.

I get into training to find I'm on my own at work too. Has everyone forgotten about me? After some lonely fitness work I phone Julie and catch her having lunch with the former Crystal Palace and England star Geoff Thomas and his wife Julie in their garden in Birmingham. I've known Geoff a long time, but we became really good friends when we were both at Wolves. He's recently been diagnosed with leukaemia. It was a real shock; I can't begin to imagine how his wife must be feeling. Thankfully they discovered his sister's bone marrow matches his and they've arranged a transfer, hopefully for January. We're thinking of you, mate.

After my one-man training session I head for Greens as usual and then to Sainsbury's to get my sad meal for one: anything chicken and microwaveable. I'm desperately trying to delay my trip home. I really hate going back to an empty house, especially at bedtime. Like most people I seem to hear every sound. I even sleep with the landing light on and a baseball bat under my bed, which might be just a little over the top, but if anyone even thought of breaking in I would do anything to defend my family. They're everything to me.

Thursday 14th

I can't wait! It's my first day back in training with the rest of the lads after a very long and very frustrating three weeks out. Being a Thursday, however, I know we won't be doing a great deal of physical work. It'll mainly be tactical stuff, working on our formation for Saturday's home game against Rotherham and listening to the manager as he gets out his fuzzy felt tactics board and shows us who'll be marking who.

We finish off with a small-sided game, but I feel I haven't really done enough so I head off for a half-hour run, followed by my usual weights circuit which takes me about 40–45 minutes. I started doing it three or four years ago but I wish I'd started sooner. My old PE teacher used to tell me weights would make me faster and stronger, but I just thought they were boring. I wish I'd listened. I don't know that I'd have been a better player, but I could have been half a yard or maybe a yard quicker – and looked damn good on the beach!

I spend a quiet afternoon cutting the grass, which I hate doing, take Molly for a walk and turn down the offer of dinner with friends – I do a great beans on toast.

Friday 15th

Another lonely breakfast – well, a lonely coffee – I don't eat breakfast. Like I said, I don't eat much at all.

After training the gaffer has his usual meeting, talking for 20 minutes or so about the opposition before he puts up the squad. I head straight to the noticeboard and there it is in big black letters on the team-sheet . . . 'Roberts'. Yes! I'm in the squad, although the best I can hope for is a place on the bench.

We go through our usual Friday morning routine of set-pieces and a young v old game. Guess which team I play for? Yup, the old'uns dream team starring yours truly, Crichts in goal, Flem, Malky, Eddy, Holty, Rivvo, Jimmy B and sometimes Squiz and the gaffer, depending on numbers. These are fiercely contested games, always close, and we keep score all through the season.

It really feels like my season starts here, and even though there's no way I'll be starting tomorrow's game I prepare for it just like any other, which means Friday nights are just for relaxing, sitting watching television with my feet up. I have to admit I'm a big soap fan, although I draw the line at *Neighbours*. Actually, what the hell am I talking about? It's like this most nights really. And they call football the new rock and roll.

Saturday 16th

Nationwide League Division One
Norwich City 2　　　　**Rotherham United 0**
Easton 9
Rivers 30
Carrow Road　　　　　　Att: 16,263

I have a strict routine on the morning of a home game, which basically involves being the father from hell. Up at 8.30am, walk Molly for 15–20 minutes to get some fresh air and clear my head, watch *Soccer AM* and shout at the kids. If the kids are fighting I go mad. I'm really grumpy, horrible in fact, just horrible. I just want a peaceful morning, concentrating on the game. I'm dead superstitious, too, so if I've scored the week before I will have the same pre-match meal, wear the same underpants, all that rubbish (I changed my underpants quite a few times last season). With no kids to scream at today, I have my pre-match meal of chicken and soup around 11.30am, have a shower and set off for the ground at 12.45pm.

I sign a few autographs walking from the car into reception and come across Bryan Gunn, the legendary Norwich keeper who is now sponsorship sales manager at the club. Gunny takes great delight in spotting that I have left the Hugo Boss label on the sleeve of my brand new club suit. You're supposed to take that thing off, are you? Julie, I'm missing you, although believe me I'm not the only culprit.

On a matchday the manager always has a 1.30pm meeting (he does like his meetings) and then finally names the team. Huge disappointment: I'm not one of the subs. To be fair I've only trained for two days, so maybe I was expecting a bit much, but I'm gutted not to be involved. So, at 2.50pm I shake all the lads' and coaches' hands and head up to the Amec box, where I'd arranged to watch the game with my mate Alan if I didn't make the bench. I slip in at the back, just as one guy is telling his mate Norwich won't get anything from the game if I'm not playing. It does my ego the power of good and you should have seen the look on the bloke's face when the others start laughing and he turns round to see me sitting there.

I hate watching us play, I become a normal fan. I try not to criticise but you do end up saying, 'Come on, better ball here, better touch there.' You get a totally different perspective and it's easy to see why fans have a go. It's not as if I think I could do any better, it's just you become more aware of things because you can see the whole picture. On the pitch you're trying to concentrate on your own game first, then you try to help other people out. I found that difficult last year when Neil Emblen got injured and I took over the team captaincy. I was so busy trying to sort out other people's games and encourage (and players do need a lot of encouragement) instead of getting on with my own job that, for the first few games, I struggled a bit.

Anyway, the game goes well and we win comfortably, 2–0, with goals from either side. Left-winger Clint Easton scores with a sweet shot on nine minutes, which I'm really pleased about because he's a great lad who's taken a lot of stick from our supporters – unjustifiably, because he never hides in a game. Then ex-Crewe forward Mark Rivers, now our right-winger, gets the second with a header on 30 minutes, which is one for the collectors' album. We're always winding him up that the reason he hardly ever heads the ball is because of his Frank McAvennie haircut. It's a bleached blonde scarecrow affair – all wiry and straw-like – and the ball just seems to just bounce off it.

It's a good result for the team but it doesn't feel the same if you haven't been involved. I'd really have liked to have played today. Rotherham have a lad called Martin McIntosh who I really don't get on with, he's always moaning. He got sent off today for a bad tackle on Paul McVeigh, but I played against him last year and he moans for fun. Even before you've jumped he's going 'Ref! Ref!' He really likes to give you the old verbals, even though you've done nothing.

That said, I must admit I'm a much nastier bloke on the pitch than I am off it. I'm your archetypal ginge. I've got a wicked temper. It takes me a lot to lose it, but I've got a right nasty streak in me when I do. I never lose it at home, but on the pitch, if someone catches me with their studs, comes straight through me from behind or deliberately uses their elbow, then I will lose it. I'm a bit like a caged lion. But, funnily enough, when I do lose it I'm a better player. Tom Walley didn't think I had that mean streak in me when I was younger. He thought I was a good player, but lacking the killer instinct. Some players become horrible as soon as they cross the white line, but something has to happen to me before the red mist descends. As soon as it does I feel as though I could run all day at 100mph. All those aches and niggles miraculously disappear as the adrenaline rockets through my veins. I'm totally focussed.

The thing is, you have to look after yourself. I wouldn't deliberately try to hurt anyone, but if there's a situation where it's either me or him, it's got to be him. You get your elbow higher than his so you're in control. If you're going into a tackle and you can see that he's going to try and hurt you (coming in with studs up or whatever) you can always be a little bit later and make sure you go a little bit higher than he does. Last year, for example, against Wolves at Molineux, I was up against Paul Ince. I know how he plays. I know he likes to get stuck in. He caught me in the first half and then there was a 50:50

ball a bit later between the two of us. I could see he was going in high, so I just delayed my tackle a little bit. He slid in and I just went straight over the top of his boot and caught him on his shins. It must have been agony, and I was surprised he didn't go off. For the next 15–20 minutes he was limping around, hurting.

It was a case of kill or be killed. I bear him no ill will, but if someone catches me five minutes into the game or one of their defenders comes right through me that pisses me right off. And that's when I think, 'Right, he's going to get it.' You mark him down. He doesn't have to get it straightaway. There are 90 minutes in the game. You play them twice a season. You'll get your chance. No doubt. Like with the infamous Kevin Muscat . . .

Off the pitch Muscat is a really nice lad. The year I signed for Norwich we went to Australia on holiday. Australia were managed by Terry Venables then and I knew two of the lads in the team, the big goalkeeper, Spider (Zeljko Kalac) and Stevie Corica, who our twins were going to be bridesmaids for. We went to one of their World Cup qualifiers and back to the hotel to wait for Spider. Terry came up and asked how I was, but Mark Bosnich and most of the other players just ignored us. Kevin was the only one who came up and had a chat, which I really appreciated and I enjoy his company if I see him in the players' bar.

Since then I've had a few tussles with Kevin. About a year later we were playing our old friends Wolves at Molineux and I landed feet first on his back right in front of the 'Snakepit', the corner of Molineux between the Barclay and City stands where lots of our more vociferous fans sit. They loved it. The ball came over the top, he was stretching for it, I gave him a little nudge and we both went down. The ref gave him a free-kick. As I got up, I 'lost my balance' and trod on his back. Fourteen stone through eight studs, you do the maths. He was in agony, but the ref didn't see it so I got away with it. Of course, I pulled him up and said, 'Sorry mate, sorry mate', but he knew. He knows what he did to Bellamy and, to be fair to him, after the game it was all forgotten. I've seen him since when we've played and had a chat with him after the game in the players bar and he always says: 'What about when you did me?'

'I never did you, you fell on the floor and I had to jump over you!'

And we have a laugh and a drink. There are no grudges.

Kevin's at Millwall now so we'll probably have another tussle when we play them in November. I won't try to do him, that's to say really hurt him, but I will let him know that I'm there – and I'm sure he'll try and do the same to me. The Norwich fans love it. They love anybody having a pop at him. And if that gets the crowd going then it's something you just have to try and do. I guess I'll do anything to be popular!

Sunday 17th

Even though the kids are away, I still wake up at 8am. So I head for a weight circuit and sauna at the gym and then meet our little striker, Alex Notman, for a lovely Sunday lunch at the Rushcutters, a gorgeous pub by the river with great food. They have a whole menu of healthy salads and pasta dishes yet, for some bizarre reason which I can't quite explain, I end up with scampi and chips. Weird, huh? Alex has been out injured for more than a year. He's a lovely lad and my new room-mate for away trips. I get on really well with him, even though in age I'm closer to his mum and dad.

After lunch we have to make our hardest decision of the day – go home and watch Liverpool v Chelsea or find a

pub showing it. With the family away it takes a millisec-
ond to make up my mind and, after a little persuasion,
Alex agrees to accompany me to Squares and watch it on
the big screen. Norwich is great because we never get any
hassle. I'd say it's a lot easier because it's a one-team city.
There are no off-limits pubs and people here are generally pretty friendly and respect your privacy: they want
to know how you are and ask you about the game, but
they don't pester you.

Wolves was the worst club I've been at for that: their
fans just didn't expect to see you out. Ever. That said, I
never go out if we've lost. I don't think it's wrong to, just
sensible not to. It's almost as if fans are in mourning. They
don't want to see you and you know you're not going to
get a good reception, so why make it hard for yourself?

Later we head up to Delaney's. You can't beat an Irish
pub for good atmosphere and we've had some fantastic
nights in there. I get on really well with Adie, the mad
manager and Andy, the owner, and the place is buzzing. I
stick to my Buds (I don't like Guinness) and very sensibly
accept a lift home from Alex's girlfriend Hilary. Thank
goodness Julie and the kids don't go away every Sunday.

Monday 18th

Aargh! I have the hangover from hell. I have to accept
I'm 35 and I just can't do it any more. Never again,
never again, never again. When I was younger I could
do it no problem – drink 15–20 pints, get up the next
day feeling great and train as if I'd not been out. Not
any more. Training with a hangover is horrible and I'm
really struggling this morning.

We split into two groups, the lads who played on
Saturday and those playing for the reserves against QPR
on Wednesday night. I'm in with the ressies so I suffer

in the company of reserve team manager, Keith Webb, for about two hours, working on passing and the shape of the team. Boring, but vital to ensure you all know what you're doing.

I delay going home by doing my weights routine, the usual sauna and jacuzzi and then finally drag myself back home to an empty house for the last time. An early night is definitely on the cards.

Tuesday 19th

I wake up and leap out of bed all excited at 7.30am; Julie and the kids are coming home today. I arrive at training at my usual time of 8.45am with a new spring in my step. I like to get in early to have a coffee and a bit of banter with the lads: I think that's what I'll miss most when I hang up my boots. And my step is even more sprung this morning because I'm playing in my first game of the season tomorrow night and I can't wait to pull the yellow shirt on again.

We don't do much in training as the gaffer wants us 'fresh as daisies' as he puts it. I have the quickest shower ever and rush home, only to find Julie's visiting friends from our Wolves days and won't be home for hours yet. Hmph! Eventually they get in at around 8.30pm, it's kisses and cuddles all round and I can go to bed a happy man with my pride and joy back home.

Wednesday 20th

Tonight can't come quickly enough. I feel I have a responsibility not just to myself to play well but, being the elder statesman of the team, I like to set a good example to the younger lads and give them as much help and advice as I can.

I always go to bed for a couple of hours on the after-noon of an evening match and this is no different: I treat reserve games like any first team game and prepare properly.

Part of this preparation is not answering the phone on a matchday – I hate the interruption and Julie knows who I will and won't speak to. But she isn't in when it rings today so I pick up and I'm glad I do. It's my strike partner David Nielsen telling me he's going back to Denmark. Tenna, his wife, has been offered a good job back home and he's been offered a contract with Aalborg. The club have been great with him, very under-standing, and given him a free transfer so he and his family can settle back in Denmark. I am really shocked – he is a good friend and had been playing so well for us. I'll miss him.

We win the game against QPR reserves 3–0 but I only play the first half, which is disappointing as my back and hamstring feel good and I need the fitness, but I've never been one to argue with the manager. Instead I watch the second half in the viewing lounge with Daryl Sutch, a former Norwich player and good mate. It's great to catch up with him again. It's also great to see little Alex Notman playing his first game tonight after a year out injured. He manages the full game, does really well and scores our first goal. Well done, buddy.

Thursday 21st

Arrgh! Wake up feeling like I've been beaten with a base-ball bat overnight. My body is aching so much it feels like I played my 50th game of the season last night, not my first – and only a half at that. Fortunately, if you've played the night before you only have to do a warm-down in training – a little light jogging and stretching – and the agony doesn't stop me being first to the noticeboard to discover my name on the list of those travelling to Sheffield United tomorrow.

Friday 22nd

My first away trip of the season, and another three or four hour bus journey, great for my back. That's the worst thing about playing for Norwich – the travelling. The players (and the fans) must spend half our lives going up and down motorways on buses. Our away form's been pretty poor over the last year or so and I think that's partly because of our location. Don't get me wrong, I love Norwich, but everywhere is a big trip from here, so we always have to leave on a Friday, stay in a hotel, different bed, different surroundings, don't sleep as well. The gaffer doesn't subscribe to this theory. He says: 'It's a fucking green pitch, it's got white lines, two goals . . .'

We leave for Sheffield at 9.30am, and there are no late-comers now Darren Kenton's gone to Southampton, so no fines. I'm not good with laptops like a lot of the lads, so I'm in the card school with Mark Rivers, Paul McVeigh and Alex Notman. I must stress there's no gambling – Julie would kill me. We play Hearts, a game I've been playing since my first club, Watford, which is probably why I always win.

We get to Sheffield around 1pm and have a light lunch, followed by a light training session, then it's back to the hotel, the Moat House on the Chesterfield Road, where we're confined to our rooms. The manager doesn't really like you wandering about or going for a jacuzzi or a swim. He wants you to conserve your energy, so you're right for 3pm the next day. You're supposed to lie on your bed, get a couple of hours' kip in before tea, then just watch some telly. God, is it boring! Especially if you've got a poky room or a poky room-mate (sorry Alex).

The manager is a fair man, but he wouldn't be pleased if he saw us out of our rooms. You'll never see a foot-baller out in the city on a Friday afternoon. It's not the done thing. Even just a short shopping trip really takes it out of your legs – although I'm more likely to have a tired pocket after a day's shopping with Julie and the kids. I don't think any of the lads would dare be seen out and about just before a big game. The gaffer's not one to cross, so the lads will make the effort not to piss him off or rub him up the wrong way by going behind his back. So, it's a quiet night in for me and Alex, a long soak in the bath to relax my muscles and bed at 10pm. Oh the glamour of it all.

Saturday 23rd

Nationwide League Division One
Sheffield United 1   Norwich City 0
Page 23
Bramall Lane   Att: 24,285

My old Wales team-mate Robert Page picks today to score his first goal for Sheffield United. Bastard. We're having loads of possession, but young Michael Tonge is playing a blinder for them and they're just about worth their lead. I make it on as a sub after 62 minutes. I would be delighted, but unfortunately I'm replacing Zema Abbey, our electric young striker who hasn't had the best of luck with injuries and now it looks like he's picked up a nasty knee problem. I don't really get a chance and we lose 1–0.

The gaffer doesn't like to criticise the players in public, but he gives us a right bollocking in the dressing room afterwards. I've had some ranters and ravers in my career and he's right up there with the best of them.

'You were second best all over the pitch,' he screams. 'You didn't pass the ball, you didn't get crosses in. You didn't compete.'

He's right. We could have got something out of the game because they weren't great. We won't get many better chances to beat one of the top teams in the division than today. It's about time we started taking them.

Sunday 24th

I am oddly uninterested in reading the papers this morning, so Julie asks me to go to Sainsbury's. But as soon as I get there I'm on the mobile.

'What was that again, love?'

'Bread, milk and bacon,' she says. Again.

I haven't got the best memory. I'm hopeless with names – faces even – and I think that comes from heading a football so often, especially in my early days when balls were that bit heavier. If you catch the ball on your fore-head, 99 times out of 100 it doesn't hurt. But if you catch it slightly wrong, on the top or side of your head, my God it can be agony. I've caught so many wrong – so wrong you can actually see stars – that it must have taken its toll.

I'm thinking of taking the FA to court, in fact. That's why I'm so thick, not because I didn't pay attention at school. It's their fault!

Monday 25th

Discipline is a big thing at any football club. At Norwich you get fined by the club for big stuff like getting sent off or refusing to eat one of Delia's pies, but there is also a whole series of fines for minor indiscretions like being late or leaving kit out on the training pitch. These go into a fund for the players' Christmas party, plus usually around £1000 goes for toys for kids in hospital at Christmas.

Thing is, being the tight sods that footballers invariably are, we have the chance to appeal against these fines and take them to court. Only trouble is, if you lose your appeal the fine doubles. We normally deal with court cases every Friday, but as we were travelling to Sheffield last Friday court is in session this morning instead. As always it's a very solemn affair, with team captain Adam Drury (the best left-back outside the Premiership and better than many in it) sitting, aptly enough, as judge and jury.

The gaffer sets out the rules at the start of the season. Leave an item of clothing out on the training ground and it'll cost you a tenner. If you're caught on your mobile anywhere at our training ground at Colney that's £50. Boots on in the building? That's another tenner, as is leaving cutlery, plates, or glasses on the dinner table. Then there's being late for training or getting on the coach back from an away game: that's a big fat £50. The gaffer hates lateness.

It's quite a laugh really. When court is in session you put the case for your defence, Adam listens to all the evidence (or at least what he can hear above the other lads shouting, 'Fine him, make him pay!'), makes his decision and says, dead quiet, 'Yeah, it's a fine.' Nobody's tried to bribe him yet, but we do all work very hard at stitching each other up.

Anyway, this morning our Scottish centre-back, Malky Mackay, has been grassed up for using his mobile by midfielders Phil Mulryne and Paul McVeigh. But he is refusing to pay the £50 fine – typical sweaty sock. Adam decides, to everybody's great delight, that Malky will have to pay. That's £20 mate. First team coach Steve Foley will have to collect it but it'll be like getting blood out of a stone.

The manager then names the team for tomorrow night's game against Wimbledon and the big news is I'm starting. Whether I'll finish or not is another matter. I feel so bad for Zema. He's worked so hard to get back from injury and now he's done his cruciate and faces another whole season out. I want to be in the side but not in these circumstances.

After training I take my son Ben to Dunston Hall's driving range to hit a few golf balls. Well, to watch him hit a few. I don't want to risk damaging my back swinging a golf club – wouldn't go down too well, I don't think.

I did, however, join him for a putting competition. Of course Dad won! I don't let him beat me! Dearie me! I don't let any of my kids win anything. Ask any sports person and they're the same – we don't want to lose anything – cards, raindrop racing. It's just something you grow up with. If you accept defeat you're not going to play to the maximum of your capability. If you think positive and think as a winner you'll succeed.

Tuesday 26th

Nationwide League Division One

Norwich City 3 **Wimbledon 2**
Francis 10 *Holdsworth 84*
Rivers 27 (pen), 56 *Leigertwood 90*
Carrow Road Att: 16,082

It's my first first-team start of the season tonight and I realise that I still get the same buzz as I did when I first started playing all those years ago.

We do very little in training in the morning and I'm home by 11.15am. I have my usual pre-match lasagne and go to bed for a couple of hours. Julie is a diamond and takes the kids out for the afternoon so they won't disturb me.

I'm at the ground just before 6pm. I still get very nervous, which is probably why I have too many superstitions to mention. Oh, all right then. If I've scored the previous Saturday I'll have the same pre-match meal and wear the same underpants. Fortunately I do allow myself (well, Julie actually) the luxury of washing them. I never play in my wedding ring, I put in on a chain and hang it on my peg before I put my boots on. I always put my right boot on before my left. When I come out onto the pitch I always untie my laces and then tie them up again. Our mascot, Splat the Cat, annoys me, because his superstition is coming up to me as I'm bent over and ruffling my hair.

'Sod off! It's taken me half an hour to get it looking that good!'

I used to be even worse: I'd have to come out third, behind the keeper, but that went out of the window last season when I was made team captain (I am now club captain). I also always have my ankles strapped before a game because I've gone over on them so many times, but last year I decided to have them strapped in the dressing room rather than walk to the physio room because then I knew I was going to play well. Obviously.

I suppose I do have one other rather silly habit – I play in boots that are too small for me. Quite a lot too small. All my shoes and trainers are size ten-and-a-half or 11, but when I play football I squeeze my feet into size nine boots. It's not really a superstition; I just can't stand loose boots. I like to feel my foot filling the entire boot. No gaps. There's just one problem: when I take them off after the game it feels as if my feet are going to burst. It's agony. I squeeze them to try to ease the pain. It's even worse if I have a hot bath or it's really cold. I must have lousy circulation. But I won't change my boots. Not now. No, my toes aren't manky or black, thank you very much, but they are a typical footballer's toes: all bent and over-lapping. Very attractive.

Other than that I'm just a normal player: I insist on Terry the kit man giving me a brand new pair of socks every game (they discolour and lose their all-important tightness). Oh yeah – and I take my teeth out. I suppose I haven't noticed any of the other lads doing that.

Everyone's got their own little routines on a matchday. Malky's is checking his hair, Clint Easton's is going on about how good-looking he is, Craig Fleming's is making sure everyone knows he was tucked up by 9pm the night before. The dressing room is buzzing with anticipation and nerves an hour before kick-off. Some of the lads play keepie-up, try different tricks, get a rub off one of the physios. I just sit there, trying to conserve my energy and focus on the game. And then, finally, we're called into the tunnel, the ref gives us the nod and off we go, to be greeted by . . . er, nothing.

This season it's a bit strange running out of the tunnel at Carrow Road because there is literally nothing in front of you. The whole of the ageing South Stand has been knocked down, and a new stand will replace it by January/February time. It has made for a bit of a weird atmosphere but the club had to do it because it was getting more expensive to maintain every year and it will give us much-needed extra capacity.

Luckily today the other three sides of the ground are full to bursting point – swelled by the 16 Wimbledon supporters – and to my amazement I play the whole game, quite some feat considering I'm blowing out of my arse after 15 minutes. We go 3–0 up, thanks to a strike against his former team by Damien Francis, and two from Mark Rivers, before giving away two stupid late goals which ensure the dressing room is very quiet afterwards. Still, we're up to seventh in the table now, with seven points from five games and two home wins. It's not a great start, but if we can just sort our away form out . . .

After mulling this over, and running the two chances I had over and over again in my head – particularly the header I put just wide – I finally go to bed at 2.30am. I find it really hard to get to sleep after a game as the adrenaline's still pumping, and the last time I look at the clock it's 3.15am.

Wednesday 27th

And I still wake up at 8am! Surprisingly the body feels good, not too stiff considering it was my first full game for a few months. I take Julie and the kids clothes shopping and come back with loads of stuff for them, but nowt for me, which Julie remarks drily makes 'a refreshing change'. In the evening I watch Man U v Wolves with Ben, who is a massive United fan. I haven't a clue where that came from, as my team is Liverpool, but tonight we're United – we're both hoping Man U will hammer them.

I hate Wolves with a passion. I had one season there in 1996–97, played 28 games for them and scored 12 goals, including four against West Brom, three of which were at the Hawthorns. I am the only Wolves player ever to score a hat-trick there and I scored in a 2–1 victory over them at home, the first time we'd done the Double over them for something like six years, and yet their fans still slaughter me whenever we play them. It's not as if I wanted to leave – Mark McGhee sold me. I was gutted when they got promoted to the Premiership. The only person I was pleased for was Sir Jack Hayward because he's a really, really nice man and he's put millions into the club. But when they were going through bad times a couple of years ago, fans were spitting at him and abusing him. I couldn't believe it. After all he's done for the club and they treat him like that. He deserves better. If I was him I'd have walked away.

Wolves fans seem to think they have a God-given right to be in the Premier League just because they've got a nice stadium. It doesn't work like that. The majority of First Division clubs have lovely all-seater stadiums. The fans do get behind you at Molineux, but they are arrogant. And Norwich fans have told me they were spat at and pushed after the play-off semi-final a couple of years ago.

So we have a little bit of a giggle in our house when we see Wolves at the bottom of the Premier League with one point after so many games. I hope they are relegated, and by the end of the Man U game Ben and I are both very happy – it finishes 1–0 to United.

Thursday 28th

I'm aching all over from Tuesday night. For some reason it's always worse two days later. I go into training early to get a massage off Neal the physio, but it does me no good whatsoever. The gaffer tells me to go and have a nice hot bath and rest my legs as he wants me to be fit to play against Forest on Saturday.

Friday 29th

I'm sitting down at the training ground enjoying a deluxe breakfast of coffee when the gaffer ruins it by calling me into his office. He tells me that Delia and Michael have received a letter from a 'disgusted' Richard from Harrogate, saying he'd seen me and Phil out the Thursday night before the Bradford game. Not this again! For me it isn't a problem as I was never going to be involved in the game anyway, but for Phil it's more serious: at least a two weeks' wages fine; maybe even a sacking offence. The gaffer says: 'I don't mind, just be honest.'

I tell the gaffer it is total bullshit and explain about the sad man on the radio after the Bradford game who said he'd seen us out on the Thursday night before the Bradford game when we were actually out the Saturday before. I'm pissed off that this bloke has written to Delia to waste her time. I'll have the last laugh though: my best friend in Norwich is David Pett of the solicitors Morgan, Jones and Pett – so Richard from Harrogate will be receiving a letter by return of post. I can't stand it when anyone questions my professionalism and commitment to Norwich City.

But I would hate for Delia to think that we'd been out like that. She's brilliant, really down-to-earth and so passionate about the club. I remember soon after she first became a director years ago she came into the dressing room to wish us good luck before a game. She was so excited and in awe of us. It was really funny. We were all sitting there going, 'My God, it's Delia Smith! She's on the telly and everything!' And she's jumping around going 'My God! I can't believe I'm here with you guys!' She and her husband saved the club from going out of business back then and have pumped in millions more of their own money since. They go to every game; they're Norwich through and through and they really deserve to see the club get promoted. In case you're wondering – no, I haven't had her over for dinner yet.

Anyway, the gaffer believes me and the matter is closed, although I am even more fired up than usual for the traditional Friday old'uns v young'uns game which finishes 1–1 today.

I then take my usual seat on the bus for the short trip to Nottingham – just three hours today. We play our usual game of Hearts, but without the usual result: I don't win. I hope that's not an omen!

Saturday 30th

Nottingham Forest 2   Norwich City 0
Johnson 30
Harewood (pen) 50
City Ground   Att: 21,058

I like playing at the City Ground: it's a great stadium and you always know you're going to get a decent game of football. I start the game and it's going well until, out of the blue, Robert Green makes the sort of howler which you know will be shown again and again. And again. Having comfortably taken a cross and waited for his defenders to push out, he prepares to hoof it upfield, unaware that former Ipswich striker (had to be, didn't it?) David Johnson is hiding in the stand behind him. As soon as Greeno rolls the ball forward, out jumps Johnson from row B, nicks the ball off him and rolls it under a shell-shocked Rob into an empty net. 1–0 to Forest.

The first thing poor Greeno does at half-time is hold his hands up and apologise. But he doesn't need to, he's saved us time and time again over the last couple of seasons. He's a fantastic keeper and if he doesn't play for England before he's 28 I will stand naked in

Jarrold's shop window. Er, or maybe I'll think of something else . . .

In the second half I have a little tussle with Forest defender Michael Dawson, who is going to be a tremendous player and will also play for England one day. He turned round and walked straight into me, then started screaming and shouting at me. He thought I caught him on purpose, but I didn't. I said: 'Hold on, you turned round and walked straight into me. I'm not going to do that on purpose, am I?'

So he thought about it and we shook hands. I'm not a dirty player. I'll put myself about a bit, look after myself, but I don't deliberately go out to smash someone in the face or anything (unless they've done it to me first!).

I have to come off after 68 minutes with a sore calf and we eventually lose 2–0 thanks to a very, very harsh penalty decision, but the gaffer is full of praise for our performance. Last year Forest battered us at their place because we couldn't combat their diamond midfield formation. But this year we matched their formation, created loads of chances and had two cleared off the line. We only had time for a very short session on team shape on Thursday but even though we lost he thought we had taken it into the match really well.

Even so the journey home seems to take twice as long; they always do when we've lost. It's even worse when you know you've played well but not got a result. I'm home by 11pm, watch the Premiership highlights and go to bed.

We've dropped to 12th in the table, with seven points from five games. Not good.

Sunday 31st

I'm up at 8.30am, as it's the first friendly of the season for Ben's team, Thorpe Rovers. I enjoy a bit of banter about yesterday with the other parents. Fans don't mind you losing if they can see you've tried hard. Ben has to come off with about 15 minutes to go in the 5–4 defeat as he is running out of steam. Unlike his old man he obviously hasn't been keeping himself fit during the close season!

Nationwide League Division One

Pos	Name	P	HOME					AWAY					GD	PTS
			W	D	L	F	A	W	D	L	F	A		
1	West Bromwich Albion	5	2	0	0	5	1	2	0	1	3	4	+3	12
2	Reading	5	1	1	0	3	0	2	1	0	7	3	+7	11
3	Sheffield United	5	2	1	0	3	1	1	1	0	2	1	+3	11
4	Wigan Athletic	5	1	1	0	2	1	2	0	1	5	2	+4	10
5	Crystal Palace	5	1	0	1	2	2	2	1	0	7	4	+3	10
6	West Ham United	5	1	1	0	1	0	2	0	1	4	3	+2	10
7	Sunderland	5	1	0	1	2	1	2	0	1	6	2	+5	9
8	Millwall	5	1	2	0	4	2	1	1	0	1	0	+3	9
9	Nottingham Forest	5	2	0	1	5	2	1	0	1	3	4	+2	9
10	Stoke City	5	1	1	0	2	1	1	1	1	4	2	+3	8
11	Cardiff City	5	1	0	1	4	3	1	2	0	3	2	+2	8
12	**Norwich City**	**5**	**2**	**0**	**0**	**5**	**2**	**0**	**1**	**2**	**2**	**5**	**0**	**7**
13	Crewe Alexandra	5	2	0	0	2	0	0	1	2	2	5	-1	7
14	Walsall	5	1	2	0	6	3	0	1	1	0	1	+2	6
15	Burnley	5	1	0	2	3	5	1	0	1	4	4	-2	6
16	Gillingham	5	0	1	1	0	3	1	2	0	3	2	-2	6
17	Rotherham United	5	1	1	1	1	3	0	1	1	0	2	-4	5
18	Preston North End	5	1	0	2	2	4	0	1	1	1	2	-3	4
19	Bradford City	5	0	1	2	2	7	1	0	1	2	1	-4	4
20	Wimbledon	5	1	0	2	4	7	0	0	2	3	5	-5	3
21	Coventry City	4	0	1	1	1	3	0	1	1	2	3	-3	2
22	Ipswich Town	5	0	2	1	3	4	0	0	2	0	2	-3	2
23	Watford	4	0	1	1	2	3	0	0	2	0	3	-4	1
24	Derby County	5	0	0	3	2	7	0	1	1	1	4	-8	1

SEPTEMBER

Monday 1st

The papers are all saying I'll be out for three weeks with a strain but they're talking rubbish, I'll be able to train tomorrow.

Go to Greens and bump into Bruce Rioch in the sauna. I quite often see him in there and I get on really well with him, so we always enjoy a good chat. Trouble is, I often see him when I'm about to get out, but I enjoy listening to him talk about football so much I end up staying in there way longer than you're supposed to! I still call him 'gaffer' and other people in the sauna look at me as though I'm daft. 'He's not your gaffer now!'

I've learnt more off him than any of the managers I've played for. Without a doubt. His knowledge of the game is phenomenal. Before I played for him, I always used to like to receive the ball to feet, just get it and give it, then get in the box. He improved my all-round game by teaching me little things like getting right on defenders' shoulders, making the right runs to get on the end of things. I'm surprised he's not got a job since he left here. I think he could have gone to two or three clubs, but they weren't right for him. He still comes to every home game and shakes all the boys' hands, even comes down the training ground to watch us.

He'd admit in his younger days as a manager he was a bit of a hothead. One thing he did at Norwich was throw a bottle of water at a wall, just above Andy Marshall's head. It cleared his head by an inch and smashed behind him. He wasn't aiming for him, but if it had hit him in the face it would have killed him! I remember another time at Crewe when we were 2–0 up with ten minutes to go and lost 3–2 and he went absolutely berserk in the dressing room after. He booted this huge heavy table which had iron legs. I swear to God, he must have broken every toe! He didn't wince or react in any way. Nobody dared laugh. We all went dead quiet, he finished his speech and limped off.

I've still got loads of time for the guy and it's lovely to see him again. But I didn't get on well with Bryan Hamilton, who joined as director of football or something when Bruce took over as manager. I remember in the first few weeks after they took over, when I was a bit overweight, I had to come off because my ankle was playing up during a pre-season friendly in Ireland. The next day in training I'm sitting there with an ice-pack on my ankle, watching the boys, and Bryan comes over to me and says: 'You've got to sort yourself out, big man. You're drinking in the last chance saloon now!' I thought: 'You bastard.' That's always stuck with me.

He was a nice enough man, but I never saw eye-to-eye with him. At the end of the day, Bryan's a big Ipswich man. After he got the sack here he went to Ipswich and the first thing he said was: 'I'm back where I belong.' Frankly, I couldn't agree more.

I still get on really well with Mike Walker, the man who brought me here. I'll always be grateful to him for that. And I'll always feel guilty because I let him down big-style – I had the worst season I've ever had that first season here. He'd paid a lot of money for me, put a lot of faith in me, said I was the final piece of the jigsaw and I just didn't perform. But he never ever said anything bad about me in the papers; he stuck by me through thick and thin. He was a right ranter and raver though – up there with the best of them. He's a right genuine man and I still speak to him quite a lot. I get on well with his youngest son David and Julie gets on really well with his daughter Ursula. Every time I play against Ian we have a chat.

I felt sorry for him when he left at the end of my first season. It was his second time in charge at Norwich and I think it's always harder when you go back somewhere. I'm a big believer that you should never go back. He had a much harder job the second time. The first time the place was on fire: the club was in Europe, playing great football, scoring plenty of goals and it was always going to be a hard act to follow. I remember watching Norwich on telly and marvelling at some of the goals they were scoring. Hopefully we can get back to that.

The gaffer likes to mix it up a little bit. He wants to play and pass the ball. People think just because he's worked with Howard Wilkinson he likes the long ball, but he likes us to pass it, that's the way it's got to be done. Especially here – it's what Norwich fans have been brought up on.

Tuesday 2nd

A very strange day at training today. Because of the reserve game tomorrow night, international call-ups and injuries, only seven able-bodied players turn up. Steve Foley, who used to be reserve team manager at Watford, takes the session and thankfully it's all ball work; he doesn't just run the testicles off us. He's a quality coach and his sessions are always very enjoyable. The calf is a bit sore, but I didn't do any real damage on Saturday.

Wednesday 3rd

Wake at 7am on hearing a commotion downstairs. Grab the baseball bat and quietly creep down, open the door to the kitchen and am confronted by . . . not a nasty-looking burglar but a demented-looking wife doing cartwheels. Have we won the lottery? No, the kids go back to school today. So mornings will be manic from now on. I make Ben his bacon sarnie and get the girls their cereal and drinks. Finally, after shouting at the girls for the twentieth time to get their school uniforms on, I leave for work at 8.30am. Phew!

Not that it's exactly chilled out at Colney today. Everyone is talking about the story in last night's *Evening News*, headlined 'HOW COULD CITY WIN? THEY EVEN FORGOT THEIR BOOTS!' I kid you not, the skip containing the whole of the first team's boots had been left off the team bus last Friday. Luckily, we trained on the Saturday morning and Terry the kitman realised it was missing. Equally luckily, we were kicking off late because the game was live on Sky. Even more luckily, the supporters' coaches hadn't left by the time Terry discovered this and frantically started calling people on his mobile. In the end the fans delivered our boots about 45 minutes before kick-off. Had it been a 3pm kick-off we would have been stuffed. Terry's a good bloke, works his socks off and always has a million and one jobs to do (hence his nickname Terry One Job). But instead of taking the newspaper article on the chin, Terry insists it wasn't his fault and is blaming the apprentices who load up the bus for him. Oh dear, there's going to be one hell of a court case when the whole squad is back.

Thursday 4th

No game this weekend due to international call-ups, so after training today we're off until Monday and the lads are buzzing – all eight of us. The downside is we train for nearly three hours, finishing off with probably the hardest session you can do – four v four on a full-size pitch. You just don't stop running and I'm totally knackered afterwards. I hope the gaffer doesn't notice quite how heavily I'm breathing, because after training he says by the time we come back in on Monday he hopes to have two, maybe three new players in. I haven't a clue who. Mmmm . . .

Spend a fun afternoon on the golf course with ex-Norwich midfield nutter Mike Milligan – a great lad who's still living in the city. Then Julie calls; we've signed the rather inappropriately named 6ft 7in striker Peter Crouch from Aston Villa on loan for three months. Great news . . . seriously. All day people keep asking me if I'm pissed off that he's coming in to take my place but, hand on heart, it's not the case at all. The Forest game was a hard one for me. I'd hurt my calf and my back was playing up. To play two games in a week is tough enough but at my age it's nigh-on impossible. I'll welcome him with open arms, but I'll still fight tooth (well, gum!) and nail for my place.

In truth, I'm pleased it's Peter Crouch because at least he's a proven goalscorer. We've played against him a few times and know what a handful he is. I would have been a bit miffed if it had been someone not as good as him. It pisses me off that the media, the fans, everyone, has been saying 'we need a 20-goal a season striker.' Well, in the four years up to last season, when I was injured for a long time, I've averaged 20 goals a season. Just because you hit 35, you don't suddenly become a bad player.

If I was 32 or 33, I don't think the gaffer would have been looking to bring in a striker at all. I think we're light in other areas. In central defence, for example, we've just got Malky and Flem and young Jason Shackell from our academy, who will be a superb player but at 20 isn't all the way there yet. So if either Malky or Flem get injured we're stuffed.

I'm not just saying this because I'm a striker, but I don't

think we've been missing sitters. We've just not been getting the chances. We had David Healy on loan last year. He scored goals at Man U, he scored for fun at Preston, and he comes here and all of a sudden he gets two goals in 13 games. Maybe other people aren't doing their job as well as they could. If you ask me we don't create enough chances: especially away from home.

Of course I'm worried about not playing as many games, but I really want the club to do well and there's no doubt Peter Crouch will improve the squad. The gaffer has assured me I still have a big part to play, but I'll have to work harder than ever if I'm going to get the 12 goals I need to hit my 100 goals target. I would be disappointed if I didn't at least reach double figures this season, so 12 shouldn't be beyond me, but it depends how much I'm going to get on now.

Crouchy's imminent arrival is the subject on everyone's lips when the lads hit the town to celebrate the birth of Malky's son Callum and Mark Rivers's baby daughter Fallon. It's not as if we need one, but there is another excuse too: Adam Drury has recently got engaged to Helen. We don't so much wet the babies's heads as drown them, well, all apart from five lads who go away to see their friends and family. I'm a bit pissed off with this: this is something we should all do as a team. As club captain I'd asked the gaffer for permission and he was all for it. He loves the lads getting together. But you always get two or three who don't join in. Gary Holt went back up to Scotland, which disappointed me a bit. Keith Briggs went back to Stockport, which disappointed me a lot, because all week he had been saying he'd be there. It does annoy me when people don't make the effort. You get fed up of asking, you just think 'sod it.'

Anyway, those of us who could be bothered to turn up had a great night taking the piss out of each other.

Friday 5th

To my huge surprise I feel quite good, probably thanks to the bottle of water and two painkillers I had as soon as I got in at 2am this morning. I feel so good I actually walk the twins to school, which comes as quite a shock to them, as walking is not normally in my vocabulary. Then it's straight to Greens to sweat the alcohol out of my system – see you in three days!

Ouch! Lunch with Julie and the painkillers are wearing off; by tea-time my head's banging badly. I get no sympathy from her so I head up for an early night.

Saturday 6th

With no game due to the international call-ups I'm free to watch the mighty Wales take on Italy. Well, the first 25 minutes anyway, before we head out for dinner with friends. Halfway through the meal I take my phone out and there are four text messages from Ben. I fear the worst, each one signals a goal for Italy. Damn! If only they'd had a striker at the peak of his game . . .

My brother and cousin actually went to Milan for the match. I was very close to joining them but, because we don't get too many weekends off, I thought it was a bit unfair on Julie and the kids. With hindsight I'm glad I didn't because they had loads of problems with the Italian fans – they were getting pissed and spat on and getting bottles and cans chucked down at them. They said the Italian police could see it all, but they didn't do a thing. Apparently, the Italians fans were even trying to stick their fingers down their throats to vomit over them. My mother really panicked when she saw it on telly, but thankfully my brother rang her straight after the game to say he was all right.

I'm a Welshman born and bred and I'm proud to say

I've played for my country 15 times. My one big regret in football is that I never scored for Wales. However, I remember once in a game against Portugal, Craig Bellamy burst through their defence and got to the byline. I'm stood in the middle of the box on my own and if he squares it I've got a tap-in. And he shoots. I fucking hammered him. After the game Mark Hughes hammered him. Gary Speed, John Robinson – we all hammered him. We didn't fall out over it, but I was pissed off.

'Fucking hell, Bellers, if you'd just squared it! You know if it was me I'd have squared it to you.'

'Robbo, Robbo I tried, I swear!'

Bollocks did he, it was a definite shot. But I'm not one to hold grudges. Bastard.

Apart from that day, actually I always absolutely loved playing up-front with Bellers. When he was at Norwich we hit it off straightaway, probably more so than anyone else I've ever played with. I can't really explain it, it was like telepathy between us. He knew where to run, I knew exactly what he was going to do. He was very, very clever: it's the old cliché, but there are some things you can't coach. And God, would he train. Bruce Rioch would have to drag him off the pitch. He was always last off. He'd still be there an hour or two after everyone else, practising his crossing or his shooting.

We were the classic big man, little man double act, a la Keegan/Toshack. We made goals for each other. That first season together, 1998/99, I got 24 goals and he got 17. And because we're both Welsh we were closer off the pitch too, although unlike me he didn't speak Welsh, which came in quite handy at times . . .

He was always a right cocky sod, though. I remember once playing Oxford and Bellers was really giving it to their centre-half, Phil Gilchrist, 'How much are you on a week then?' and they beat us 2–1. We're all sitting in the dressing room after and Gilchrist opens the door and shouts: 'How much are you on now then, you little fucking prick?' I'd heard Bellers saying it so I knew what Gilchrist was on about, but the rest of the lads were a bit bemused, to say the least.

I remember falling out with him myself once on a pre-season tour of Ireland after my first, dismal season at Norwich. He was top scorer that year and said something to wind me up and I shouted: 'Fuck off Bellers, you're just a one-season wonder mate!' He still likes to remind me of that, six years and £10million later.

It wasn't just me, he would piss everyone off every now and then. He denies this story now, but the lads were so pissed off with him once they locked him in the coach toilet. He was stuck in there for about 45 minutes before they eventually let him out, but only after he'd signed a piece of paper agreeing not to be such a cocky little bastard from then on.

That's Bellers, but it's a shame we didn't have longer together (after two seasons with Norwich he was sold to Coventry) because I think he made me a better player.

I wish I could be a bit more like he is, mentally, but I'm not that confident. I don't know why: after all, I have got 240 goals in my career. I think to be a truly top class player you have to have that slight cockiness. But I can't do it. I wish I could be an arrogant so-and-so, and not give a shit what anyone thinks about me. But I do. And I let it get to me. Even after all these years I can still get upset by what's written about me in the papers or what fans say. If I got told by a third party that someone thought I was a right arrogant bastard then it would worry me to death.

It's not that I want to be everyone's friend, but I'm not a big-time Charlie and I would hate people to think that of me. So would Julie. If we go out for a meal and I'm a bit withdrawn with the waiters because I haven't played well or I'm worried about my game she hammers me and tells me not to be so rude. After the last home game I was walking up Carrow Road with Julie and three teenage lads walked past. Apparently the middle one said 'hello Robbo' and, because I didn't say anything back to him, his mates were taking the piss out of him. Julie said 'oh the poor lad,' but I hadn't heard him. I felt dreadful when she told me. I was so close to running after him to apologise. I wish I had done. So if you're a 14-year-old lad reading this and you recognise yourself, I'm sorry mate. I'm really not an arrogant bastard, I just didn't hear you.

Sunday 7th

Ben's football season starts today so no more quiet, lazy Sundays. Thorpe Rovers' first game is at home to Hellesdon and they win 7–1. Ben plays at centre-half for the first time and does really well – watch out Malky and Flem!

Ben used to play on the right wing, or as a centre-forward, but Thorpe Rovers haven't got anyone to play at centre-back this year, so that's where he is today. He takes to his new role like a duck to water. He's tall like me and he reads the game really well. He's an intelligent player, and he really enjoys it, which is the most important thing to me.

I think he'll be a decent little footballer but I'm not sure whether he wants to make a living out of it. He's talented at a lot of things and is really into F1 – he tells me he wants to be an FI mechanic! – as well as golf, tennis and long-distance running, so he's not putting all his eggs in one basket. As long as he tries his best at whatever he wants to do, that's good enough for me.

He's a great kid, very kind, but it must be hard for him

and the girls. Being a footballer is not a normal job and I can see other parents and players watching him play football, saying 'Oh that's Iwan Roberts' son' but he doesn't show any pressure.

I'm not one of these parents that stands on the touchline and shouts. I just let him get on with it. I wouldn't push him, but if he wanted to become a footballer I would back him 100 per cent. My parents never pushed me. My dad took me to games all over north Wales when I was younger and they were both brilliant, but not once did they say 'Come on son, you've got to go here today.' It was purely down to me and they backed me all the way.

If I hadn't become a footballer I'd have probably joined the police force. The place I'm from is like Great Yarmouth but on a smaller scale (and a bit nicer). Very quiet. All my schoolmates joined the Army but I don't think it would have been for me. Or, if I'd been clever enough, I'd have been a PE instructor at school. My great mentor in life has been my old PE teacher, Iolo Olin. I'm still friends with him now. He helped me as much as my dad. He picked me for the school team and got me into the local men's team, Harlech Town, in the Caernarfon District League, as he was the manager. I must have been about 15 and it really helped me mature, really shaped me as a player. It was a hard league and I was up against men of 30, so I think it toughened me up and made me a lot stronger. That's where I first learnt to look after myself.

Monday 8th

I don't often look up to people, but I have to look up to Crouchy! He's a bit of a pole, not too much meat on him. But he said some really nice things about me in the paper at the weekend, about how I'd had a great career and I could be someone that he could learn from, and I thought that was a really nice touch. He didn't have to do that.

Anyway, my job as club captain today is to show Crouchy around, introduce him to everybody and welcome him to the team. He seems a really nice guy, quite quiet though, shy even. He's not had the happiest of times at Aston Villa, so I'd imagine his confidence is a bit low.

Anyway, we're chatting outside the dressing room and, out of the corner of my eye, I can see the gaffer coming towards me and he's really buzzing. He comes over, all smiles, and says: 'Robbo, I can't keep it in any longer . . . we've got Darren Huckerby coming in from Man City this afternoon for three months on loan.'

'Jeeezus!'

We played against him at Forest last year and he tore us apart with his pace. I think he's very, very good. Hats off to the gaffer and the board, they've gone out on a limb. It's going to cost the club a few bob to get these two in and everybody knows that, but it'll be great for the team. The lads are really buzzing when they hear the news.

Tuesday 9th

Hucks needs no introducing to the rest of the lads. He might not be playing for Man City at the moment, but we've all come up against him at some point and we know what a great player he is. He's blisteringly fast and he's got the ability to do the unexpected. Surprisingly, he's really quiet off the pitch. People think he must be like how he plays – all swagger and talking at 100mph – but he's very laid-back. A real player's player. There's certainly no hint of the big-time Charlies when he arrives at training this morning.

Wednesday 10th

Get a letter this morning from the bloke who wrote to Delia about me and Mullers in the pub before the start of the season, apologising and saying he was a big Norwich fan and that he didn't mean to upset anyone.

I watch the Wales v Finland game at home with Ben. It's on BBC Wales and the poor lad doesn't have a clue what the commentators are saying. He's a big Wales fan even though he was born in England, so he's English really, like his mum (although she was born in Cyprus and spent 13 years in Cardiff, which is good enough for me). Ben would qualify for Wales because of me and his grandparents. Ah, one day . . .

I remember the first time I got into the Welsh squad, aged just 17, I was so excited . . . and dead nervous. We played Israel away. I was sat next to Mark Hughes on the plane, and he never spoke a word to me. I was so excited, thinking 'I'm sat here next to Sparky Hughes!' I eventually plucked up the courage to speak to him.

'Er, what was playing for Barcelona like?'

'Yeah, it was all right.'

And that was that. We sat in silence for another three hours.

It was the same with Ian Rush on that same trip. He was my ultimate hero, although Kenny Dalglish runs him close. I didn't know what to say to him. I was a quiet little mouse in the corner. Me and my mates Malcolm Allen and Kenny Jackett, who both played with me at Watford, were a bit freaked out. There were guys who were legends, people like Neville Southall and Kevin Ratcliffe, welcoming us into the squad. They played for Everton who were winning championships and cups in Europe and Southall was the best keeper in the world. There's me from the backstreets of north Wales mixing with them. I was gobsmacked.

My first actual cap was against Holland at Wrexham. We only lost 1–0. I was up against Gullit, Van Basten and Rijkaard, and was completely in awe of them; a bit like Eva and Chase when they met Westlife, but possibly more embarrassing. I was already in awe of most of my team-mates, but these guys were world superstars. For the first five minutes I was running round like a headless chicken with a grin the size of The Hague on my face. Then I realised that if I carried on like the stupid teenager I was, smiling and desperately trying to work out whose shirt I could get at the end, I would be dragged off after 20 minutes. I played for 80 minutes, so I can't have disgraced myself, although I didn't get any chances.

Thursday 11th

After training today the gaffer says he hasn't seen me strike the ball with such power, accuracy and such a devilish attitude for a while. I was busting the back of the net and it felt good. Maybe it's the new signings. They've given us all a lift, but I guess there's a bit of a 'I'll show you' attitude. The extra competition certainly forces you to dig deep and get more out of yourself. I'm back on the bench for Saturday's game against Burnley though, as Crouchy is straight into the side.

Friday 12th

The day Terry the kit man has been dreading. He's up in court this morning for the scandal of the missing boots and – just to make him sweat that bit more – we're leaving him till last. The court was baying for his blood for trying to blame the youth lads for leaving the boots off the bus to Forest, but to be fair to Terry on a matchday he does have a million things to do. Terry pleads guilty, then tries to change his plea. Too late, mate. He's fined £25 by a very harsh Adam. The lads, however, decide this is too much, so we reduce it to £15. And after training Malky and I put a smile back on his face: I give him a tenner and Malky gives him a fiver to cover the fine. Who said the Welsh and the Jocks were tight?

We've signed Scottish international right-winger Kevin Harper on a month's loan from Portsmouth, which is great news as Rivvo's still injured.

Saturday 13th

Nationwide League Division One
Norwich City 2   **Burnley 0**
Crouch 58
Roberts 90
Carrow Road   Att: 16,407

What a buzz! My first goal of the season and it feels as good as my first ever goal. As a striker the relief you feel when the ball hits the back of the net is incredible: it's much more relief than anything else. It's like a massive weight being lifted off me today, and not just me but everyone in the ground – the players, the staff, the supporters. We were 1–0 up, still with a couple of minutes to go and Burnley were putting us under a bit of pressure. I make it 2–0 and it's Goodnight Vienna, the game's over.

I'd come on for Crouchy after 69 minutes – which is ideal for me at the moment. Apparently he had cramp in his calves. What calves? He'd worked his socks off for me to come on when their defence was tired and, a minute into injury time, Darren Huckerby set me up and I scored.

Hucks did really well, rolling the ball across the face of

the goal for me – he set it up on a plate for me really – and I knocked it through the keeper's legs. Nice. I knew I had loads of time because the defender marking me had gone to close down Darren and left me totally unmarked in the box. But, still, all sorts of things go through your mind in that split second. Do you have a touch? Do you have a couple of touches to make sure, or do you just hit it first time? I hit it first time. First and foremost I wanted to hit the target. To be honest, I would have preferred it to go either side of the keeper but I'll settle for it going through his legs. I charged straight over to Hucks and said: 'Cheers mate, I needed that one.' He could have gone for it himself, but he was very unselfish. He just smiled and said: 'Well, hopefully, there'll be a few more of them to come before I go back.' He's been superb, and in those 20 minutes we had on the pitch we just clicked instantly.

When I get back into the dressing room, the gaffer starts taking the mick: '. . . and well done Robbo, who got his first goal in three years!'

Cheeky sod. I've not really been one to go through lean spells, but someone says it was my first in seven months. I suddenly realise I can't remember my last goal for the club. I ask Dave Carolan, the fitness instructor, and Steve Foley but they can't remember it. It's not until I get in the car afterwards and say to Julie: 'Do you know, I can't remember the last goal I scored for Norwich?'

Quick as a flash, Ben pipes up: 'Sheffield Wednesday, away, last season.'

Cheers, Ben. Yep, seven months. Jeez that's a long time. Still, that's me up to 89 with Norwich now . . . only another 11 to go!

In the evening we go out to a charity ball at the Great Witchingham Cricket Club and I'm inundated with well-wishers, people coming up to shake my hand. I'm on a complete high, but I can't have more than a couple of drinks because I've got training tomorrow.

Sunday 14th

Not the usual post-match day of rest: we're in training because we're playing Gillingham on Tuesday night. But hey, after my goal yesterday I'm not complaining. In fact training is a breeze this morning – it's amazing what a goal does for your confidence. If I'm honest, I had started to question whether I could still play football at this level. I'd really started to wonder whether I was past it but it's all up there in your head. When things aren't going well for you, you question everything, especially yourself, and the self-doubt creeps in. Confidence is such a big part of this game. In the afternoon I take Ben to Horsford for Thorpe Rovers' second game of the season. Ben's wearing his new Puma boots, given to him by Robbie Savage. It does the trick: we win 8–2 and Ben gets man of the match.

Monday 15th

All the press are at training this morning, wanting the usual quote or gossip before the game tomorrow. And for some reason, this morning, they all want to speak to me! I don't mind – I get on well with most of the local press – and I'm more than happy to do my bit this morning.

Tuesday 16th

Nationwide League Division One

Gillingham 1	**Norwich City 2**
King 40	*Francis 28*
	Crouch 67
Priestfield	Att: 8,022

Wow, I feel a different player tonight. It's the goal on Saturday. I'm not tense or worrying about making sure I'm getting hold of the ball before the murmurs from the crowd start. I'm more relaxed so I'm playing better. The pressure isn't completely off, but I can start to enjoy my game now. If you're uptight you tend to be a bit rigid, a bit awkward, the ball bounces off your shin or your boot.

I had been really looking forward to the game tonight: I love night games. You get to go to bed for a couple of hours in the afternoon, then wake up really refreshed, like you could run all night. I wish all our games were in the evening.

As it is I only get 15 minutes as we beat Gillingham 2–1 but I feel brilliant, and recording our first away win of the season is a great way to end a day which had started so badly.

We were due to leave Norwich on the coach at 9am but I got in early as usual and I could tell by the look on the gaffer's face that something was up. He was fuming and asked me to get all the boys together. Apparently, yesterday Terry got all the skips together ready to put on the coach, then when he turned up this morning one of them was missing. He eventually found it, but in the light of the Forest boots incident someone is seriously taking the piss.

The manager is fuming and says he's got an idea who the culprit is, so we all look at Crichts. Paul Crichton, our reserve goalkeeper, is renowned as a bit of a practical joker but, to be fair, he's not daft enough to do something like this. He'll cut up your socks and put Ralgex in your underpants, but he'd never take the match boots off the bus. That's deadly serious. That's a sackable offence. I have no idea who it could be.

Anyway, the gaffer says as soon as he finds out who it is he'll hit them with the highest fine available – two weeks' wages. I wish he'd said to the person he suspects, 'I think it's you and if I catch you, then you're going to get it,' because I think that would put a stop to it.

The last thing he says is: 'We put this fucking away thing to bed tonight!'

Which we do, and now we're up to seventh in the table, and there's a great atmosphere on the coach on the way back. I don't think the gaffer would have minded if one of us asked to stop at an offie and get a few cans in for the journey back but none of us ever do. Gone are the days when you'd stop for fish and chips and six bottles of Bud. These days it's all Lucozade and water. The last time we did was when we beat Wolves in the play-off semi-final at Molineux a year ago. That was quality. I must admit I got totally legless. I wouldn't have even minded a twelve-hour journey back that night.

Wednesday 17th

Big news: San Jose want me! I receive a surprise call from a good friend of mine, Trevor James, who has his own soccer school in LA. He's worked for Major League Soccer and knows a lot of people and says there are a couple of teams keen to get me out to play in the States. San Jose Earthquakes, in particular, want to take me now on loan until the end of October. So I've got a big dilemma. My contract with Norwich runs out next June and I would love to go to America. On the other hand, I'd love to stay here in some kind of coaching role. If I can't, it's not a problem – they don't owe me a living – but I'd just like to know so that I can plan my future. I don't want to be left high and dry come next May.

San Jose want me for their last seven League games of the season and then for the play-offs at the end of October. If I settled out there and did well, maybe they'd offer me a two-year playing contract. But I can't see the gaffer letting me go at the moment because we're doing well. While Crouchy's here I'm always going to be on the bench and get thrown on for the last 15–20 minutes. But there is a real buzz about the club at the minute and I've still got a lot to do here before I pack up playing. If I can win promotion with Norwich then I'll have finished the job – achieved what I set out to try and do. I think I'd prefer to finish my season here, but I'm really tempted by the prospect of playing out there next season and I don't want to blow that by turning them down now.

The other thing is, going to the States would be six weeks without Julie and the kids and I'd miss them desperately. I don't know what to do. I might talk to the gaffer on Monday. I don't want to do it before the game, mess with his head. If we get a win on Saturday he'll be in a good mood and I'll have a word with him then. See what he says about a coaching role after I hang up my boots.

But I have to consider the well-being of my family. We've not discussed money, but I could be looking at a two-year contract, which there's no way I'm going to get here. I think, on average, players in the States earn $150,000 a year, which goes that much further as it's cheap to live out there. That would be a fairly big drop from my salary here, but at 35, where am I going to earn that kind of money? Lots of people at First Division clubs are only on £1,000 a week now: that's just the way the game's gone. The money just isn't there any more.

I've got a fair idea of what the club can and can't afford and when they bring players in, what they are on. There is a strict wage structure, so when I renegotiated my contract four years ago I knew I couldn't go in and ask for stupid money so I didn't. I could have gone to Nottingham Forest or back to Huddersfield, but it would have meant uprooting the family again and I didn't think it was worth it for the sake of a few extra thousand pounds a year. The family are well settled here and the grass isn't always greener.

The only place I would have gone is Cardiff. About two years ago they offered £200,000 for me. I only found out through the papers. I was in Cardiff with the Welsh squad and the local press cornered me in the hotel and asked if I knew that Cardiff had come in for me. First I knew of it! I was seriously tempted. Julie's from there, I would have been close to my mum and dad, who are getting older and don't get to see their grandchildren that much. I could have done some media work for BBC Wales (I'm fluent in Welsh – it's my English I have trouble with) and I wouldn't have had to do so much travelling. But the gaffer wouldn't let me go. He said: 'I can't replace you for £200,000. It's an insult.'

I accepted it. I enjoy it here and I like living here. We're more settled here than any other club I've ever been at. Norwich is a safe, small, friendly city. In ten minutes I can be at the training ground, in the city centre, at the club, on a lovely beach, on a boat on the Norfolk Broads. And the weather's mild too. The gaffer knew I wasn't going to kick up a fuss or hand in a transfer request.

So I signed a two-year extension to my contract in September 2001. No agents involved. David Speedie used to be my agent. I played up-front with him for Leicester and we used to be best buddies. When I was negotiating my previous contract in 1999, he told me not to sign for Norwich, that he had Forest and Huddersfield interested. But, at the end of the day, he couldn't produce anything on paper to say I'd be signing for Forest on this date for this much a week. So I could have got injured in training, never played again and not got a penny.

'Speedo,' I said to him, 'Norwich have offered me a decent contract, two years on decent money, it's guaranteed. Julie likes it here, the kids are settled here, so I'm going to sign.'

We fell out over it. I can remember the first home game after it all came out in the local press, the Barclay End sang 'David Speedie, what a wanker, what a wanker' for about 20 minutes. I had a little smile to myself about that.

I've only spoken to David a couple of times since. I was very disappointed in the way he treated me.

So when I signed my last contract with Norwich I knew I didn't need an agent. I knew I wasn't going to get something stupid like £6,000 a week so there was no point asking for it and jeopardising a two-year deal which, at 33, was what I wanted. I wouldn't do that anyway. I've been on the same salary, just about, since I joined Norwich seven years ago. At Leicester I was on £800 a week – and they were in the Premiership at the time – but it wasn't until I went to Wolves that I got a big salary jump. It's a lot of money, especially compared to what most people get, but compared to what the lads in the Premiership are on it's chicken-feed. But I'm happy.

I think I was probably always one of the highest-paid at the club, but not now – even without the new boys. I think Damien Francis must be on a few quid, and Phil Mulryne because the board pushed the boat out and were desperate to keep him. But I don't know how much other players are on and I wouldn't ask. People actually think all the Norwich players are on £10–15,000 a week. I know we live comfortably, but I'll still have to work when I've finished playing. I can't retire at 35, 36, like a lot of Premiership players can. But people still think if you're a footballer you must be a millionaire and have four houses.

It does annoy me when people moan that footballers get paid too much. I was sat in the sauna once and this lad came in and said I got paid too much. I said: 'So what are you going to do if someone offers you £2,000 a week? Would you turn it down? Of course not. If another firm offers to treble your wages, wouldn't you be tempted to join them?'

People ask me how much I'm on all the time. Cheeky bastards. I think they're all right and then, after two minutes, they say: 'So how much are you on then?' I'm like: 'Listen mate, you've just killed yourself. I thought you were all right, but I've got no time for you now.' They always say: 'Well, I don't mind if you know how much I'm on.'

So, to all those people can I just make one thing quite clear: I don't fucking care how much you're on. I don't want to know!

Thursday 18th

Training's short and sharp today. The gaffer's starting with the same team that beat Gillingham on Tuesday night – no surprises there – so they take on the rest of us who, tonight Matthew, are going to be Stoke.

We follow this with a seven v seven game over half a normal size pitch. I'm not saying Damo's daft but, as one of the captains, he's allowed first pick. He's standing there thinking and says: 'I think I'll go for one of our centre-halves.'

Malky and Flem look at each other, wondering which of them it will be, when he finally says: 'Adam.'

Adam Drury? Our left-back? Damo, you muppet.

Friday 19th

The journey to Stoke is a nightmare. We set off from Colney at 1.30pm and are still nowhere near our destination at

5pm, when we all thought we'd be there around 4.30pm. The poor bus driver just keeps finding more and more traffic jams and gets hammered for it from the lads. Of course it's not his fault, but try telling that to 18 frustrated footballers who spend half their lives on this bloody coach. Luckily I've brought the DVD of the first series of *24* along. Only another eight hours to go . . .

Saturday 20th

Nationwide League Division One
Stoke City 1   **Norwich City 1**
Noel-Williams 36   *Huckerby 67*
Britannia Stadium   Att: 10,672

Returning to the Britannia Stadium reminds me of one of my scariest football memories. I was at Leicester at the time. We played Stoke in the play-off semi-finals in 1996, beat them 1–0 at our place and the score was 0–0 at their place, putting us through to the final at Wembley. I didn't play, but at the final whistle I went running onto the pitch in my suit to congratulate the boys. When I turned round I saw there were fucking thousands of Stoke lads coming over the fence.

I shat myself. I went running straight up the tunnel, but some of our players like Neil Lennon and Muzzy Izzet were penned in the corner. The Stoke supporters wouldn't let them get near the tunnel. There was a cordon of riot police and dogs to prevent them getting at our players. But all some of our lads were wearing was their slips – they'd thrown their shirts and shorts into the crowd and they were standing there in their socks, boots and slips. It was scary.

The only other incident that's really bugged me in my

career occurred when I was at Wolves, although it contin-
ued for my first year here at Norwich. I used to get letters
every month or so from someone in Northampton saying
stuff like 'You ugly bastard, I'm going to stick a knife in
you'! I just used to rip them up and put them straight in
the bin. I was never really scared, because they didn't
mention Julie or the kids, just me. But I was baffled. I've
never been able to work out what I've done to offend
someone in Northampton. The bizarre thing was,
whoever wrote them actually had quite nice handwriting.

It does get to you sometimes. You wouldn't be human
if it didn't. I remember one game against West Brom, as
I retrieved the ball, someone shouted 'Oi Roberts, your
missus must be so fucking ugly 'cos you're an ugly
bastard.' You can't retaliate though. I'm not a fighter
anyway. I can't remember the last time I had a fight. I
don't want to spoil these good looks, do I!

Anyway, I have plenty of time to mull all this over on
the bench today as I only get ten minutes at the end.
Gifton Noel-Williams gives Stoke the lead in the first half,
but we play pretty well in the second half and Hucks'
equaliser gives us a 1–1 draw. Not a bad result, but not
a great one either and we've dropped a place in the
League, to eighth.

Sunday 21st

Out on the pitch and putt course with Ben by 8.30am,
before heading to Greens for 45 minutes on the treadmill as I didn't get much of a run-out yesterday. In the
afternoon Ben's team play against a team called
Sheringham and one of our Academy scouts is down to
watch the opposition's big centre-forward. I'm delighted
to report that Ben, in his new role as centre-half, hardly
lets him have a kick. Thorpe win 6–3 so they are top of

their division after three games – unlike his old man's team. I am a very proud dad as I help take down the nets.

Monday 22nd

Footballers get that Monday morning feeling too, you know, and today is no exception. The lads who played on Saturday have the day off but, as I only had my ten minutes, I'm in. Boo. The first team are off on Wednesday as well but I'll be playing against Northampton reserves. I'm feeling very much part of the reserves right now. Bloody hell, it's only Monday morning.

I also feel really stiff for some reason, but manage to get through training without pulling a muscle or doing my back in.

The only good thing about being in with the reserves is being there to witness the unveiling of midfielder Ian Henderson's latest 'new week, new haircut' monstrosity: an astonishing creation which features ancient Aztec fertility symbols carved into one side of his head. Or something. Apparently he'd travelled all the way to Luton on Saturday to get it done. Why I'm not sure – my local butcher's in Brundall would have charged him half the price.

Tuesday 23rd

It's hard to tell if autumn's arrived or Colney is just its usual forbidding self. I'm told the training ground is the highest point for miles around so there's nothing to stop the winds sweeping in straight from Siberia. That I can believe: even in summer you're surprised when you get back into Norwich city centre and discover everyone else is sweating it out in 85 degree heat.

I'm really feeling my age today: of the reserve team for

tomorrow's game at Colney I'm the oldest in the side by nine years. Nine years! We have a lad of 21, Alex, on trial from Newmarket for a few days and he's very nervous so I take him under my wing. I could be his dad. Talking of which, I spend a hectic afternoon visiting every toy shop in Norwich in preparation for the twins' birthdays tomorrow.

Wednesday 24th

I'm woken at 7.10am by two very excited little girls who want to open their hundreds of pressies. Ironically today is the one day I don't have to be at the training ground until 12.30. When I get there, Keith Webb informs me I'll only be playing the first half in the reserve game, which is fine by me as I'm only really playing to keep up my fitness. I'm even happier to just play the first 45 by the time half-time arrives and we're 1–0 down. I watch the second half with two old (team)mates Rob Newman and Mark Walton who've popped down to Colney for a chat. They must have been impressed: we end up losing 2–1 and having summer signing Keith Briggs and promising trainee Greg Crane sent off for professional fouls! Back home I console myself with a big slice of birthday cake.

Thursday 25th

I don't know if he does it on purpose, but the gaffer is always a bit moody on a Thursday. He'll say things like: 'You fucking think this is easy-ozy, I'm not getting the right vibes off you.'

He likes his little mind games: he doesn't want us thinking it'll just happen, we'll turn up and win. He's Jekyll and Hyde. He's great at praising the lads at other times, he just likes to keep us on our toes.

Every Thursday the gaffer gets us working on the team

shape for Saturday's game. He always likes to play 4-4-2 but Palace – our opponents in two days' time – play 4-3-1-2, with Andy Johnson just off the strikers. The gaffer's plan is that our back four will pick up Palace's front three. He doesn't want one of our midfielders to drop deep and pick Johnson up, that'd mean one of their midfield players would be free. The coaching staff have a little green pitch with little magnets and they show you where they want you to be when the ball's in certain positions.

So the gaffer says: 'I want the two full-backs to push on, one midfielder will bomb on, one will sit back. I want Hucks to make runs into the channels, I want Crouchy to peel off to the back post and Eddy (right-back Marc Edworthy) to put the ball in for Crouchy.'

He talks about the system for about 15–20 minutes before we go out and try it out for real. So the team that's likely to start lines up in their usual 4-4-2, and he gets the rest of us to play against them in the formation that Palace play.

Normally the first team do this against the youth team, but as they're at college today the lads who played in the reserves on Wednesday have the honour of posing as Crystal Palace – which is why we haven't got the day off. Again.

After a masterful display disguised as a Palace striker I pick Ben up from school and drive to Wembley Arena to see 50 Cent. Not sure who's more excited, Ben or me. I'm a bit wary about trouble and smell a few funny cigarettes but the concert is fantastic. Ben says he saw at least two people older than me.

Friday 26th

Still completely knackered after arriving home at 1am. Ben is already up and having a bacon sandwich when I crawl out of bed at 7.15am.

At training we have our usual, 'And now, live from Norwich, it's Fines of the Week!', session featuring Adam Drury as judge and jury. First up: Paul Crichton and Keith Briggs. Charge: caught with their boots on (but thankfully, not pants down) in the dressing room at Colney. It's only a tenner fine but Crichts isn't happy. The judge allows him to present his case for the defence which is, in a nutshell, that reserve team coach Keith Webb had given him permission. I'm no legal expert but I believe what then followed was a case of Webby committing perjury, followed by a swift doubling of the fine to a massive £20 and Crichts being absolutely disgusted with the frailties of the East Anglian justice system.

Having watched all this, Keith Briggs sensibly decides to pay the £10.

After court has been adjourned, as always on a Friday before a match, we go out to practise our set pieces for about 20–25 minutes. We have a list so you know exactly where you are supposed to be for all our corners, free-kicks etc and theirs – who you're supposed to mark, where you are in the wall. For example, depending on which of us is on the pitch at the time, either Crouchy or I will always be second man in the wall, because of our height, alongside the two wide players and one of the central midfielders.

So in training on the Friday we get into our positions and then they'll get someone to whip a couple of corners in. As I'm still in with the reserves today, when the lads are practising taking corners I'm a defender trying to stop them scoring. Then we swap it round and I'm trying to score against them. The gaffer really wants the boys at the back (and Crouchy) to win every header; he doesn't want them giving away any free headers – he thinks if that happens on the Friday they'll take it into the game on Saturday.

We haven't really got any signals for set pieces. A lot of clubs will bounce the ball twice if it's to the back post, once if it's going near post. They'll put two hands up, one hand up, all sorts of signals, pull their socks up if it's a short corner. You look out for them. But other teams get to know them, because they get you watched a few times before they play you, so we don't really bother.

We just go back post, especially now we've got Crouchy, the tallest man in football. In him and Malky we've got two good headers of the ball. We let them scrap it out with the two lads marking them, then if we can get a header on goal then all the other lads have got to react and hope to get a tap-in. There's probably less margin for error in going to the back post. The problem with the near post corner is if you don't put a good ball in the man in front clears it or, if you overhit it, the keeper just comes and gets it. If you knock it back post at least you can see the flight of the ball, run onto it, take a step back or whatever.

We finish off with our usual small-sided game: oldies against young'uns, and it's thoroughly satisfying to hammer them 4–1. Ha!

Saturday 27th

Nationwide League Division One
Norwich City 2   **Crystal Palace 1**
Huckerby (pen) 37   *Derry 1*
Mackay 88
Carrow Road   Att: 16,425

God, my back is agony this morning. It's been stiff for a few days now and I'm a little bit worried about it. My achilles tendons are both really sore too. I'll have to have a couple of painkillers before the game: they'll sort me out.

Early on we have a couple of friends come round who we haven't seen for ages. At least that's one good thing about not starting the game today: I can relax and enjoy their company. If I'd been starting I'd have been sitting quietly on my own in another room, hating the intrusion.

You could say the game starts well. 30 seconds. Holty. Shot on goal. Well saved. But you could also say it doesn't start too well. 74 seconds. Bang. 1–0 to Palace. Which is a bit of a shocker. Shaun Derry takes it well, but we didn't close him down and he had too much time to pick his spot. It's a good strike though, right in the top corner, and it knocks us back a little bit.

We have to score before half-time and on 37 minutes Hucks wins a penalty, which he then decides to take himself. This raises a few eyebrows on the bench as Holty was taking the pens in training yesterday.

I asked Holty after: 'Did you not fancy it?' But he said he didn't get time to get the ball. Squiz was there, Harps was there but Hucks said there was no-one going to take it but him and rightly so. Strikers should always take pens. They're used to scoring goals. It's a shot on goal for nothing. 1–1!

In the second half they have a little spell where they peg us back a bit. It isn't one of Crouchy's better games, but he's allowed an off day every now and again. I am desperate to get on and try to score the winner, so I go and warm up with 25 minutes to go. I eventually get on with eight (count 'em!) minutes left.

If you're coming on as a sub you have to try and make an impression. The lads said the gaffer had a bit of a pop at Zema after the game at Bradford. He came on about 6–7 minutes before the end and the gaffer said he hadn't really made an impact on the game. But it's hard to do something in six or seven minutes. You don't even get into the pace of the game. You're breathing out of your arse. All the other boys are into it. People see you and think you're running round like a blue-arsed fly, but it's not until you get your second wind that you feel okay. Anything less than ten minutes and you don't get a chance really.

Still, I'll give it my best shot. The gaffer just tells me to get hold of the ball. He hates it when the strikers give it away when it's played up to them, if they have a bad touch or the defender nicks in front of them. He wants us to take the pressure off the defence so they can push up, the midfield can push up, and we can pin them in their own half, put pressure on them and get crosses in.

We've just got a corner and I say to the gaffer: 'Put me on and I'll score from it.' He does, but I don't. I am inches from getting my head onto the ball, though, but I was definitely having my shirt pulled.

Then, with four minutes to go, I have one of those chances you don't get very often in a season. In the 86th minute I find myself in acres of space, 15 yards out, with the ball dropping right at my feet. I could take a touch but I see the keeper diving so I think I'll just hit it first time the other way. Incredibly, the ball hits his foot and he saves it. I blame Flem. He'd made a little darting run and I was so gobsmacked by this it put me off! Looking back, I still wouldn't take a touch because by that time I'd have got closed down. I did everything right: you've got to hit the target. If you hit the target then you've done your job. The keeper dived early but the ball hit his foot. The bastard.

In a match you don't get time really to dwell on your missed opportunities. Obviously there's disappointment for a split second, you have your head in hands for a couple of seconds, but then you have to say to yourself, come on, get on with it.

Oh well, at least I had a hand in our second, winning goal, two minutes later. Eddy puts a great diagonal ball straight onto my head and instead of heading it back in towards goal I see Mullers peeling off, so I head it down to him. He crosses it to Malky and, bam, it's in the back of the net. Bedlam! And some noise at last from our fans.

They were so quiet today it was eerie. I couldn't believe how subdued it was, probably the quietest game at Carrow Road I can ever remember. Everyone on the bench was talking about it. Even weirder was that we as a team were quiet too. Normally, you can at least hear the players shouting. But there was nothing. As far as the crowd goes, if the Barclay Stand don't sing then nobody does really. I don't think the other sides sing, they just moan! Maybe today it was because the sun was in their eyes down the Barclay and they were squinting. It gets quite hard to see from that end. We'll have to turn the ground round.

I think the fans were as shocked as we were at the early goal and it probably knocked them for six, but that's when you need them to get behind you. You go to places like Newcastle and Leeds and it's like, 'Fuck!' It's worth a goal start to them. Our fans proved they could do it when we went to the play-off final two seasons ago at Cardiff. I spoke to people who work there and they said that was the best atmosphere they'd ever had. It was unbelievable: a sea of yellow and green. If our fans can do it then, they can do it again.

Away from home it's not a problem – you get your hard-core 1,500–2,000 who go week in, week out, and they sing for the full 90 minutes, and usually louder than the home fans. Here, for some reason, they're just really quiet. I couldn't understand it today: we'd won our three home games and taken seven of the last possible nine points, so why not get behind us from the start? I can understand sometimes it takes a spark on the pitch to get them going, but we'd made a couple of good runs down each side and were unlucky not to score. Obviously after we got the penalty they got behind us, but they've got to do it from the first whistle: they don't know how important they are.

To be honest I think some of them come for a whinge and a moan. That's why I feel really sorry for Easty (Clint Easton), our midfielder who was instrumental in getting us to that play-off final but has had fits and spurts of form since. If they spent half the energy they use up having a go at him on getting behind the team then who knows what could happen?

I had it in my first season. I can understand it because I was shit. I remember playing Bradford at home, I hit the post when I should have scored and we lost 3–2 or something and I'm walking into the tunnel, the whole crowd is booing, and I'm thinking 'just get in the dressing room.' I know they are booing me. And there's one geezer by the tunnel who goes: 'You fucking donkey Roberts, why don't you fuck off back to Wolves?'

I thought: 'Fucking hell. What have I come to here?'

Flem gives as good as he gets. He shouts back 'fuck off' when he gets abused. I've only done that once that I can remember. There's a fella who sits just to the right of the goal in the River End – sorry, Norwich and Peterborough Stand, otherwise known as the 'Nice and Peaceful' for obvious reasons. He just hammers people. He hammered me about three years ago: 'Retire Roberts, you're past it,' he'd scream at me. He's hammered the gaffer, Holty, Rivvo, everyone at some stage. 'Come on Rivers, join in. Come on Norwich, you've only got ten men with him on the pitch!' He's one of these bitter twisted old men. 'Shut up you prick,' I shouted back at him once and he's not had a go at me since.

But it's not really in my character to do that: I get more embarrassed than anything else. I remember once coming out of the players' lounge with my son and getting booed by a group of lads. Ben was only about six or seven and he started crying.

'Dad, why are they booing you?'

'Cos I'm not playing very well, mate.'

We just rushed to the car. I can understand why they do it but it doesn't help, it makes matters worse. If they channelled their frustrations into positives that would help us no end.

Booing does make you angry, but in a way it kind of works. It's not pleasant, but it makes you think 'fuck them' and 'we'll go out and show them in the second half.'

The mad thing is, if I was a supporter I think I'd probably be a boo boy. I don't slag players off when I'm watching from the stands, but I do shout quite a bit. I'll be like: 'Come on! Jeez, you could have done better there. Put a decent cross in.' So really I'm just one of them. I'd probably be one of these whinging old sods. Scary.

I definitely feel like a bit of a whinging old sod after the match today, and I say to the lads that I think the gaffer could have given me a little bit longer today. Julie says the same when I get in the car. Last year if it wasn't happening for me I'd be taken off with 20–25 minutes to go, so I am a bit peeved that I only got eight minutes today. But it's not my style to say anything and in the end it was a good three points today: it keeps everything bubbling. We were eighth before the game and to see us jump into fourth is a massive lift for everybody.

Sunday 28th

Had an early night last night, despite the win. I hate going into training hungover and reeking of alcohol and we have a full session today ahead of Tuesday's game against Reading.

When I arrive at Colney I discover Neal Reynolds in a bit of a mood and he shouts at me when I ask him what's up. Malky walks in and asks if I'd read the local Saturday night sports paper, The *Pink' Un* (why Pink when we play in yellow and green I don't know). Apparently there's been a story criticising 'The Fridge' (Neal's nickname is because he's so big, not because he's especially cool) for not getting players back from injury quick enough.

Now, The Fridge is a great guy and a top quality physio and I don't think there's any justification for the *Pink' Un*'s story, but he isn't half easy to wind up. So our reserve keeper, Paul Crichton, is injured at the moment. We all enjoy winding up The Fridge, but Crichts likes winding him up more than anything. So he's lying on the couch and The Fridge put the interferential machine (it's some kind of painkilling machine that sends electric shocks through the body) on Crichts' leg. Except it's the wrong leg. Crichts whispers to me to go and tell the gaffer. So I tell Keith Webb, who sprints into the office to tell the gaffer. And, sure enough, the gaffer saunters in.

'All right, Crichts?'

'Not bad, gaffer,' Crichts replies, dead casual.

'How's the leg?'

'Obviously me good one's great 'cos it's got the machine on it. But the other one's killing me!'

The Fridge doesn't see the funny side.

After training I go to get a KFC for the kids and the lad behind the counter recognises me.

'How did you feel when you missed that chance then, Robbo?' he says.

Here we go.

'It's just one of those things, isn't it?' I reply. 'You've

got to hit the target. It's not as though I missed the target, the keeper saved it.'

The cheeky bastard then says, even more loudly: 'When are you going to have a race with Huckerby then?'

'It wouldn't be a race, would it? I'd piss him!'

Loads of people are ear-wigging by now and I'm so embarrassed. I'm willing him to just give me my stuff and let me go.

Unfortunately, Ben's team got hammered 8–2 by Drayton this morning while I was training. Apparently he got really upset because a couple of his team came off laughing and joking which pissed him off a bit. He felt they didn't care. I don't know – Chase is so competitive she was barging little girls out of the way at her birthday party when they played musical chairs. Ben's so competitive he gets upset when his team-mates don't take it seriously enough. They both hate losing. Where can that possibly come from?

But I have always tried to teach my children that you can't win everything. After all, even Manchester United lose a few. Ben cheered up after I reminded him of that. Anyway, Drayton are probably the best team in the league, but I was disappointed I couldn't be there for him this morning – if there was one game I'd like to have seen, it was that one.

I don't really get involved with Thorpe Rovers. I don't like to step on their toes. The manager, Mick, has asked me to take training a couple of times which I don't mind at all, because that helps me with my coaching badges. I'll shout encouragement to the boys but I won't offer my opinion on who should be playing. There was a time last year where they kept taking Ben off – even when he was having a good game – and he got a bit disillusioned. But he stuck it out. You can't get involved. Can you imagine how big-time Charlie I'd look if I started making suggestions or complaining that I thought my son had been unfairly overlooked? To Thorpe Rovers I'm just Ben's dad, which is the way I like it. You can see the people from all the other teams going, 'Hey, it's Iwan Roberts' but nobody at Thorpe gives me any hassle. I get on well with them, they do a good job.

In the afternoon the girls have their birthday outing to the International League for the Protection of Horses – a fantastic pony rescue centre. They've got a baby Shetland pony there and they've only gone and named him after me. He was born the day before the play-off final. Apparently they didn't have a clue what to call him, then they watched the match and saw me score. He is tiny. Still, at least he isn't a donkey. I had my picture taken with him but he was very unimpressed, as though it was an imposition and he'd rather continue eating his hay. And he had all his own teeth. Bastard.

Monday 29th

Confidence is sky high in training this morning. We're all buzzing and you can really tell the difference. Training's a lot sharper, no-one is scared to have a shot and overall the quality is so much better. We can't do a lot though because we're missing three key players. Flem's struggling with his back. He scraped through a late fitness test on Saturday and did well to get through the game – in fact I thought he was outstanding. So he's gone to see a back specialist today. Adam has got problems with his glute and is going to see an osteopath this afternoon. Meanwhile, Harps has got a bit of a hamstring twinge so as a precaution he doesn't train. Fingers crossed for all of them.

Worst of all, we have to wait until tomorrow for the gaffer to name the team for tomorrow's match against Reading. I want to know now.

Tuesday 30th

Nationwide League Division One
Norwich City 2   **Reading 1**
Huckerby 17   *Forster 24*
McVeigh 87
Carrow Road   Att: 16,387

Yes! Flem has declared himself fit, but the gaffer is still
sweating on Adam and Harps, so he's in and out of the
treatment room every five minutes. They are both 50:50
and will have fitness tests at 9.30am. Fifteen minutes
later it's obvious neither of them are right for tonight,
which gives the manager a real headache. Harps has
been fantastic down the right wing since he arrived and
Adam is always one of the first names on the team-sheet.
It's a big blow, especially as we are a settled side on a
good run.

At 10am the gaffer announces the team and we find out
that teenage starlet Jason Shackell, whose normal position is centre-half, will replace Adam and Phil Mulryne
will replace Kevin. Phil's the best passer of a ball we have
at the club and I always feel we play better when he's in
the side.

Even though I'm only on the bench again, I head home
for the usual couple of hours' kip at about 1pm. I get to
the ground about 6pm for my usual routine of sorting
out tickets and reading the programme before the ous is
something of an understatement. Driving into the car
park, somehow he doesn't see Ian Henderson's car and
drives straight into it. Crunch! Needless to say, being the
caring lot we are, he gets hammered for it.

The less said about the game the better really. Let's just
gloss over it and say it wasn't our best performance of
the season – and believe me, the manager let us know

about it at half and full-time. We'd taken the lead through Darren Huckerby, but conceded a bad goal, which Malky came straight in at half-time and held his hands up for. Fair play to him. I came on for Crouchy with 15 minutes to go but barely got a touch. Thankfully, we got the three points with a late goal from Paul McVeigh.

The relief at grinding out a good result despite a poor performance means a few of the lads decide to go out and celebrate. Naturally, being club captain, I feel obliged to go. It's a great night, with loads of fans celebrating and wearing their shirts with pride. It may not have been a classic but we're up to fourth now and the city is really buzzing.

Nationwide League Division One

Pos	Name	P	HOME					AWAY					GD	PTS
			W	D	L	F	A	W	D	L	F	A		
1	Sheffield United	10	4	1	0	13	4	3	1	1	7	6	+10	23
2	West Bromwich Albion	10	5	0	0	12	3	2	1	2	5	7	+7	22
3	Wigan Athletic	10	3	1	0	4	1	3	2	1	10	5	+8	21
4	**Norwich City**	**10**	**5**	**0**	**0**	**11**	**4**	**1**	**2**	**2**	**5**	**7**	**+5**	**20**
5	Sunderland	10	4	0	1	9	4	2	1	2	8	6	+7	19
6	West Ham United	9	2	2	0	3	1	3	0	2	7	5	+4	17
7	Nottingham Forest	9	3	1	1	9	4	2	0	2	7	7	+5	16
8	Millwall	11	3	2	0	8	3	1	2	3	7	10	+2	16
9	Cardiff City	10	3	1	1	12	3	1	2	2	7	9	+7	15
10	Reading	10	2	1	1	6	3	2	1	3	8	8	+3	14
11	Burnley	11	2	0	3	7	8	2	2	2	9	10	-2	14
12	Crewe Alexandra	9	3	0	1	5	4	1	1	3	4	8	-3	13
13	Gillingham	11	2	1	2	7	8	1	3	2	5	10	-6	13
14	Walsall	10	3	2	1	10	6	0	1	3	2	5	+1	12
15	Stoke City	11	2	2	1	7	5	1	1	4	6	10	-2	12
16	Derby County	10	1	1	3	6	10	2	2	1	5	6	-5	12
17	Crystal Palace	9	1	1	2	4	5	2	1	2	9	8	0	11
18	Ipswich Town	10	2	2	1	9	6	1	0	4	5	10	-2	11
19	Preston North End	9	3	0	2	10	7	0	1	3	3	6	0	10
20	Bradford City	10	1	1	4	6	12	2	0	2	3	5	-8	10
21	Coventry City	8	1	2	1	6	6	1	1	2	6	8	-2	9
22	Rotherham United	10	2	2	2	5	6	0	1	3	1	11	-11	9
23	Watford	9	1	2	2	7	7	0	0	4	2	7	-5	5
24	Wimbledon	10	1	1	4	9	15	0	0	4	4	11	-13	4

OCTOBER

Wednesday 1st

Doh! I feel shocking. I think I might have overdone my sense of duty last night. My darling gorgeous sweet beautiful wonderful wife Julie lets me have a lie-in. Finally emerging at 10am, I decide a sauna will banish the booze from my body. But I only get five minutes down the road before realising what a ridiculous idea that is, turning round and heading straight back to bed.

Thursday 2nd

Hmm . . . the gaffer's in an unusually chirpy mood today – and on a Thursday, too. It's pissing down but I keep expecting him to start warbling *Singing In The Rain*. Could it be anything to do with his winning the 'Manager of the Month' award? Surely he knows he's for the chop now . . .

Before training he calls us all together and thanks the staff and players for helping him win the award, but it's no more than he deserves after a great month for the club. Would you believe, he's the first Norwich manager to win manager of the month since Mike Walker ten years ago?

The lads are all feeling fresh after our day off yesterday and training is excellent: really enjoyable, high quality, which means the gaffer doesn't have to shout at us once. Either that, or he's already started on the champagne!

Afternoon trip to the 'Back Man', otherwise known as the 'Jigsaw Man', who clicks it all back together once every six weeks. Lovely.

Friday 3rd

Just what the 'Back Man' ordered – a five-hour coach trip. Oh joy. We're playing Wigan tomorrow so we leave at 9.30am and finally get there at 2.45pm – just as the last pack of cards is falling to bits. We were going to train at Bolton's training ground but as it is late and we've been on the coach so long the gaffer just takes us for a jog and a stretch round the hotel grounds.

The gaffer still hasn't named the team as we've got a few injury worries. Briggsy is rooming with Crouchy and he thinks he's really struggling with an ankle injury he picked up in training yesterday. But I saw Crouchy walking round earlier and he looks fine so I'm sure he'll be all right.

A night in on my own beckons as my usual room-mate, Alex, is injured and, although we've got an even number of players, Hucks likes rooming alone.

Saturday 4th

Nationwide League Division One

Wigan 1	**Norwich City 1**
Liddell 25	*Roberts 63*
JJB Stadium	Att: 9,346

God! I wake up feeling absolutely zonked. The fire alarm kept going off half the night. I looked out of my window, but there were only three people outside and no smoke or flashing blue lights so I did the right thing: went back to bed, pulled the duvet up high over my head and tried to get back to sleep.

I'm looking forward to playing at the new JJB Stadium: it looks fantastic, much better than the old one. I played there a few years ago and it actually had dog shit on the pitch. I'm also looking forward to seeing Mum and Dad, who are making the trip, especially as it's my dad's birthday today. Happy birthday Dad! I'd love to give him an extra-special present: a goal.

I go for the usual Saturday morning walk with the rest of the lads and find out I'm playing: Crouchy's ankle is still playing up. So it's a mad scramble for the phone. I can't get through to Mum and Dad but eventually Julie gets hold of them and reassures them that the six messages I've left are good news.

We get to the ground at around 1.30pm and I sort out my mum and dad's tickets. They're so chuffed I'm playing. Unfortunately, we're absolutely shit in the first half and the gaffer really lets us have it at half-time.

'Two thousand people have travelled all the way up here to support you lot and you've shat on them. I spoke to a couple of fans who said it would cost them £100 to come along and support you today. Now get out there and sort it out.'

He doesn't have to say any more. He is right: it's a lot of money for one day out and we've got to realise the amount of effort people put in to come and watch us. We owe it to them – and ourselves – to perform.

The second half is a lot better. The gaffer brings on Easty for Damo, who I feel a bit sorry for as he was playing out of position out wide on the right, when every game in the centre of midfield he's been outstanding. I think Mullers would have been better out there; he could be our Beckham and I'm a bit surprised he hasn't tried him out there.

But at least we start creating chances. I have a few. Darren dinks one to the far post and I go to head it, convinced I'm going to score, but it just goes over my head. I jumped too early. I was so tempted to just punch it in. Then I hit the bar with a 20-yard left-foot shot, which I'm gutted about. As it came over I just thought 'Hit it as hard as you can'. I didn't realise until afterwards that the keeper had fallen down running backwards so I could have picked my spot. I thought then 'It's going to be one of those days.' Then I had a shot that the keeper parried. It's the most chances I've had in a game for a long, long time.

Then, finally, I score. I know where Mum and Dad are sitting – in with the Norwich fans – so I run straight towards them and I can see my Dad jumping up and down, dancing in the aisle. I'm celebrating with all the lads jumping on top of me, and I find myself screaming: 'Dad, Dad, sit down. Remember you're 61 now!' And I'm thinking: 'Bloody hell! I'd better not score another one!'

I am surprised to last the full 90 minutes, unlike poor old Easty who doesn't have the best of games and – having come on at half-time – is subbed in the 89th minute. The first 15–20 minutes I was blowing a bit, but I'm lucky I'm up-front with Hucks who runs here, there and everywhere. He has the pace and experience to know exactly where to run and when to go, and I don't do half as much running as I would have two or three years ago. It's fantastic playing with him!

But to be honest, with 10–15 minutes to go I was gone. Afterwards Doug Livermore asks me how I feel and I admit I'm completely bollocksed.

'Yeah, you looked tired,' he says, 'but we had to keep you on for the set-pieces.'

I can understand that. Whenever Wigan won a corner or free kick I had to go back and mark Matty Jackson, the former Norwich skipper, or one of their big centre-halves. If we'd had another 6ft 2 or 6ft 3 centre-forward on the bench I don't think I'd have finished the game.

I would never signal to the bench that I was tired. Subs are their decision, but I wouldn't have been pissed off to have been taken off today. At that stage I think fresh legs would have bettered the team. We could have played balls into the corner and, with Rivvo upfront, used his pace to turn Wigan a bit more, push up further. As it was in the last 5–10 minutes we were under a bit of pressure, but we held out and I am delighted to get another 90 minutes under my belt – although I probably would have been sick if I'd had the energy.

Overall we are pleased with the point. Wigan worked hard and closed us down really well. Plus, mine is only the second goal they've conceded all season at home and they beat Fulham in the Worthington Cup. They're a good side. Crouchy was one of the first to congratulate me after the game, which was good of him.

I was booked in the first half of the game. I thought the ref had yellow carded me in the first half for the foul, but it turns out he booked me for my reaction because I threw the ball down. Stupid, I know, but I didn't agree with the decision. Matt Jackson was running back towards his goal, I cut across him, his ankle hit my knee and he went down. That's not intentional. Then a few minutes later Jacko caught me on the back of the leg. But I got my own back in the second half when we both went up for a header. I won the ball, but accidentally caught him with my elbow and split his head open. I directed the header to Hucks, who beat four players, played it back to me and I scored. Double bonus!

Five minutes later we had to stop and get the physio on to deal with the blood. I asked Jacko what the matter was.

'You did it when you scored the goal, didn't you?'

'You were nowhere near me!'

'No, with the header.'

'Oh yeah, sorry mate. I didn't even realise I'd caught you.'

Jacko annoyed a few of the boys during the game. As soon as he shouted 'Ref!' the ref would blow up. Then in the first half Flem gave a free kick away – it was a tackle from behind although I thought he got the ball – and Jacko came running up for the free-kick shouting: 'Fucking hell, ref – is that his freebie? You should be booking him for that!'

Flem just lost it and shouted: 'Fuck off Jacko!'

But we would all have done the same: Jacko was just trying to get the most for his team, and they all went and had a drink together after.

I would have gone too – I like Jacko – but it being Dad's birthday I meet up with my parents and we sit and have a chat on the team coach. If I'd gone to the bar I wouldn't have had as much time with them. Dad is delighted with his other birthday present. Eva and Chase had told Julie that Taid's (that's Grandad in Welsh) pyjamas were a bit tatty – so we got him some new trendy ones. You need a good set of pyjamas in north Wales!

We eventually leave at 5.50pm because the gaffer, Malky and Mullers are all late, so that will be fines of £50 all round. We're looking good for the Christmas party!

The journey back seems to take ages, even though I'd scored and I won at cards. As usual. I finally get home at 10.15pm, starving. Should have had something on the bus. The kids have waited up to see me and are really excited I'd scored. Well, the girls are for five minutes, then they go and watch *Friends*.

Sunday 5th

Get up extra early to read all the papers – all right, just the bits that mention Norwich's veteran Welsh striker! There's even a decent photo of me in the *News of the World*. Wonders will never cease.

Monday 6th

Training is cancelled due to lack of interest: everyone's playing in the Norwich City golf day on the coast at Gorleston. There are 31 teams, each comprising a former or current Norwich player and three people who have paid to play a round of golf with us. All organised by Mr Norwich himself, former Sheriff of the City and goal-keeping legend Bryan Gunn.

I'm not bad at golf, I suppose, despite The Day I Nearly Died. I can laugh about it now, but only after years of counselling! Me, Gunny, Flem and Phil Grice, a pro golfer, were playing golf together in a tournament at the Sprowston Manor Hotel in my first season at Norwich. Me and Gricey got fed up with waiting for Flem to take his shot on one particular par five so we walked about 50 yards up the hill, chatting. All of a sudden, I heard an anxious shout of 'Fore!' A split second later, bang, the ball hit me on the side of my head with a huge crack and knocked me down. I fell flat on the floor, with my bag on top of me. Gunny came running over immediately. 'Do we get a drop shot then?' I was touched by his concern.

This fella ran over from 300 yards away and told me to get straight to the doctor's. I was so dizzy I couldn't even carry my bags. Poor old Flem carried them: he felt so guilty, bless him. The doctor took my blood pressure and made sure I didn't have a fractured skull. I was so lucky. Mostly because Gunny and Flem are such dozy bastards. As soon as he hit the shot Flem panicked. He just froze, he didn't shout 'Fore!' It was Gunny. He looked at Flem, as if to say 'Are you going to shout?' and when he finally realised he wasn't, at the very last minute he shouted 'Fore!' And that indecision probably saved my life. If I'd heard the shout a second before and turned round, the ball would have hit me in the temple and could have killed me.

It put me off golf a bit, and I still love winding Flem up about it. I'll have to make sure I'm playing behind him today.

Before the big tee-off, Gunny and I have a little argument about my handicap (he's put me down as 14 but I want 16 as it is incredibly windy). I win and head for a bacon sandwich but decide it's not worth the effort when I see Malky's at the front of the queue!

My main aim today is just to beat former Norwich psycho Mike Milligan, but when I return to the clubhouse with 36 points I realise I'm in with a shout of winning the Top Canary trophy. Not only that but my team-mates Pete, John and Mike, have also played well and we are looking good for the team trophy with 87 points. Relaxing after a hard-earned (it was a five-and-a-half hour round!) pint in the bar after, I find out I've won. Yes. Get in there! I'm just worrying about the usual chants of 'bandit' and 'cheat' that will accompany me picking up this much-coveted trophy when I hear that my team have won the whole tournament. Shit, I'm going to get slaughtered! So I grab my trophies from a very pissed-off Gunny and leg it.

(May I just point out how very, very much I enjoyed writing the above!)

Tuesday 7th

My mate who's a Wolves fan (well, I'm only human – you can't hate them all!) just texted me.

'I thought I saw your name on a loaf of bread this morning but I looked again and it said Thick Cut.'

Cheeky bastard. It seems a good time to mention how far Mark Lawrenson's gone up in my estimation, after his joke at the weekend: 'What time do Wolves kick off? Every 10 minutes.'

Quality. I always thought Lawro was a bit of a prick before that. Great player, mind.

I have a new role today: taxi driver. Briggsy has had a smash in his car and wants me to take him to training for the next two weeks. We have a crap day's training: half the lads are away at Southend for a reserve game and, despite wind so strong it puts you in mind of Malky after a kebab, we're not using the indoor arena supposedly built for us to train in when the weather's bad. Bring on the snow; at least it will get us out of this hurricane.

Wednesday 8th

We expect a hard session today as we've got tomorrow off, and boy we are not disappointed. Loads of running, loads of sweat. Feel oddly good at the end of it, though, but decline a night out with the lads in favour of taking my wife to see *The Italian Job*. Pick and mix or a pint? It's a close call, but it's no wonder I've got no teeth!

Thursday 9th

Thank God we've got a day off: the legs and back are a bit stiff today. The girls have got the day off school because they're off to the BBC studios in London to audition for a modelling job, so I mooch around all day before taking Ben to football training.

My daughters' portfolios are amazing. Chase looks like a 15 year-old, which is scary. Eva looks exactly what she is – a pretty little girl. I do feel a bit sorry for Ben sometimes. Julie's got these big wooden frames, the size of a door, with little frames in which she's filled with pics of the girls. Poor old Ben sees it and says: 'Oh, so I'm not part of this family any more am I?' Bless him. Horrible woman, his mum!

Friday 10th

There's a new lad at training today. Oh no, sorry, it's the gaffer. He's been away since Saturday. Obviously not abroad since he's as white as ever. Malky is upset with me as court was already in session when I helpfully reminded fine collector Steve Foley about him and the others being late back onto the coach at Wigan. Like Malky wouldn't be the first to tell – we don't call him 'Busy' for nothing!

Me, Adam Drury and Flem then head off to meet with the club's chief executive Neil Doncaster and club secretary Kevan Platt to discuss the team's bonuses. Believe it or not, we've had the same bonus system ever since I've been here. I didn't realise Flem was such a good negotiator: he should be working for the UN!

The club have been brilliant – they want to sort it out because they know it's well overdue and the meeting goes well. Hucks has been really helpful, too, even though he probably won't be here in two months. You just get the feeling he really wants to help the lads – suggesting what we should ask for, telling us what other lads he knows are on.

We want the club to base the system on League position, so if we're in the top two we get a certain amount, if we're in a play-off spot we get a bit less and so on, until, if we're in the bottom few, we don't get anything. It's a lot of money, and I don't take it for granted, but I also happen to know that some players in this division are on £1,500 a win. We don't want to screw the club, we want to get promoted. But if, having got promoted, we were then relegated the bonuses would drop by 15 per cent or whatever. You see, we do give a little bit!

Saturday 11th

Our game against Coventry has been called off due to international call-ups. We would normally have had the weekend off but, as we've got a massive game on Wednesday, away to West Ham, the gaffer gets those of us not called up for European Championship action in for a really good, really enjoyable training session.

In the evening a few of the lads meet up at a local hotel to watch the England v Turkey game. As Julie went out on the lash with Marc Edworthy's and Hucks' wives last night, she has very kindly told me I have permission to join them. Which is just as well, since I have already invited former Norwich team-mates Chris Llewellyn and Daryl Sutch to join us!

I know I'm Welsh, but I'm rooting for England. Wales lose to Serbia but it doesn't really matter as we are now in the play-offs because Italy won anyway.

Sunday 12th

It's bacon sarnies for me and Ben this morning before watching Thorpe Rovers beat Dereham 3–1; Ben getting the 'Man of the Match' award (no champagne) in the process. Damo's got us free tickets for the Mystique concert this evening (his cousin is in the band apparently). Cheers, Damo. You've made two little girls very, very happy.

Monday 13th

I'm well pissed off when the gaffer names the team to start on Wednesday night – I'm not in it. Crouchy is. The gaffer can tell I am annoyed – my face gives me away straightaway. So, as we walk out after the meeting, he pulls me aside and says: 'We've got a lot of games coming up and I'm thinking of starting you on Saturday at West Brom because I think that'll be a more physical game for us.'

Fair enough. I get on well with the fella. I might not agree with all his decisions but I'm not going to rant and rave and fall out with him. I'll accept it. But I'm 35, I'm club captain, and I think I deserved to find out beforehand. If I was 17 then fair enough, but I've played nearly 600 League games. I was really excited. West Ham away is one of the biggest games of the season. Ben is going down with some of his friends, it would have been a chance to play at a really nice stadium against a good side, and my confidence is sky high after my goal. Most of the lads thought I'd start. I'm disappointed I'm not in the team, but even more in the way the gaffer's handled it. I feel a bit let down to be honest. And if Crouchy scores on Wednesday, will I really get a game on Saturday?

Babysitting duty this evening as all the wives and girlfriends go out for dinner and a show. The gaffer's missus is brilliant at organising trips like this for our partners. It's great, makes them feel included, part of the team. Maybe the gaffer should take a few tips from his missus!

Tuesday 14th

Did my good deed for the week today. My prize for winning last week's golf tournament was a lovely Wilson golf bag. I knew that Terry the kit man had had his eye on it and, seeing as I don't play that much, I gave it to him. I thought he was going to cry.

Wednesday 15th

Nationwide League Division One
West Ham United 1   **Norwich City 1**
Edworthy (og) 6   *Crouch 62*
Upton Park   Att: 31,308

The coach arrives at the hotel at Waltham Abbey on the outskirts of London at 11.30am. With relatively close evening games we always head off on the morning of the game and spend the afternoon in a hotel. Hucks is rooming with me but our room stinks, as if the cleaner had used our loo, so we decide we can't stay there and end up in a bigger room with two massive double beds. Must try that again.

Hotels usually lay on a buffet of chicken, spag bol, rice, etc for lunch and then we sleep until 4pm, before our usual walk around the grounds. Then I like to get to the stadium early, have a look at the programme (to see if anyone has come up with another way of saying 'veteran striker') and, if possible, have a bit of a wander round. It's not always possible. At home you obviously have the run of the place, but I remember playing for Leicester at Blackburn once when I'd got my mum and dad player's lounge tickets. I was in my tracksuit and asked a steward where the lounge was and he asked if I'd got a ticket. I said no and he said, in that case, I couldn't go in. I said: 'But I've just played out there! D'you not recognise me? Do you not have tellies or read newspapers or your programme? Surely the fact that I'm wearing a Leicester City tracksuit is a bit of a clue?'

He let me in.

I don't get a chance to test out the Upton Park stewarding tonight as, thanks to the London traffic, we don't arrive at the ground until 6.30pm, just over an hour before kick-off. I hate to rush before a game, so maybe it's as well I'm not starting. Who am I kidding? Upton Park has changed beyond recognition since I was last here with Leicester. It's a fantastic stadium with a great playing surface and I'm gutted I'm not going to be running out on it, especially as Ben's here with all his mates.

We do okay in the first half, backed by an incredible support of over 2,500 of our fans, who just don't stop singing. On six minutes Marc Edworthy scores his first goal for Norwich, but unfortunately it's in the wrong net. There wasn't much he could do about it though. Then Hucks goes off just before half-time with an ankle injury and Rivvo takes over up-front and does well, especially considering he's coming back from injury.

As I make my way back to the bench after half-time, the gaffer tells me 'get yourself going'. Excellent, I'm on here. So I go and warm up for five or ten minutes, look at the clock and see there are just 15 minutes of the second half gone, so I sit down. We completely dominate the second half and score when Harps sends a great ball over for Crouchy who meets it with an equally impressive header. We go mad on the bench and it feels like there's only one team going to win this game (that's us, by the way). Damo hits a post, we're creating chances and I can't wait to get on. Maybe if Crouchy tires. Yes, the gaffer's signalling to the bench. Oh: Mullers on for Harps. Ah well, still time.

I feel sorry for Easty, who is sat next to me on the bench. He knows I'll get on before him, so after the gaffer sends Mullers on he says: 'I might as well take my pads off and go for a bath then.'

I try and cheer him up but he's pretty down after being subbed as a sub at Wigan. He's always chirpy though.

'Hey, I got the biggest cheer of the afternoon,' he said when our fans cheered his number being held up on Saturday. I wish they wouldn't barrack him so much.

Ten minutes to go and the gaffer tells me to get ready. So I put my shin pads in, strip down to my shorts and shirt, freezing, waiting for the shout. The problem is the gaffer stands a few yards away from the bench and just gets so engrossed in the game. So I wait. And wait. To be fair, we're looking good. Two minutes to go. Am I going to get on? The gaffer gives me the signal, but the ball doesn't see it and stubbornly remains in play for another agonising 60 seconds. I finally get on, a full minute to make my mark. But now we've decided to make sure we leave with a point. We win two free-kicks in good positions out wide right at the end, but instead of putting the cross in Mullers and Marc keep the ball in the corner. Why do we do that? There's a minute to go, how often do you see the opposition break away and score in that situation? But the gaffer has told them to keep the ball up there and, to be fair, we'd have taken a point before the game.

So we just kill the game. The fans hate it, they go mad. It winds the opposition up and it bloody well frustrates me too. I'm on for 62 seconds and I don't touch the ball once. Afterwards the lads joke: 'Oh but you got your appearance money.'

But that doesn't bother me. I'd rather get 20–25 minutes and no appearance money. At least you get a chance to have an effect on the game then. If I start my appearance fee is £500. If I come off the bench and play it's half that, even if I only get on for a minute. So financially it is worth it, but that's not what you're thinking about when you're on the bench. In the dressing-room after Harps comes up and says: 'Fucking hell Robbo! Is the gaffer on half your appearance money or what?!'

I wish. If he got a fiver for every minute I'm on I might start two games in a row one day.

I know David James quite well from our days at Watford together so I get his shirt afterwards for Ben. David is a nice guy and signs it for him. I don't always swap shirts at the end but if you know someone really well you might ask them. I remember asking Tony Adams, who I've played against a few times, for his shirt after a friendly at Arsenal's training ground at London Colney.

'No problem,' he said, 'would you like this one or one with my name on it?'

I said I'd prefer one with his name and he said he'd send it up. Tony, mate, if you're reading this, it never arrived. You seem to be a really nice fella, so I'm sure you just forgot.

Most players are happy to swap. Not the Brazilians though. I played against them for Wales in Cardiff about four years ago. In that situation you give your shirts to the kit man and he takes them into the other dressing room and if they want to swap they do and if they don't they don't. None of them wanted to swap with us! On the pitch I'd gone up to Silvinho, who I'd also played with in this friendly with Arsenal, so he sort of knew me. But he said: 'I'm really sorry, but it's my international debut so I want to keep it.'

Which was fair enough. But by the time I looked round everyone else was off the pitch. I was gutted. Everyone wants a Brazil shirt, don't they? Three lads did manage to swap shirts: no surprise that Bellers was one of them. Must have been his pace . . .

I have got a few shirts though: Larsson when he was at Feyenoord, the Portuguese centre-half Couto, Koeman – not Ronald, though, the other one. One of my favourites is Rudi Voller's Germany shirt. I always thought he was outstanding, but, unfortunately, when we played Germany I was only on the bench. Gavin Maguire was marking Voller and got his shirt at the end, so afterwards I beat him up, mugged him and gave him my poxy German number 18 instead. Either that or I told him I was gutted, that Voller was one of my heroes and he just gave it to me.

'I'm not fussed, you can have it,' were his exact words.

I've only got about half of my Welsh shirts: I've given the rest away, either to family or for charity auctions. But I'd never give away my caps. I don't know whether it's the same with England, or whether the Welsh FA are just really hard up, but you don't get one for every game, you get one for the whole season. I've got five at home and I treasure them. It's the way they're made – red velvet with gold stitching. They're lovely. Shamefully I've only got one shirt on display: the others – and the caps – are festering away in a bag in the loft. I must dig them out and give them to Ben.

Thursday 16th

I am officially the 'Best Dad In The World'. Ben got back late from the game last night and at 7.10am this morning he's sitting, head in hands, miserably slopping his breakfast into his mouth when I casually toss David James's shirt onto the table (avoiding the milk naturally). His whole face just lights up. You live for moments like these.

It'll be interesting to see what the gaffer says tomorrow. If he says he's got to start Crouchy against West Brom because he scored yesterday then I'll be well pissed off and mention that I scored against Wigan. It's not as if there were just two days between the Wigan and West Ham games, it was 10 days later, so he couldn't argue that I would have been tired. It's always hard to drop someone when they've scored – impossible, even – but he did it to me. He keeps saying that if people take their chance they'll keep their place in the team. I took my chance and I'm out, so he's contradicting what he keeps telling us. It will make it harder to believe him next time.

I'm looking forward to taking Ben football training later . . . I could do with a game.

Friday 17th

Mum and Dad are coming to the game tomorrow so, touch wood, they'll get to see me playing again. I hope so. The West Brom fans hate me. But for some reason, touch wood, they're a team I've always done well against – whichever club I've been at I've always scored against them. Especially at their place: twice for Huddersfield, three times for Wolves. So the crowd will be wound up. I enjoy it. You must be doing something right if they're always on your back.

Unfortunately, when I pull into the Colney car park and see Hucks in jeans and T-shirt I know immediately that he's failed the fitness test on his ankle and won't be travelling.

It's a long old journey to the Copthorne Hotel in the centre of Birmingham. Luckily I have my usual stash of Haribo jellies, but make a conscious effort not to eat them. Because – whisper it – I might be playing tomorrow. Anyway, I've got a couple of packets of McCoys in my bag in case I get peckish. I share them with Mullers and Flem.

The boys all bring magazines and newspapers, sweets and crisps to share on these long, tedious away trips. Except Malky. He's fucking unbelievable. He's so sneaky. He'll buy mags but keep them in his bag until the journey back. So he'll read all the other boys' stuff on the way there, but on the way back he'll get out his own mags and read them. *OK! Hello* – all that sort of stuff. Yes, he is quite girly for a big, hulking centre-half. He spends ages blow-drying his hair just so, and he has all these creams . . .

Anyway, it really annoys Mullers that Malky won't share his mags with the rest of the lads but asks to read Mullers's *FHM*. So they end up chucking bottles of water at each other. Mullers squirts Malky. Malky goes to do it back but misses and it goes all over Steve Foley. Oh shit! Steve takes it well.

Malky and Mullers love each other really. It's daft, I suppose. Because we room together, stand naked in the shower together every day, spend hours on buses together, I probably know some of these players better than I do my own brother. Having said that, while I do wish Hucks was with us as we'll miss him tomorrow, tonight I'm glad he isn't – he snores like a train!

Saturday 18th

Nationwide League Division One
West Bromwich Albion 1   Norwich City 0
Koumas 35
The Hawthorns   Att: 24,966

Big news: I'm starting! With Hucks not playing I'm on my own up-front with Rivvo and Harps playing off me. Respect to the gaffer, he's as good as his word. And, to be fair to him, I am probably better suited to playing against West Brom than West Ham – it's going to be a battle because they're a big, physical team.

For the first 15–20 minutes I barely get a touch, and I'm just working my way into the game when, on 35 minutes, Jason Koumas scores a wonder-strike from 20 yards out. It's 1–0 to them but we're still looking good.

Five minutes later I've got the ball in the net myself. I hadn't been getting quite as much stick as I had expected from their fans, but I was still hearing plenty of 'Judas bastard' and 'Wolves scum'. So when the ball hits the back of the net I'm right in front of their fans and I'm about to go over to give it large with the old fingers behind the ears when I see the linesman flagging.

'Oh, you bastard!'

Offside. I look back at the fans and they are all laughing.

Then, just before half-time, I get booked. Me and Koumas are running towards the ball, he cuts across me, catches his ankle on my knee and goes flying. The linesman's flag is straight up.

'Are you fucking sure? Do you really think I meant to do that?'

'Well I think you meant it.'

'Excuse me? You think I meant it, you THINK!'

Initially the ref doesn't give it but then he comes over and awards the free-kick and says to me: 'Ah that's two now.'

'Two what?'

'Two fouls you've given away, so I'm booking you.'

Some refs you can talk to, some you can't. I've never had this fellow before and he is a typical schoolteacher type: 'No, you can't talk to me. I'm the boss.'

Thing is, if it's a foul then it should be a pen because it was in the box. Ha! My blood's boiling.

I run up to the ref when he blows for half-time. I'm only going to chat to him, but someone stops me. When we come back out for the second half he's standing with his assistants so I go across and shake hands. He says: 'No, we're all right Robbo, don't worry.'

As if!

In the second half I'm working hard and feeling good – even though my goal was disallowed it's given me a boost – when I glance over and see Crouchy warming up. I'm like: 'Fucking hell, there's only five minutes gone!'

If I was having a bad game I would have understood but I'm not. It affects your game when you see someone warming up: there's that sinking feeling and you know if you give the ball away or don't quite control it, you're off.

Time's up. I look over again and Crouchy's already stripped off. So, when the board with the number nine is held up I walk off slowly, only half-jogging when I near the touchline. I'm bitterly disappointed and I try not to let it show, but I think the gaffer knows I'm not happy. He can tell by the way I use my walk.

I just don't think it's being very fair. When I come on as a sub I'll get ten minutes if I'm lucky, whereas Crouchy gets 30 minutes. If it had been 70 minutes and it still wasn't happening and we were still 1–0 down I could accept it. But after 50–55, especially after my 62-second cameo at West Ham, I'm cheesed off. I grab a seat on the bench next to Easty. He'll understand.

West Brom go on to win 1–0 but at full-time they are booed off by their fans. We get a standing ovation from our 2,000-strong support. That says it all. I'd hate to play for West Brom because of the way they play. For most of the second half they couldn't get out of their half. Every time they got the ball they just banged it up front. Malky and Flem were outstanding at the back for us. They won their headers, we picked up nearly all the second balls and we were straight back at them. But if that style works for them, who am I to judge? When they got promoted two years ago I think they won 20 games 1–0. They are big lads, so you look at them and think there's only one way they're going to play. And I suppose they did win.

It all kicks off in the dressing room afterwards. The gaffer moans at Holty, accusing Jason Koumas of being stronger than him. Koumas, who's not the biggest of players, had won two or three balls and the gaffer is shouting: 'Fucking Jason Koumas! Fucking Jason KOUMAS winning tackles!'

Referring to one of the tackles, Holty retorts: 'It was a two-footed challenge.'

But that just makes things worse.

'Fucking two-footed challenge?'

It was a nasty challenge, and Holty's got a big gash on his ankle. Holty's honest, he wouldn't dream of doing that to somebody. He always goes in to try and win the ball but sometimes you have to be a bit cuter than that.

Then the gaffer has a bit of a pop at Easty for being a joker before the game – when he was just being his normal self. Then he bollocks us all for them being stronger as a team. I disagree. So does Harps. He throws down his boots and shouts at the gaffer that he's talking bollocks, which takes the gaffer aback a little. I try a more softly-softly approach.

'The reason they've won is because they've scored a wonder goal, their keeper's made a great save from Flem's shot and I've had a goal disallowed. But we've outplayed them for the second half, our fans have applauded us off and they've been booed off – that says it all. All right, there might have been instances in the first half where Koumas has won two or three tackles but that's not why they won.'

Mullers and Holty say their piece, too. The gaffer had gone bright red, ranting, raving and swearing. But he calms down and we talk about it and it's good. After we've all had our say, he takes a step back and thinks about it for a few seconds and all credit to him for taking on board what we said. It's good to get stuff out in the open, it shows we care.

Sunday 19th

We're in for training this morning – not a punishment for yesterday, but our usual post-match routine when we have a game the following Tuesday. It's a nice, easy warm-down to get the lactic acid out of our legs. The lads are in a good mood, despite the defeat. We think we were a bit unlucky not to get anything out of the game. I watch a video of my goal and am horrified and disgusted to discover that I was nowhere near being offside.

Spend a quiet evening glued to *Dream Team* and American football.

Monday 20th

Every day we vote for who we think was the worst player in training. The gaffer's got a yellow rugby shirt with a drawing of a baby in a nappy on the front and a donkey on the back. The worst trainer has to spend the next session wearing it, to the delight of his team-mates.

Young Jason Shackell gets it today but I think the gaffer is a bit upset by this – all morning he kept shouting to me: 'The yellow jersey's coming your way, big man!'.

But I scored three goals in the little game at the end and pulled myself out of the mire.

I find out from reading the local paper that I'm probably back on the bench for tomorrow; the gaffer's told the press that Crouchy will be starting. I haven't got a problem with not playing but I am slightly put out that I have to find out by reading the local rag.

Go to Chase and Eva's school parent evening and I'm proud to report they both get glowing reports – they must get that from their mum.

Tuesday 21st

Nationwide League Division One
Norwich City 2   **Derby County 1**
Roberts (pen) 81   *Taylor (pen) 61*
Mulryne 90
Carrow Road   Att: 16,346

It's a foul evening: swirling winds and torrential rain, but thankfully it holds off while we're warming up. I'm on the bench again as expected. Rivvo and Crouchy are up-front. Rivvo used to play up-front for Crewe and he did well there when he came on against West Ham, so I think the gaffer doesn't want to disrupt the team formation too much.

The Carrow Road crowd are really quiet tonight. It's not surprising, I guess, since we're not giving them anything to shout about. Derby could have been two or three up after 20 minutes. They hit the post and have a couple of half chances. We're just not at the races and I don't know why. Worryingly, it's not the first time it's happened this season. Then, just before half-time, Harps lunges in for a mad two-footed tackle on Argentinian defender Luciano Zavagno and is sent off. No complaints. And, as daft as it sounds, it's probably the best thing for us. It gets the crowd going, and all the players.

At half-time the gaffer decides to stick with the formation, leaving two up-front, which I think is very brave. He could quite easily have thought 'We're down to ten men so I'll take the point.' And in the second half every player lifts their game by 15 per cent – it just shows how fit we are as a squad. They take the lead from a penalty, but we still run and harry and win more second balls, despite being a man down. It's hard work for the two front boys because they have a lot of ground to cover and they look tired as the half progresses. I know I probably won't get on for more than 10–15 minutes but I make a point of carrying on warming up so the gaffer knows I'm ready whenever I'm needed. I normally go out, warm up for five minutes and sit back down, but I must have been out there for 20 minutes tonight before getting the nod with 16 minutes to go.

Again, it's another brave move by the gaffer. He's

bringing me and our young England U19 striker Ryan Jarvis on together. Jarve has an exceptional start. I set him up with a nice little one-two down the right-hand side and he takes it into the box with a great touch and shoots, but the keeper saves well. Then he makes a great little run down their left-hand side and tries to whip it back to me but it's cut out.

Then we win a penalty. A chance to salvage a point and keep our unbeaten home record intact. Just nine minutes to go. Rivvo has taken both our pens this season and scored both, but he's off. Lucky for me! I look round and none of the lads fancy it so I grab the ball. I'm feeling the pressure because with ten men you're know you're not going to create too many chances to get back in the game.

I'm talking to the ball as I slowly walk up and put it on the spot.

'Please go in, will you? Go in, go in, go in.'

I sound like Mrs Doyle from *Father Ted*. I missed one here about three years ago against Blackpool. Smashed it against the bar. And suddenly that's the only thing going through my mind.

'Don't hit the bar. Keep it low. Get over it, don't lean back.'

I point the arrow on the ball towards goal. I always put pens to the keeper's right, but I'm suddenly struck by a moment's indecision as I walk back to take my run-up. Shall I change? No, put it to his right. So I do. And he saves it. Shit! Head in hands time. Oh no. But hang on, what's this? The ref has blown his whistle for something. Says the keeper moved early. Yes! A chance to redeem myself. I go straight for the ball. Thankfully none of the lads come up and ask if I want them to take it: that would put more pressure on me.

But I don't feel as nervous this time. I make sure the

Mitre logo is facing me – I don't know why but I always do. Maybe it's because I'm so anal about being tidy. Then I make sure the little arrows are pointing north, south, east and west. As I walk back I'm feeling a little bit cocky. I'll show you this time. I won't miss this one. I put it straight down the middle and he dives. Keepers normally do – the majority of pens get put to either side and if the keeper just stands in the middle and the ball goes in the corner he looks a right idiot.

I'm relieved more than anything when the ball hits the back of the net. I've scored the goal that's got us back in the game. As soon as I hit it I knew. I saw him going early. I knew as soon as I made contact that I'd hit it well and I wasn't leaning back so it wouldn't go over. He dived the same way as he did for the first one, so if I'd stuck to my routine he'd have probably saved it again. To be honest the plan wasn't to go down the middle – it was just to smash it as hard as I could. If he'd saved it he'd have gone in with it.

I'm buzzing now. It's very close, but I think this goal may indeed be better than sex. All the boys rush over: Holty, Mullers, Damo, Jarve. The gaffer loves all the boys celebrating together. I run away to the crowd, banging my chest in relief, as if to say 'yep, the old ticker's still going!'

Scoring puts an extra yard in my stride and makes me sharper because I know I've done my job and I can relax a bit more. I love scoring in the first 5–10 minutes of a game for that reason. If you've gone a few games without a goal and you don't score in the first 30 minutes or so you get more tense, but then things bounce off you, you have a bad touch. Scoring chills me out straightaway, my touch is good and I'll try different things.

I look around and see that the Derby players are gone. They've had it, they're totally deflated, whereas we've got stronger as the game's gone on. We're still going for it. In the 90th minute Damo heads the ball down to me and I manage to get in front of the defender and lay the ball off to Eddy. In turn, he makes a great run and picks out Mullers on the edge of the box. Me and Eddy both follow the ball in – Mullers has his back to goal so it would be easy for him to lay it off to one of us – but instead he turns and shoots. As soon as I see the ball leave his foot I know it's a goal. I go running straight to the fans, giving it loads, before suddenly pulling up and thinking I'd better go and celebrate with Mullers. Well, it was him who scored! By now, everybody bar Malky, Flem and Greeno has come up celebrating. I give Eddy high-fives and Damo a cuddle for putting me in with the header. We never kiss. Well, no tongues, anyway. You'd get a slap. I might snog Mullers after in the dressing room though!

As if this game isn't mad enough: in the last minute Zavagno punches the ball into our net from a corner. To concede an equaliser now would be disastrous. I'm a bit panicked for a second as some of their players are celebrating but a split-second later I see the ref's not giving it. It was blatant. Hand of God 2! I wouldn't do that. I'm just glad the ref was in a decent position. Two seconds later the whistle goes and, with the surreal way this game is going, I half-expect the ref to abandon play due to a spaceship landing behind me, but no, it's the final whistle.

Absolutely everybody's in the dressing room after: the lads who haven't played, all the staff. Everyone's congratulating everyone else, giving it high-fives, loads of noise. I shake the hands of everyone who's played, as does Holty and the gaffer says:

'Second half was different class, boys. You worked your bollocks off. The fitness came through again, but you've got to start playing from the first minute. You can't keep hoping your second half performance will bring you through, otherwise you'll get a slap in the face at some point.'

I switch on my phone to find hundreds of texts from my, er, mates, saying they thought my arse was twitching on the pen. Yes lads, it was! Steve Foley says I showed loads of character taking the second one. Loads of character and not looking at the fans: I think I might have asked someone else to take it if I'd seen their faces . . .

The gaffer doesn't want anyone going out on the town before our home game against Sunderland on Saturday, so I head straight home for a sandwich – ham on white with butter, since you're asking – and a bottle of Lucozade.

Julie tells me she didn't watch the penalty. Well, she watched the first one, but for the second she buried her head in her hands. It's hard for her: she knows what I'm going through. After Derby's penalty tonight Ben said: 'Well, that was a pants penalty!'

Julie said: 'What d'you mean?'

'Well, he blasted it straight down the middle!'

So, when I retook my penalty, Julie asked him:

'So where did your dad put it this time?'

'He just blasted it straight down the middle!'

'So was that a pants penalty then, Ben?!'

Ben went a bit quiet.

'No no, it was the best one taken, Mum.'

Watch the pen again on *Sky News*. Yeah, he definitely moved too early! At about 12.30am I try to go to bed, but I'm still buzzing, so I get up again and watch the Major League Baseball final. I love basketball and American football, but I don't really understand baseball. It passes a couple of hours though before I eventually calm down enough to sleep.

Wednesday 22nd

Wake up at 7am because I can't wait to read the papers. We get *The Sun* and *Evening News* delivered but because I scored Julie will get up and buy the *Eastern Daily Press (EDP)*.

The papers are full of George Burley moaning about the re-taken penalty, but the keeper, Lee Grant, must have moved because the first one was a decent pen, right in the corner. He's not the biggest lad in the world and for him to get that far he must have come a little bit forward. If Greeno had saved Taylor's pen and they'd given him a chance to take it again, Burley wouldn't have complained.

These things really do tend to even themselves out. For the disallowed goal I scored against West Brom I was half a yard onside. It was a perfectly good goal and would have put me one closer to the magic 100 goals mark.

I'm not really worrying about that at the moment, there are still 32 games left so I've got a fair chance of getting the nine I need. I've started four games – only finished two though – and scored three goals, so I'm delighted at the moment. If I can keep plugging away hopefully I'll be quite close. I think I'll do it. I feel so much better confidence-wise than last year. Last year was not a grind exactly, but it was hard work and I didn't really enjoy my football. Things didn't happen for me. This year the new boys have given everybody a lift, especially Hucks. Playing with him has done me the world of good.

If anything, the papers today are too kind to us. They say we deserved the three points, which I think is a little harsh on Derby – they played well and if it wasn't for Greeno we could have quite easily lost the game. A point would have been a fair result, but I don't think we could have complained if we hadn't got anything out of the game. They outplayed us in the first half and they still had a few chances in the second.

We're just not starting games at the right tempo. We chat about it in training this morning, after watching the first 15 minutes of last night's game on video. We didn't get close to their players, they won most of the second balls – in the first half they won 39 and we won 29 – and we didn't turn them enough in the first 15 minutes. If you turn them and have them running back towards their own goal, you get throw-ins in the final third. We didn't really put many passes together and the service to the front two has got to be better. Most of the balls they played into their striker Daniele Dichio were played into his chest, so there was no way Malky was going to win them: if he or Flem had tried it would have been a free-kick. But we just floated the ball in to our front men, which is a hard ball for a centre-forward to either bring down or flick on because you're running backwards while the centre-half's coming forwards to meet the ball.

We've got to lift it all over the pitch, not just from half-time. Hucks says he thought we showed Derby too much respect. We're a better team than Derby, we've got better players; the League table doesn't lie. We should have been at them from the first minute, especially because we were on our own patch and with the home record we've got. We sat off them. Watched them. We should have rattled into them. You have to earn the right to play and we're not doing that at the minute. We're just turning up and expecting things to happen. Giving the ball to Hucks or Rivvo and waiting. They can't beat three or four men every time they go on a run so we all need to lift our game. Mullers says no-one was making themselves available. We like to pass the ball in little triangles but there was none of that until the second half. At the minute we're getting away with it, but the gaffer leaves us in no doubt about what's expected Saturday: he wants us to turn up the heat for the opening 15 minutes and really fire the crowd up.

Thursday 23rd

My two little princesses have gone to the ball. Well, school disco. Dressed to the nines. They look so grown-up I half think they might be heading to Time, a local nightclub. They've been yabbering on about which boys from year six they like. I'm dreading the time when they're old enough to date.

I take Ben to training as usual. I know there are lads out there on the pitch who watch me play on a Saturday and while I'm standing there watching tonight I think: 'I bet you really give me stick on a Saturday, and here I am watching you play now and you're absolutely hopeless. You sit there howling at me every Saturday but just look at the state of you!'

I hate it when people come up and say: 'You should have scored today!'

'Yeah,' I think, 'and I'll come and watch you do your job tomorrow!'

Friday 24th

Great news. Hucks has declared himself fit to start tomorrow so he'll be the only change to the side that beat Derby. I sound out the gaffer and his assistant, Dougie Livermore, about the vacant youth team coaching job. I really fancy it, as I enjoy working with the young lads we have at the club. They ask my advice and confide in me and I like that. The gaffer is honest and says he thinks it will go to someone with a bit more experience, but tells me to give my CV to the Academy director Sammy Morgan. Fine, except I haven't got a CV, so I'll have to butter up Julie to help me put one together on the computer.

Actually, I think the job might be a bit too early for me anyway. I did say this could be my last season, but I'm really enjoying my training and football at the moment and there's a real buzz around the club which is great to be a part of. In an ideal world I'd be offered another contract here when my current one runs out next June and then take a coaching role after that. I'd love to stay here for the rest of my life. But that's in an ideal world . . .

America's still in the back of my mind, although I still haven't talked to the gaffer about it yet. I'll leave it until the New Year. I don't want to play in the Second or Third Division because it's a lot more physical and I'm getting slower with every year. I don't want to have to prove myself and win people over all over again. Of course, that's the risk with the US too, but the majority of players out there are in their mid-thirties. There's a different outlook. If I was struggling in games then I would definitely consider hanging up my boots. But I'm not, and, sure, a new contract could mean another season of coming on for ten minutes, but a coaching job could be my life for the next ten years. Decisions, decisions.

I think about stopping playing quite a lot. I'll be sad because it's been my life for 18 years. It'll be strange. I've been talking about it with Mike Milligan and Neil Adams and they really miss the dressing room banter. It'll be like coming out of the Army and having to live on civvy street. I'll have to adapt. We footballers are weird people. Quite thick-skinned.

I think people are very wary of footballers, especially in big groups: they get the wrong impression and think we're all big-time Charlies. But it's not like that – at least not here, we're more like an extended family. I see the boys every day. We fall out, but next minute it's all forgotten and we're laughing about it. We don't hold grudges; you can't. It would be daft. If I thought Malky was at fault for the goal on Saturday I'd tell him. We can't fall out about it, it's just my opinion.

It would be so strange playing on the same team as someone you detested, who you wouldn't even give the time of day to. I've heard about feuds at other clubs, but it's never happened to me and I can't imagine that here. I've seen fights in training and in the dressing room – but it's all heat of the moment stuff: passions run high. I remember Marshy (Andy Marshall) and Mullers having a fight a few years ago after the first game of the season away to Barnsley. Mullers blamed Marshy for a goal and Marshy wasn't having it so they started having fisticuffs and we all jumped in. But the next day it was all forgotten.

I feel I could say anything to people like Malky, Mullers, Alex, most of the lads really. Having said that, I'd never tell them I was depressed or down. I suppose you just have to get on with it. I'd never turn up and say I was feeling a bit under the weather either. I used to confide a lot in Peter Grant, especially that first season when I was having a bad time. He was a smashing fellow. I got on really well with him and his family. He'd been there, seen it, done it, everybody had so much respect for him. It's that closeness I'll miss most. It'll be the end of an era when I stop and I'm dreading it; it'll be like chopping my hand off. It actually scares me more than turning 40.

Court's in session today and Easty's in the dock for not bringing cakes in on his birthday on October 1st, surprise surprise. His pockets are so deep we expect him to fish a lump of coal out of them. He has absolutely no defence (even if we'd been interested in listening) and is fined £20. The Fridge goes before the court for putting one of the pain-relieving machines on Hucks' good leg (sound familiar?), and his assistant, Peter Shaw, is up for putting a machine on Cricht's leg and forgetting to switch it on! Both somehow manage to plead their case and escape with warnings.

I am dreading tomorrow as Julie and the kids are off to Euro-Disney. To have fun and eat loads of sweets. Without me. For five whole days!

Saturday 25th

Nationwide League Division One
Norwich City 1   **Sunderland 0**
Francis 32
Carrow Road   Att: 16,427

Drop the family at the train station at 8.30am and run down the platform waving to them until I run smack into a post. It looks like I did it for a joke but, to be honest, I never saw the bloody thing! The kids appreciate my 'deliberate clowning' and almost wet themselves laughing. Chase seems tough but she cried her eyes out at leaving her daddy. I could tell Eva and Ben were upset but they didn't want to upset me by showing it. I wish I could have gone; I'm already looking forward to picking them up on Wednesday night.

Anyway, must focus on this afternoon's game. It's a big test for us as Mick McCarthy has really turned Sunderland around and we've still got our 100 per cent home record to protect. I watch Wales beat Italy in the rugby World Cup to take my mind off things. I love the game and used to play for North Wales at under-18 level but switched to football as rugby's a bit rough for me! Phone Julie to check they've arrived safe at Heathrow. Now I can prepare for the game.

We take the gaffer's advice on board and start well, deservedly taking the lead through a cracking left-foot drive from Damo. It must have been even sweeter for him as the gaffer was taking the piss out of him before the game, asking when he'd last scored. Ah, the gaffer's old mind games work again.

The crowd are brilliant, really getting behind us. I only get seven minutes, so I can't really do a great deal. I feel under a bit of pressure as we're only 1–0 up and they're pegging us back a bit and if you make a mistake they might get an equaliser. If you come on when you're losing there's no pressure, just the potential to be the hero. I almost get a chance – which would have been a carbon copy of my goal against Burnley – when Hucks squares the ball to me but it's just cut out by the centre-half. I do manage to get myself booked though.

Earlier on, one of their players got injured so we put the ball out. For some reason the ref decides to restart the game with a drop ball, which their left-back Julio Arca should have just kicked back to us, but he took it and started running. Mullers never even made any effort to try and win the drop ball, as he thought – like everyone else in the stadium – that he'd give it back to us. To be fair to Mick McCarthy someone in the crowd shouted that to him and he turned round, looked apologetic and said: 'I'm not playing out there, am I?'

So I said if I got on I'd have to try to leave a bit on him in revenge – which I do with a crunching tackle. So that's my third booking of the season: two more and I'm suspended. I'm going to have to try and get them in for Christmas! Not really. I'm not clever enough to work out when I need to get booked to ensure I can't play Boxing Day. I know some players who have done it, but I've never missed a Boxing Day or New Year's Day match.

Arca was all right actually. I've played against him a few times, so I had a chat with him as I came on and he said 'You all right Robbo?' 'Fine thanks, mate, and you?' 'Ooh I'm breathing out my arse,' he said (nice to see an Argentinian with such a good grasp of the language). I said: 'You was first half 'n' all, weren't you?' He said: 'Yeah, I couldn't believe it – we played half-decent for ten minutes and then all of a sudden we're 1–0 down!' You have to take people how you find them and he's always been good with me. Still had to take him out though!

In the dressing room after we're all buzzing. That's seven wins out of seven at home. Long may it continue. Right, I'm off to get slaughtered.

Sunday 26th

Ouch. Got in at 2.15 this morning. The clocks went back too. But I still leap out of bed at 7.30am to check the papers, and there it is in black and white – we're third in the League, two points off top spot. Nobody's running away with the division at the moment, so if we keep working hard we should hopefully stay in the top six and make it into the dreaded play-offs.

Mick McCarthy's as good as gold in the papers. He says we're a good side, with a great home record and at the end of day we deserved the three points because we were better than them. I love people like that. I played against Mick when he was at Barnsley and Man City and he was a hard man, but a really nice fella. He's the sort of man I would love to play for because of how he is and how he talks about his players. Yesterday I was coming out of the physio room and he was in the middle of sorting out some tickets but he took time out to have a chat.

'You still carrying on? Playing well?'

I spend the morning ringing little Alex to see what he's doing but his mobile's off and he's still in bed at 2pm. Eventually I drag him out to the Rushcutters for a bite to eat and some hair of the dog. This single life's not all it's cracked up to be. It's too much like hard work.

I phone Julie four times. Yes, they are having a great time without me.

Monday 27th

The first team are off today and the gaffer very kindly gives me the day off too – I thought I'd have to be in training as I'm playing the first half in the reserve game against Spurs tomorrow.

So I take a little trip into the city to pick up a watch and, let's be honest, bask in the glory of people still buzzing about the game. Well, might as well enjoy it now as shopping is a 'mare when you've lost.

I spend the afternoon trying to buy some sleep from Sainsburys, before my old friend David comes to stay with me as he's playing in my friend Philip Browne's golf day tomorrow – as I would be if I wasn't playing for the reserves. Lucky sod.

We have a quiet night in with a takeaway talking football and golf. I can't face alcohol. I hate drinking in the house anyway, so I could never be an alcoholic. I won't even have a Bud watching football. I think drinking's boring unless it's a party or a night out. Julie and I just have squash or Lucozade.

Tuesday 28th

I would so much have preferred to have trained with the lads for a couple of hours this morning. Instead I have to wait until 12.30pm for the Spurs reserve game. But I suppose the gaffer wants me to get my match pace. I haven't played a full game since Wigan, more than three weeks ago.

Despite myself, I enjoy the match. We draw 1–1 and I get a good sweat on. Then when Dave gets back from the golf we head for a great pub called the Garden House for some food and a few drinks. It's probably just as well I didn't play today: Dave and I are very competitive and have had some right battles on the golf course and tennis court. He has beaten me at golf, but never at tennis. Ever.

The other reason I'm delighted I didn't play (yeah, right) is that I won the competition two years ago and my prize was having to get up and sing the first song on the karaoke. I hate anything like that where I have to stand up in front of a room full of people I don't really know. I'd much rather play at the Millennium Stadium in front of 80,000. If it had been left up to me, I'd have sung Tom Jones' *The Green Green Grass of Home*. But it wasn't. I had to sing *These Boots Are Made For Walking* and believe me I proved that not all Welshmen are born singers. The next year someone told me: 'If you par this hole you've got a good chance of winning'.

So I bogeyed. They reckon I did it on purpose. They were right.

Wednesday 29th

What's worse than having a hangover? Having a mate with a hangover staying with you. Bleurgh! We're both up early though as I can't lie-in and Dave has to get off back to Leeds. Rather him than me. Oh, hang on, I've got to drive to Heathrow to pick up Julie and the kids at 10pm.

I set off at 3pm and get there at 7pm – you could say I'm looking forward to seeing them. At the airport I suddenly realise I haven't eaten all day so I head straight for the healthy option – two KFC chicken sandwiches and chips. Not ideal for a professional athlete, but my stomach is in a hurry. Then I grab a couple of hours' kip back in the car before seeing my pride and joy walk through arrivals. Ben's first: all manly hugs now he's 12. Kisses and cuddles from all the girls though. It was worth the wait.

Thursday 30th

I should be knackered after getting home at around 1am, but training is excellent this morning. The lads are all very sharp and the session's enjoyable and high-quality. The gaffer gives us his usual Thursday morning 'I don't want you lot getting complacent' bollocking. No chance of that. We all want to keep our unbeaten run going, even if it is only two games. We could be top of the League come quarter to five Saturday if other results go our way.

Friday 31st

Ho hum. Yet another visit to Birmingham's Copthorne hotel, our venue of choice when we play a Midlands side. We arrive after four-and-a-half back-wrenching hours on the coach.

Marc Edworthy isn't fit so Harps goes to see the gaffer and says: 'I played right-back for Portsmouth last year a few times, so if you're struggling for a right-back I can play there. I don't mind.' The gaffer says: 'Thanks very much. That's what I want to hear.'

Then he announces that Gary Holt will be right-back, so it's obviously a case of 'Thanks very much but you stay where you are!' It was a good gesture on Harps' part though and one which shows our team spirit.

The gaffer tells me I'm on the bench tomorrow. I'm really looking forward to it as I know a lot of Walsall's players and their manager Colin Lee. Colin was my last manager at Watford and sold me to Huddersfield for £250,000 all those years ago. We fell out at the time, but have since buried the hatchet. We got on well when he was my coach at Leicester and at Wolves and it'll be good to see him again. In fact, it's a bit of an ex-Wolves' reunion: it will be great to see Neil Emblen again. He's probably my best mate in the game, having played with him at Wolves and then Norwich. I'm also good friends with Simon Osborn, even though I only played with him for a year at Wolves. And, of course, I'm looking forward to catching up with Steve Corica. My mum and dad are coming to the game too, so I'm going to be very busy.

It's an early night for me, as I feel as though I have the flu coming on. I had a flu jab after last week's game and there's always a small amount of the bug in the jab, so hopefully that's it.

Nationwide League Division One

Pos	Name	P	HOME					AWAY					GD	PTS
			W	D	L	F	A	W	D	L	F	A		
1	West Bromwich Albion	15	6	0	2	13	6	4	1	2	10	7	+10	31
2	Wigan Athletic	16	5	3	0	9	4	3	3	2	12	9	+8	30
3	**Norwich City**	**15**	**7**	**0**	**0**	**14**	**5**	**1**	**4**	**3**	**7**	**10**	**+6**	**28**
4	Sheffield United	15	4	1	2	14	7	4	2	2	10	9	+8	27
5	Sunderland	15	5	2	1	10	4	3	1	3	9	7	+8	27
6	West Ham United	15	3	5	0	10	5	4	1	2	8	5	+8	27
7	Ipswich Town	16	5	2	1	18	8	3	1	4	11	14	+7	27
8	Nottingham Forest	15	4	2	2	17	7	3	1	3	11	11	+10	24
9	Reading	15	4	2	2	13	9	3	1	3	10	9	+5	24
10	Millwall	16	5	2	1	12	5	1	4	3	8	11	+4	24
11	Crewe Alexandra	15	5	1	2	12	8	1	2	4	5	11	-2	21
12	Cardiff City	14	3	2	1	12	3	2	3	3	11	12	+8	20
13	Preston North End	15	4	1	2	12	8	2	1	5	8	11	+1	20
14	Walsall	15	4	2	1	12	6	1	2	5	5	10	+1	19
15	Coventry City	14	3	2	2	10	9	2	2	3	11	12	0	19
16	Burnley	15	3	1	3	11	10	2	3	3	12	18	-5	19
17	Watford	14	2	4	2	10	9	2	0	4	6	8	-1	16
18	Stoke City	15	3	3	1	10	7	1	1	6	7	13	-3	16
19	Crystal Palace	15	2	3	3	11	12	2	1	4	9	12	-4	16
20	Gillingham	15	3	1	3	8	10	1	3	4	6	13	-9	16
21	Derby County	16	1	2	5	9	16	2	3	3	7	12	-12	14
22	Rotherham United	16	2	3	3	5	9	0	4	4	5	16	-15	13
23	Bradford City	15	1	1	6	7	15	2	2	3	7	10	-11	12
24	Wimbledon	15	1	1	5	10	18	1	0	7	5	19	-22	7

NOVEMBER

Saturday 1st

Nationwide League Division One

Walsall 1   **Norwich City 3**
Birch 9   *Henderson 52*
                       McVeigh 60
                       Crouch 64
Bescot Stadium   Att: 8,331

God I feel rough. My body aches, my throat is sore and my head hurts. Marc Edworthy and Keith Briggs have missed the trip due to flu, but I'm not going to let it stop me from taking my place on the bench. I do feel a bit daft getting off the coach at the Bescot Stadium, though, as I'm laden down with presents from Julie for Simon and Embo's kids.

I'm actually quite happy to be on the bench today as it means I can spend ages chatting to Embo. Sorry, warming up. Out on the pitch our lads are absolutely brilliant, as are our fans, but we still go in at half-time 1–0 down, thanks to one man, their keeper James Walker.

At half-time the gaffer is calm: 'I've nothing to say, boys. Just keep playing like that in the second half and we'll win.'

How right he is. It's a pleasure to sit on the bench and watch us play the second half. We are outstanding. We don't panic, we keep patiently passing the ball, creating chances and our movement's great. But now I'm itching to get on because I know there are goals out there. We are creating so many chances that I know I've got at least half a chance of getting on the scoresheet. We score three excellent goals – Hendo, Squiz and Crouchy – and it's only their keeper who stops us from getting seven or eight.

The gaffer finally tells me to get myself warm so I go for a 25-minute gas with Embo before suddenly realising there's only five minutes to go. Then, just before the gaffer can take Crouchy off, he gets sent off for a second bookable offence, so he takes Hucks off and chucks me on for four minutes.

And in that four minutes I score a hat-trick! Oh all right, I get a couple of touches. You can't really do anything in that amount of time, but when you're 3–1 up you've got nothing to lose either, so you do try stuff you normally wouldn't – a little trick rather than just an easy lay-off. Not something like a bicycle kick, that's not in my locker. The only time I've ever pulled one of those off was in training at Watford, when I was 18 or 19, and it flew into the top corner. I'd never try it now. I'd have to go up in stages and probably break my back landing. Crouchy's good at it – I've seen him do it three or four times in training.

I think he was a bit unlucky to get sent off, but it might be good news for me . . .

Sunday 2nd

Spend a rowdy morning cheering on Wales against New Zealand in the rugby. We've got England in the quarter-finals. Bring it on! Ben's game is cancelled due to a waterlogged pitch. The lads are all disappointed, but us parents are all delighted we won't have to stand out in the pissing rain and can watch Leicester take on Blackburn instead.

Like all my previous clubs, except for Wolves, I still have a bit of a soft spot for Leicester. Mostly because of Brian Little. He signed me from Huddersfield and when Julie and I first went to see him to talk about a possible deal, he totally charmed us. We came out of the meeting and Julie said: 'Oh, you just have to sign for him, he's lovely.' I consider my current gaffer a good mate and have so much respect for him, and still get on really well with Mike Walker and Bruce Rioch, but I would have to say that Brian was the nicest man I ever played for. That's probably my only criticism of him: he was maybe a bit too nice. He was so softly spoken and just didn't have it in him to ever shout at anybody. I remember making my Leicester debut at home to Wolves. By half-time we were 2–0 down and we got booed off and I thought 'Fuck, what have I signed up for here?' We're all sat in the dressing room and I'm thinking 'Shit. He's going to go mad.' I'm waiting for the tea-cups to start spinning. He turns to us and says: 'Listen lads, I'm going to do something now that I don't like doing . . .' (Just get it over with, will you?) He points and says: 'You two boys come off and have a rest. I'm going to put these two boys on, okay?' That was it. He made two substitutions, didn't shout, didn't lose his cool at all. I was amazed. But you know what? We went out in the second half and worked our way back into the game and I scored twice on my debut to get the draw. He was very clued up on his football too. If anything he preferred the long ball, but I think that was more to do with the personnel we had – it probably suited us better. Anyway, his style must have worked because we got promoted twice while I was there. He will always be one of my favourite memories.

Monday 3rd

I'm very jealous this morning as the lads who played on Saturday get a morning off to relax at Greens. The rest of us join the youth team and Webby for a good session, despite the usual Arctic gale. I'm feeling great when I see my good friend Terry the kit man carrying a pair of extra-long tracksuit bottoms. After six years with Norwich City I still have to wear my own tracky bottoms to away games as the club ones are too short for me. So I'm thinking 'Fantastic, I'm finally getting my own pair.' But Terry tells me they're for Crouchy. What? I've been here, sweating blood for this club for six years, and he's been here six weeks and he gets a pair! Terry looks very embarrassed.

Julie started her part-time job today helping out at the club's warehouse in the run-up to Christmas. She's a diamond and has done everything from working on a market stall to being a hairdresser. Apparently she bumped into Terry in the afternoon and saw Crouchy's tracksuit bottoms so she gave him a piece of her mind too. I swear I had nothing to do with it.

In the evening me, Malky, Holty and Mullers attend the Fans' Forum at Acle. The club are very good – they do regular roadshows all over the county and always take a board director, a commercial guy and a few players to meet the fans. These events can be a bit hairy, but as we're doing well this season there are no awkward questions: everyone just wants pictures and autographs, which we sign until our wrists break 90 minutes later. Thankfully no-one asks me to take my teeth out for a photo. It really bugs me when fans ask that. 'Do you want to paint a clown face on me as well?' I'll happily whip them out if they want me to have a picture with their kid who's lost his or her front teeth as well. I don't mind that.

Tuesday 4th

It's the gaffer's birthday today so he brings in the obligatory cream cakes for all – although it has to be said they are a bang average selection.

Old age hasn't mellowed him, though – he's furious this morning and rightly so. He sets very high standards and expects everyone to keep them but the young lads have let their standards slip and haven't cleaned the dressing, physio or weight rooms for the last few days. All players have to do these sorts of jobs, it's part and parcel of your apprenticeship. But the gaffer only has to shout once. A couple of hours later we could eat our dinners off the floors, they are that spotless.

The gaffer's very tidy. There's a table in the middle of the changing room at Colney and people always leave always loads of crap on it. He hates that, so before his meeting every morning he clears all the stuff off. So me and Crichts have been putting everything on there over the last few days: skips, hangers, dirty washing. He's not cottoned on yet. The gaffer's like a little old lady: if there's a piece of paper on the floor he has to pick it up and put it in the bin, he has to tidy up and dust things off.

The lads are getting on The Fridge's nerves. He's losing it a little bit. Malky, Flem, Crichts and Mullers wind him up every day. They squeeze his shoulder and ask him if he's all right. He hates it. Malky strokes his shoulder and he flips. So Mullers strokes his other one, saying 'Don't be like that.' This afternoon The Fridge loses it and walks out. He sits in the canteen for 30 minutes and doesn't start treatment until 2pm, an hour later than normal.

All hell breaks loose this afternoon. After walking Molly I sit down to read the *Evening News* which has a massive story saying that Hucks won't be staying after his loan runs out. His agent is quoted saying: 'Let's be realistic about this. Darren is a player with Premiership aspirations and unless the club can guarantee him Premiership football then he's never going to stay – that dictates everything. And unless they are playing Premiership football then they won't be able to afford him. I don't think any

team in Division One could afford him.' Asked about
Hucks saying he'd really like to sign for us, his agent is
quoted as saying: 'Obviously he's going to say that. He's
not going to bite the hand that feeds him.' I'm just thinking 'That's a bit harsh' when Hucks rings.

'All right, mate? Have you seen the paper? I just came
out of Sainsbury's and saw the billboard and went 'fucking hell'.'

He's furious so he asks me if I've got the gaffer's number
so he can set the record straight. Julie gets on really well
with the gaffer's wife Sandra, so she has the number.
Hucks is really shocked; some of the things that were
said were well out of order.

I meet up with him and Harps later to watch the Man
U v Rangers game and he tells me he's had a right go at
his agent and phoned the *Evening News* to put his side
of the story.

It's not a mad night – we've got another big game
Saturday against Millwall – so we just have a couple of
pints and head home soon after the final whistle.

Wednesday 5th

Day off. Spend £80 on the last fireworks left in the city
(£80 for five minutes!) and have coffee with Julie in the
warehouse.

There's a big article in the *Evening News* today by
Hucks. 'I was upset with the comments that were made
by my agent yesterday,' he says. 'He's got his opinions
about where he wants me to be but at the end of the day
I will decide where I want to go, not my agent. I also
think it's an insult to say that Norwich City aren't a big
enough club to sign me. No player is bigger than the club
in my opinion.' And he goes on. 'Why wouldn't I want to
sign for a club that's two points off the top of the First

Division? We're playing well and me and the missus like it here.'

I feel really sorry for him. Obviously Darren's agent wants him to play at the highest level he can, but who's to say he won't be playing in the Premiership with Norwich next year?

Fans are always asking me whether we're going to sign him. Hucks himself has told me on many occasions that he just wants to be happy where he's playing and how much he loves it here. He settled in straightaway, he gets on with everyone, he loves the club, the fans love him and he's not even been here two months. That's a massive part of being a successful player. If people take to you it relaxes you and gives you confidence. I think Harps would love to sign too. Crouchy's settled in well, but I think he wants to have another crack at Villa. He's young and has had a taste of the Premiership. Plus we don't know whether Villa would let him sign for us, even if he wants to – they must have had decent reports on him playing for us and they're down among the dead men right now and haven't scored many. They may need him.

But I'm pretty sure Hucks wants to stay. He knows he'd have to take a big wage drop and he's prepared to. He just wants to be happy. He doesn't think he'll play for Man City again while Kevin Keegan is manager, and he doesn't want to have to go back there and train with the youth and reserves like he was doing before.

But there are all sorts of rumours flying around that Wigan also want to sign him and that they're willing to offer him £20,000 a week. I don't know what he's on at Man City: I heard it was £18,000 a week, and I guess he'd have to cross that bridge if it came to it. But I think he really wants to be here, where he knows he can be happy and appreciated. He's been at Man City for three years and not been playing; he's been training all week and not getting anything at the end of it. Here, he trains every day knowing he's got a game to look forward to at the end of week. He wants to play. His wife's settled here too. She loves it and gets on really well with the other wives, which is a massive help. It's very hard to focus on your game if you feel responsible for your family's unhappiness.

I think the board have got to realise we've got a better chance of getting promotion if they can keep Hucks, Crouchy and Harps here until the end of season. But you can't expect the club to push the boat out too far. There are plenty of clubs who have done that and are now struggling financially. Norwich were 24 hours away from bankruptcy when Delia and Michael first took over and they (and the rest of the board) have worked very hard to ensure we're never in that situation again. Some clubs, like Leicester and Ipswich, have been caught short by paying Premiership wages to their stars and then going into administration when they are relegated back into the First Division. The thing is, administration has enabled them to wipe out their debts and start spending heavily again, which gives them a huge advantage over the other clubs in the First Division, like us, who are struggling to spend within our means.

Having said that, this year no one team is running away with the division. It's up for grabs and you have to speculate to accumulate. We've played the majority of the top teams and have nothing to fear from them. I think we have as strong a squad as anyone in the division now. We had a decent chance when we got to the play-offs two years ago, but I think we've got a better chance this year if we can keep this team together.

It's a scary equation, but life's a risk. It's easy for me – it's not my money. It's easy for any Norwich supporter to say 'We've got to sign Hucks.' It's not their responsibility.

But this is a very, very well-run club. They've got some very good people in charge who, first and foremost, will make sure that this club is still going to be here in 50 years' time. In an ideal world Hucks will stay, Crouchy will go back, I'll get back in the team, get my 100 goals and we'll get promoted!

So, back to the fireworks – this time in the back garden. God, it's scary. I'm not the most safety-conscious of men. The fireworks are falling over, flying everywhere, landing mostly on the pile of dry leaves I'd swept up that morning. The catherine wheel falls off the fence and goes running round the garden. Of course, the more danger involved the more the kids love it, especially Ben.

'Brilliant. Do that again, Dad!'

Thursday 6th

Our summer signing, Canadian international Jim Brennan, trains today for the first time after injury, which is great to see and a real boost. He's a good player.

Then the gaffer calls us together to go through Millwall's team for Saturday and tells us Kevin Muscat will be playing so hopefully I'll get ten minutes. The thing with Muscat is he's such an aggressive player that you can quite easily get him sent off.

The gaffer says he's not sure if Andy Roberts will play, which is my cue for a bit of brown-nosing (oh God, I'm just as bad as Malky!). I get on really well with Robbo, who played for us on loan from Wimbledon a couple of seasons ago, and spoke to him yesterday, so I happen to know Robbo thinks he's going to start.

Actually, I get quite a bit of inside info from friends on opposing teams. Subtly, of course. I'll go all round the houses, round the world, to get it. I'll start with something like: 'So, will you be warming up with me tomorrow, mate?'

'Oh no mate, I'm starting.'

If he's not playing I'll say: 'What's he making changes for when you won on Saturday . . . surely he's got to play same team?'

And he'll fall right into the trap. 'Oh no, so-and-so's playing here, so-and-so's playing there . . .'

The gaffer tells us that Millwall manager Dennis Wise has been on the radio in London, saying: 'We've got Norwich Saturday, they're a good side at home, with their 100 per cent record, but they're a nice team.'

Nice? Nice! He's calling us soft. So the gaffer has marked our cards. We're fired up as he intended. Whether Wise actually said that or not I have no idea . . .

Friday 7th

The Fridge-baiting is reaching new levels. This morning he was giving Marc Edworthy a hamstring massage when Malky walked in and started touching him and The Fridge stopped work immediately.

'Right, that's it,' he said. 'Sorry Eddy, I'm not treating you until Malky leaves the room.'

Of course, Malky stayed there another ten minutes, so The Fridge stormed off again after training.

It's the worst thing you can do. If you show that they're getting to you it'll just get worse. The gaffer has a little chat with the lads and tells them to take it easy but, as Flem says, it's worth the fine . . .

Talking of which, there are quite a few this week due to roadworks at Colney Lane – the only road into the train- ing ground, which means you have to go all the way round and back the other side. There are about seven players who have to pay the obligatory £50. They don't bother disputing it, as the gaffer's such a stickler for time. It's going to be one hell of a Christmas party at this rate.

I feel a bit sorry for Easty, as the workers were having a laugh with him the day he was late and told him the road was closed and he had to go another way. When he got there, their colleagues told him that road was closed too. He tried to explain to the gaffer, but didn't get anywhere.

The gaffer might have high standards, but they can also be double standards when it suits him. After the Wigan game Malky was late getting back on the bus and said in his defence that he'd only been late because the gaffer was late too. The gaffer's defence was that he was talking to the chairman outside and he saw Malky, Squiz and Mullers standing around outside too. So they're providing each other's alibis. Well, nothing's come of it and I think that's wrong. So, of course, Malky goes in to see the gaffer – with his apple – and warns him I'm on the case.

'Robbo's going to try and get us collared,' he says.

I'm sure Adam will help me get them, even though he is just a nice quiet lad, especially for a team captain. He just gets on with his job, no airs and graces. He never has a bad word to say about anyone. I can't imagine him ever shouting at anyone, even if they were having a 'mare of a game. He leaves the ranting and raving to Malky and Flem.

The gaffer pulled me aside at the start of the season to talk about the captaincy. He told me I would be club captain, which is basically social captain. The team captain sorts out all the tickets for away matches and we work together on things like the rota for players' personal appearances. I get all the money together: £20 each towards the kit man for Christmas, the canteen ladies etc. It's the hardest job in the world, like getting blood out of a stone, especially with some of them. You know who you are, Flem and Mullers! But because I wasn't going to be playing every game he was thinking about making Adam team captain and wondered what I thought. I told him I thought Adam would be a fantastic choice.

The way Adam goes about his training and plays the game makes him such a great example to everyone. He gets the best out of people by performing the way he does every week. Simple as that. We all have so much respect for him. We call him the 'Silent Assassin' because he'll go straight through you, even in training. He's caught me a few times. Nothing malicious: he just trains the way he plays.

The gaffer always says: 'I wish I had another ten like you, Adam!'

He's like the gaffer's adopted son. The gaffer does it to wind Adam up as well. He says things like: 'Breakfast was all right this morning, wasn't it Ad?'

'See you at tea tonight then!''

Adam is mortified. He knows the boys are going to hammer him. The gaffer's done it to me in the past: 'All right, son?' he'd say.

He does it to get a cheap laugh. And he gets it, obviously.

Saturday 8th

Nationwide League Division One
Norwich City 3   **Millwall 1**
McVeigh 11   *Ward 90*
Henderson 13, 30
Carrow Road   Att: 16,423

Had a lousy sleep last night. I've been struggling with the flu all week and my coughing was so bad last night that Julie was tutting. I would have gone in the spare room but it looks as if it's been burgled. Great pre-match preparation.

I walk Molly down by the River Yare and it completely clears my head – and almost works on my lungs. Then, when I get to the ground, I reveal that Andy Roberts has let slip they're fielding the same team as last week. Cheers Robbo!

The papers are making a fuss about our 100 per cent home record: seven wins in seven and the only team in the country yet to lose or draw a home game. We try to keep it low-key, but it definitely adds pressure. It would be an unbelievable season if we went all season unbeaten at home, but if and when we do lose at least the pressure will be off.

We don't start as well as we did against Sunderland, but on 11 minutes Paul McVeigh nets a 25-yard curler and you can see all the Millwall players deflate like someone's stuck a pin in them. Then two minutes later young Ian Henderson blasts in a superb header – one I'd have been proud of – after another brilliant run and cross by Hucks, who else?

Now we're in cruise control. Hendo follows it up with a superb volley 15 minutes later – again set up by 'that man'. I'm really, really pleased for Hendo. He works so hard at his game and is always asking questions, really keen to learn. His volley showed great technique. He had to keep it down as it was quite a high ball and he was effectively side-footing it, which takes a really strong ankle.

We're passing the ball extremely well and we're a pleasure to watch. I'm almost drooling sitting on the bench. There's a period in the second half when I lose count of the passes we put together. Muscat is very, very quiet – the worst he's ever played here – I think the crowd have really got to him. I didn't see him before the game, but the crowd are keen to let him know what they think of him, singing virtually non-stop that they think he's a merchant banker or a James Hunt.

Unfortunately, by the time I get on we've taken our foot off the pedal. At 3–0 up with 11 minutes to go we're content to just keep the ball. I can understand that, but I'm a bit narked. If we carry on playing as we have been we could score a few more. They are there for the taking. As it is we concede a very late goal from a free header.

Chatting to Andy Roberts afterwards he says it's a massive blow for them that their young lad Robinson got stretchered off after 19 minutes. He tackled Hucks and fell awkwardly. I was proud of our fans for applauding him off, some even gave him a standing ovation. In the dressing room Hucks tells me he's going to write to him, wishing him all the best and hoping he gets back soon. Hucks was just too nimble for him, turned him too quickly.

I was delighted for Flem today, because he finally got his name sung by the Lower Barclay.

'One Craig Fleming, there's only one Craig Fleming.'

He's the ultimate unsung hero (well, up until now!) and has been one of the most consistent players for Norwich since I've been here. He's been so unlucky never to win the 'Player of the Season' award. I won it two years ago when I was top scorer but he could have quite easily pipped me to it. He was more consistent than I was that season, but goals always stand out. I'd love to see him win it this season – if anyone deserves it it's him.

So I was chuffed for him this afternoon. He always says to me: 'Fucking hell Robbo, you go out there, miss a sitter and they'll sing your name. I go out there, keep a clean sheet, score a goal and I'm lucky to get a clap!'

In the second half he went on a bit of a mazy run, and they sang his name again. You could see he was made up. Bless him.

The gaffer is less happy. He's disappointed with their late consolation goal and has a go at Briggsy, but I don't think it was really his fault. Holty had a chance to pass the ball forward but instead passed it back to Malky. Malky hit a ball to Briggsy, but the ball bounced up in front of him so he had to take two touches, which meant the Millwall lad had time to close him down and force a corner.

Squiz had another great game. He's probably the best footballer at the club. He's got two great feet and he's cute upstairs too. He learnt his trade at Tottenham and you can tell. He's grown in confidence in the last two years. When Bryan Hamilton was manager here he tried to get him to go to Burnley, so he's done really well to get from there to where he is now. He's worked hard on his weight and fitness and it's paid off, he looks tremendous. Last year he played the majority of games up-front – which I think he prefers – but that left-hand role suits him down to the ground because he can come inside and have a shot on his right foot, but he can also cross a mean ball with his left. He's not as quick as he'd like to be but he can use his skill and cleverness to take people on and create out on the wing. This season he's been dancing round defenders. Actually what am I talking about? He's a rubbish dancer. He's got big, wide Hobbit feet, about the size of our dining table. Malky says he should be in *Lord of the Rings*.

Have an enjoyable night out with Julie, a few of the lads and Andy Roberts and his wife Leanne, who's expecting their first child in March.

Sunday 9th

Poor Ben is ill so won't be playing football today. On the upside, this means we can cheer on Wales against

England in the quarter-final of the Rugby World Cup! It's a great game. Wales are 10–3 up at half-time, but do I ring anybody to gloat? No. But surprise, surprise, as England start to take control in the second half, my phone starts vibrating like it's going to explode. Lads, you're all extremely childish. Okay, so we eventually lose the game 28–17, but we outscored you 3–1 on tries. Sweet Chariot my arse. No wonder everybody hates the English! In the end, I can't bear to watch and go out to clear up leaves. I was like that for the Wolves v Sheffield United play-off final last year. I was that desperate for United to win I went and got the lawnmower out. There was hardly a blade of grass left by the end of the game.

Spend an amazingly glamorous afternoon hosing down the patio and getting in a KFC for my wife – Julie says she's got a cold but she may be slightly hungover (she doesn't normally drink very much but she had a few bottles of Smirnoff Ice last night!) – and falling asleep in front of the telly.

Monday 10th

Train on my own as the lads who played on Saturday have another cushy relaxation session at Greens, while the rest are working on team formation for the reserve game tonight. I decide against a crossing and shooting session with myself and do a 25-minute threshold run – which basically means you have to keep up the same good pace constantly – before joining the rest of the lads in Greens where, surprise, surprise, they're all lounging around in the jacuzzi.

Find out that Peter Reid has got the sack from Leeds. I feel sorry for him – I think he's a good bloke who found himself in an impossible situation. I'm also a bit worried the gaffer might be poached. He won the old Division

One title with them as a player and any fool can see what a great job he's doing here.

Tuesday 11th

Get in early to do my weights session, even though I'm not playing as much these days and I know today will be a hard, physical session as we've got tomorrow off. We're doing great, but then during a crossing and shooting session we all suddenly get sloppy, which irritates the hell out of the gaffer. I don't know whether we are all still tired from the weekend, but we're even more knackered a few minutes later when the gaffer stops the session and makes us all do a fast lap round one of the training pitches. Everyone has to get round in 60 seconds or we all have to do it again. We all make it in time, thank God. Funnily enough, everyone has their shooting boots on after that. I think Hucks is genuinely shocked.

Fair play to the gaffer: he's had a look at the video of Millwall's goal Saturday and says: 'Briggsy, I'm sorry, I did you an injustice the other day. I apologise.'

He's good like that.

Bump into Flem in the sauna at Green's later and we head off to meet Adam Drury at the club to talk to chief executive Neil Doncaster and club secretary Kevan Platt about the bonuses. They should be sorted soon.

Wednesday 12th

I had arranged to play golf up at Dunston Hall with Terry and little Alex, but when I wake up it's cold, wet and miserable and, wuss that I am, I hate playing in the rain. Luckily, Terry doesn't fancy it either and Al's heading down to London this afternoon with Neal Reynolds to see yet another specialist about his ankle, so he's not too fussed either.

So, with a whole day free, I decide to break with tradition and go looking for Christmas presents in advance rather than panicking at the last minute. Like most blokes, though, I'm hopeless so I end up meeting Julie and her new workmates for a coffee at the warehouse instead.

Call Darren Eadie to invite him to dinner on Saturday night: he and his wife Kelly have just moved back from Leicester and he's very bored. I was gutted for him when he had to retire through injury: he was a fantastic player and a legend for Norwich. He does a bit of work for Sky now and then and has started working for the club on matchdays, although knowing him he'd probably be happiest just fishing every day.

In the evening, Malky and I have dinner with two couples who won a competition to have dinner with us. Must have been the booby prize! Luckily they're mad Norwich fans and it's a very pleasant, easy night, mostly talking about the new stand. Every time you look at it they've added something new to it. The old one was a bit of a dinosaur. I never went in it, but apparently the toilets were a shambles. It'll be amazing when it's finished. We've had a great atmosphere all season but it's been odd with only three stands.

It does make a difference to the players. Malky says that when we played West Ham at Upton Park he felt great and knew he was going to have a good game, just because of the surroundings. I'm the same with my kit: if the shorts are nice and baggy I feel as if I'm going to play better. It's like the smarter you look the better you perform, because you feel better in yourself, and I think it's the same kind of thing with the new stand. It will add to that pride.

Thursday 13th

With Crouchy suspended, I find out I'm starting against Watford on Saturday! I feel like a teenager again.

Then the gaffer does his usual 'You're getting complacent, lads' Thursday talk. Gaffer, I can assure you that we're not. I'm 35, I know what he's doing. He's trying to keep our feet on the floor. There are still 29 games to go. But I think the younger players might be more nervous after his speech. And anyway, we have the perfect incentive for Saturday. Not only do we have to keep our fantastic 100 per cent home record going, but if we do we will go two points clear at the top of the First Division. The last time Norwich City were in that position, well, let's just say it wasn't this century!

All right then, it was five years ago to be precise, and what a massive boost it would be for us to be top again. And you know what, the way we've been playing we deserve it. We've won our last four games – tough ones too – and we've played a lot of the top sides away from home. But going top could be a poisoned chalice. The media would start to take more notice of us, but I think it suits us not to have people talking about us. They're always talking up the West Hams and West Broms, or you'll see people like Neil Warnock mouthing off. Let them. We'd be chuffed to bits if we went top of the League, but we'd just get on with it.

Phil Mulryne has failed a fitness test so Clint's back in the side too. He'll be looking forward to getting one over on his old club, as will I. I've scored in my last four games against Watford at Carrow Road – touch wood, a run that I hope I can keep going on Saturday. It's always nice to play against your old club and I was at Vicarage Road for five years, although most people I knew back then have moved on – or retired!

I started there as a 17-year-old trainee. It helped that I

knew Malcolm Allen from playing against him in local leagues back in north Wales and that the youth team manager, Tom Walley, was a Welsh-speaker from Caernafon. Back then Watford were a very up and coming club: Graham Taylor was manager and the squad included John Barnes, Luther Blissett, Kenny Jackett and Tony Coton. We'd finished second in the League in 1982–83 and got to the FA Cup final a year later, losing 2–0 to Everton.

Graham Taylor is scary, although he's an absolute gentleman. When I see him now, the first thing he does is ask how my mum and dad are. But back then everybody feared him: England players, senior pros – they all shat themselves when he walked into a room. No one would dare cross him. He used to throw cups of tea around and all that.

But I have much to thank him for. He gave me my debut when I was 17 and a bit, against Ipswich of all people, who had the then England international Terry Butcher playing for them. Terry was really nice, talking to me all the way through the game.

'How old are you, son?'

'Is this your first game?'

'Good luck with your career.'

He didn't clatter into me once, as he could see I was young and nervous. We drew 0–0 and I played the full 90. I did all right, winning most of the balls in the air, and really enjoyed it, although I didn't really get any chances.

We were due to play Arsenal on the Monday after that and I would have started my second game, but I was a bit of a silly boy. I went out with Tim Sherwood and a couple of the other Watford lads on the Sunday night, the only time in my whole career I've ever gone out the night before a game. We went out in St Albans, about 15 miles away, but the stupid thing was we weren't even drinking, we just had a few orange juices in the pubs. Unfortunately, someone Tom Walley knew was out that night and saw us.

We got to the training ground the next morning and one of the lads said: 'Tom knows everything about last night.' I shat myself: I knew he'd have to tell Graham Taylor. I was shaking for about an hour, thinking: 'How am I going to tell my mum and dad I've got the sack? After everything they've done for me, driving me to games all over north Wales and coming down for my debut.'

After leaving us to stew for a bit, Taylor pulled us in one by one and tore strips off us.

'I could sack you on the spot if I wanted to. You've given me every reason to. But I think everybody deserves a second chance in life and this is yours.'

He fined us two weeks' wages and dropped us from the team.

I ended up staying there five years although I only played 50 games, scoring nine goals, so I'm not sure quite how big an impression I made on the Watford fans. Having said that, I did pick quite a moment to score my first ever goal: coming on as a sub at half-time against Man U and scoring the winner. At Vicarage Road. Me being a massive Liverpool supporter and scoring the winner against Man U . . . it was a dream come true. I didn't sleep at all that night: I went to bed about midnight and just lay there waiting impatiently for the paper shops to open.

But it was quite hard to get a regular place in that side with players like Dean Holdsworth, Luther Blissett and Paul Wilkinson all established pros. So I had to move on . . .

Anyway, we have our usual tactics meeting after the gaffer's motivational moan. Apparently Watford's right-back isn't the biggest lad, so when Greeno takes a goal-kick the gaffer wants me to go and stand on him. Then he wants me to flick the ball on into the centre for Squiz, who will go inside me and play the ball into the channel for Hucks. Normally from Greeno's goal-kicks I like to stand to the left, as I find it easier holding the lad off with my left hand. Even though I'm right-handed, I just don't feel as strong using it and taking the ball into the centre as when I'm using the left to do it. It feels like driving on the wrong side of the road. But it's the opposite with crosses. I prefer crosses from the right-hand side so I can direct my header to the left. So now you know.

Keith Briggs wins today's yellow jersey at training. Justifiably so, as he had a shocker – although the gaffer ran him close! He joined in today and was desperate for me to get the jersey. He was whispering it to all the lads, just trying to take the heat off himself, maybe. But naturally, being the great bunch of lads they are, they know quality when they see it and yet again I end up without a single vote. I don't think I'll ever win it – unless the gaffer starts threatening the others with fines.

Friday 14th

I feel about 80 this morning. My achilles tendons again. I cheer up when Malky gets fined a tenner for messing about in the physio's room. Everyone has a smile about that. I feel even better when us oldies beat the young'uns again in training – extending our lead at the top of the table by a massive six games. And I scored a hat-trick. Oh God, it gets boring winning all the time . . .

I am really excited about the game tomorrow. I feel like Eva and Chase waiting for Christmas. Delia and Michael join us for lunch at the training ground and are very complimentary about how we've been playing and how it's all going. All right, Delia is even more like a kid waiting for Christmas than I am. They are such good people, I really hope we can do it for them.

My brother Elfyn, his wife Viv and daughter Grace are coming up tonight. Viv and Grace are going Christmas shopping in the city tomorrow – ah well, at least my brother has volunteered to come and cheer me on!

Saturday 15th

Nationwide League Division One

Norwich City 1	**Watford 2**
Jarvis 88	*Fitzgerald 34*
	Cox (pen) 81
Carrow Road	Att: 16,420

All those weeks when I was on the bench I've felt fine on the morning of a game. Fantastic, in fact. This morning, just because my back knows I'm starting, it's gone all stiff. I feel like my body's ganging up against me. I also got woken up last night at 11.15pm by three chatterboxes – the twins and Grace – combined age less than half that of mine. I was not best pleased.

The day does not improve. We lose the game 2–1 and with it our 100 per cent home record and the chance to go top of the table. We don't play well, but do enough to deserve something from the game. In the second minute their goalie makes a point-blank save from a Flem header. If that had gone in I think we'd have gone on to win it. I didn't play as well as I have this season – and I didn't have a single chance either, which was disappointing. And we had another Premier League ref, who obviously didn't want to be there – some of his decisions were shocking and on another day we could have had two penalties.

I'm gutted. The only bright spot comes when Wales get a fantastic 0–0 draw in the play-off in Russia, giving us a great chance to qualify for Euro 2004.

Sunday 16th

My body aches all over this morning after playing the full 90 yesterday, and the weekend from hell shows no sign of improving. Poor Ben's team lose 5–1 to Drayton, probably the best side in the league, then we discover poor Chase has an abscess in her gum. Luckily our neighbour is a dentist so she gets her some antibiotics. Eva seems to be all right at least! We invite little Al round for a late Sunday roast to cheer him up.

Poor sod. Alex has known for months that he might have to call it a day as all the ligaments in his ankle have gone. He went to London the other day with The Fridge, only to have a second specialist confirm he could do nothing. He was on painkillers and couldn't train or anything without them. A lot of players take Voltarol for niggly pains, but with something like your ankle you've got to think about your future quality of living. I've no doubt he'll get arthritis. It's a real shame for everyone, especially as he's only 23. He's got so much ability; it's such a waste. He says he's going to stay in Norwich for the foreseeable future as he likes it here.

After lunch me and Al head out for a few drinks at Delaney's. Well, it is manager Andy's birthday.

Monday 17th

Julie's organising a Christmas party for all the players' wives and girlfriends. She was on the computer the other night sorting out all the details and this morning she gives me a big bunch of envelopes to give them to all the lads for their other halves. Oh no! I hate this. I don't want them to think I'm busy or she's busy – I'd get hammered for it, it's the footballer's cardinal sin. Malky's always busy: if there's anything to be done with the press, he's there like a shot. But she's just dead organised and I think it's great that she bothered to organise a Christmas party. So I sneak in early and put the envelopes on their places before they get in to make sure they get them.

We have a good chat today. The gaffer still isn't happy with the performance on Saturday and lets us know it. But a few of us speak our minds. One thing I really like about the gaffer is he doesn't take it personally if you don't agree with him so we can have a good debate and get it off our chests.

I'm still really stiff, really feeling every one of my 35 years this morning, so I opt out of training and go for a 20-minute run with Mullers and Eddy who are returning from injury. The run does the trick, although I'm sure the hot bath I enjoy afterwards is even more helpful.

Tuesday 18th

The gaffer's in a much better mood today, laughing and joking like normal. He reads us an article the England rugby coach Clive Woodward has written in *The Times* about how to handle pressure. We all feel pretty positive afterwards.

Training is excellent and I feel fully recovered today. Just as well, as we have a two and a half hour session, although thankfully it's all with the ball which makes life easier. At the end the gaffer joins in our small-sided game. Wrong move! He does keep himself extremely fit, but today he has a beast. He should have stopped at half-time, but he perseveres and it just keeps getting worse and worse until he wins the yellow jersey, much to the lads' delight. We will all be bright and early for training on Thursday when he has to wear it. Thursday is press day too – so we've told him he has to wear it even when he's speaking to the media. Ha!

Wednesday 19th

It's looking just like any normal Wednesday morning: take the girls to school, head off to Green's for a couple of hours and bump into Flem and Crichts. Then, bang, out of the blue Flem offers to buy me a drink. He's not daft though – it's way too early for a pint, so a coffee it is. It's not that he's tight, he just squeaks when he walks. Flem's favourite saying is 'every pound is a prisoner'.

Dig out one of my old Wales shirts to wear as a lucky charm this evening. Me and Ben are glued to the telly from 7.30pm, willing them to beat Russia. The atmosphere at the Millennium Stadium is electric – but not as good as when Norwich were there two years ago! Sadly Wales lose 1–0 so Russia are going to Euro 2004, not us. And I'm not getting a free holiday with BBC Wales or the papers to cover it. Gutted.

Thursday 20th

Still thinking about the chat I had with my friend Trevor last night. He was over from LA so he came and watched the game with us. He thinks there's a very strong chance of me playing out in the States next year if I don't get a new contract with Norwich, so on Sunday he is going to sound out a few coaches for me.

Ben runs cross-country for his school and is trying to improve so I take him to meet my mate Neil Featherby, who used to run for Great Britain. Neil's great with him and draws up a training plan for him. I might follow it too. Like father, like son: Ben's not the quickest, but very good at lasting the pace! I was hopeless at the 100 metres.

Friday 21st

It's an early start for one of our longest away trips of the season, to Preston. We leave at 9am, are lucky with the Friday traffic and get to Blackburn's training ground at around 2pm. Whenever we're up this way Blackburn are kind enough to let us train at their impressive academy. The pitches are first class.

Everyone is stiff getting off the coach, which reassures me that it's not just because I'm getting on a bit. The gaffer names the team for tomorrow and, as I suspected, I'm not in it. I didn't play too well last Saturday so I can't say I'm surprised he's recalled Crouchy.

Spend a quiet night in watching *Children In Need* on the telly.

Saturday 22nd

Nationwide League Division One
Preston North End 0   Norwich City 0
Deepdale   Att: 14,775

We're all up early and downstairs to watch the Rugby World Cup final. Of course me, Malky, Mullers and Holty try to wind everyone else up by cheering on Australia, for obvious reasons, but I have to admit it's a very exciting game and I'm pleased for them. Apart from the fact that Flem will now be unstoppable with his 'How Great England Is' speech. Yawn.

On paper it looks like it's going to be a tough game today: Preston's home record is played eight, won seven, drawn one. And that's how it turns out. We ride our luck a little and are under pressure by the time I come on with seven minutes to go, although it's still 0–0. I've only been on five minutes when Paul McVeigh crosses an in-swinging ball from the left straight to me. I manage to get a glancing header on it and it's heading right into the bottom corner until Jonathan Gould makes an excellent save and tips the ball round the post for a corner. Damn.

But it's a great point for us, away from home. The gaffer baffles me a bit after, though. He says we played better than we did against Watford last week. I disagree: I think the result has masked the performance. I'm not saying we played badly, but we were under pressure for long periods of the game. We got through it with a little help from our fans, we had fantastic support once again today. Thanks a lot – it really helps us.

Home by 10pm for an early night.

Sunday 23rd

Ugh! What a horrible day – cold, wet and bloody miserable – and we're training because we're playing Coventry on Tuesday night. To make it worse, I have to give a grinning Keith Webb £20 as I bet him England wouldn't win the World Cup. I wish I'd stayed in bed. It's a good session though and I end up enjoying it.

Surprisingly, Ben's game against Attleborough is still on, despite the five billion gallons of rain over the last few days. Ben survives both the floods and a 4–1 drubbing, although at the end he is so caked in mud that I nearly give him the bus fare home. In the end I relent but make him sit on my big coat so he doesn't get muck all over my nice leather seats. Back home Ben heads for a nice hot bath and I head for Greens to try and warm up in the sauna.

Monday 24th

It's a quiet day's training because of the game tomorrow. The gaffer gets us working on our set-pieces as we don't score enough goals from them. It's vital we get back to winning ways tomorrow night and stay in the top two or three in the table. But confidence is high at the moment, and why shouldn't it be? We've got an excellent home record and we're picking up points away from home – not something we've been terribly good at in recent seasons.

In the afternoon disaster strikes when the screen on my mobile dies. Imagine: a footballer without a mobile? That's like not playing golf. Worst of all I can't get to any of my numbers and, being the technophobe that I am, I've only saved them onto my phone, not my Sim card, so now they're gone forever.

Thankfully, I get a nice new one from our old sponsors, the Digital Phone Company, before heading off to watch Fulham take on Portsmouth with my old Welsh team-mate Chris Coleman, now manager at Fulham. He's a really funny bloke and was always great to have around the dressing room. He was tipped as a favourite to get the sack and I'm delighted he's doing so well and proving all the pundits wrong.

Tuesday 25th

Nationwide League Division One

Norwich City 1	**Coventry City 1**
Henderson 35	*McAllister (pen) 49*
Carrow Road	Att: 16, 414

It's going to be a long day, not helped by my long drive back from London last night. We train as normal, but are finished by 10.45am, so I go through my usual routine of walking the dog and getting a couple of hours kip.

I'm on the bench again, but I'd have loved to be starting. The conditions are ideal: it's raining, the grass is wet and I'm just itching to get on. Have a quick chat with three former Leicester team-mates, all now at Coventry – goalie Gavin Ward, Julian Joachim and first team coach Gary Mills, who is the best crosser of a ball I've ever played with. He made me a fair few goals when I was with the Foxes – all from right-back. Top bloke.

Once again, we're not playing too well, but the work rate is there. Hendo heads us in front after about 30 minutes, but Coventry get back on level terms about five minutes after the restart when Flem is adjudged to have handled in the area and concedes a penalty. The ball just hit him and I don't think he could do much about it, but these things happen. Gary McAllister (still going strong at 38 so there's hope for me yet!) scores from the spot and, to make matters worse, Malky gets sent off for a second bookable offence. Coventry are playing well and have a couple of chances to nick it, but we hang on for the draw. I get on for about eight minutes, but don't get any chances.

Not a great night, then, but we're still second in the League. Finally go to bed about 1am.

Wednesday 26th
As usual the haves (those who have played last night) can have a day off while the have-nots (as in those who have not played) have to take on the youth team at Colney. The gaffer tells me I can have the day off if I want, which is nice of him, but I tell him I'd rather play and keep my fitness level up.

What was I thinking? When I turn up at Colney it's blowing a gale and chucking it down, and I'm calling myself every name under the sun by the time I realise we're not even going to play in the indoor arena. I could be home watching the telly! Luckily, after 15 minutes of trying to chase down balls which are flying through the air at 168mph, Keith Webb decides perhaps it would be a good idea to head inside after all.

In the afternoon I bump into a very depressed-looking Hucks at Greens. He tells me he doesn't know whether he is coming or going. Literally. He's really missing his family, who are still living most of the time up in Manchester, and just wants to get his future sorted. His loan spell is due to end in a couple of weeks but I don't know whether we've got the money to offer him anything. He's really down and says, again, how much he loves it here, as does his wife Lindsey. I know what he's going through. When I first came to Norwich I was in a hotel for four months and only saw my family at weekends. I found it really tough and, surprise, surprise, it showed on the pitch. He knows he didn't have the best of games against Coventry; I think all this uncertainty is bound to affect his form.

Thursday 27th

I'm feeling really stiff this morning – the artificial turf of the indoor arena is a great surface to play on, but it really takes it out of your legs. Everything aches. So much so, in fact, that I'm very close to getting the yellow jersey in training – now that would put a big smile on the gaffer's face. But I manage to grind a good performance out of my poor, aching body in the very last game and only get one vote, from Keith Webb. That doesn't bother me because he wouldn't know a good player if he ran up to him and slapped him in the face. Which, funnily enough, he'll have the chance to prove. if he votes for me again.

After training Julie and I are invited to the launch of a website called Safe, to highlight the dangers of the internet to children. I have to present some certificates to a group of children who have designed their own website – which is excellent by the way. I'm seriously considering asking them for a lesson in how to use a PC. One little girl is a massive Norwich fan and just can't stop crying when she meets me. Bless! I've never really had that effect on anyone before and I'm not quite sure what to do. Very sweet.

Friday 28th

After training we get a visit from the chiropodist. Poor, poor woman. I really don't envy her having to look at – let alone touch – the nasty, swollen, bruised, sweaty, manky feet us footballers have. She cuts our nails, gets rid of all the dead skin built up by constantly wearing boots and gives us a lovely foot massage. Bliss.

I have a sneaky feeling that, come 5pm tomorrow, we will be top of the League for the first time in five and a bit years. Bring it on!

Saturday 29th

Nationwide League Division One

Norwich City 1   **Crewe Alexandra 0**
Huckerby 38
Carrow Road   Att: 16,367

For once I'm pleased I'm not starting today. Normally I'd rest up and prepare the same, whether I was a sub or not, but being on the bench today means I can sneak off at 10am to quickly cheer on my two gorgeous daughters who are representing their school at cross-country running.

Theirs is the first race in the Acle and District School Cross-Country Championships and I am proud beyond belief to be able to say that Eva beats 50 other girls and wins it. She's got a great running action. By the end I'm really hoarse from shouting. Her little face is all red and her little heart's pounding. Chase is great and comes straight over when she finishes to give her sister a big cuddle. I don't care if I play or not this afternoon; it's already been a great day.

Back home, my mobile goes.

'Robbo, it's me.'

'All right, Hucks mate?' He sounds panicky.

'Robbo, where's the nearest hospital? My little lad's really poorly. He's been sick and he's not talking, he's just lying there.'

It's his youngest lad, Ben, who's only two and looks like an angel. Lindsey has brought their two boys down for weekend. So I ring the Fridge and ask where the best place is to take the little lad, then call Hucks back and tell him to take Ben straight to A&E at the Norfolk and Norwich hospital, just outside the city, and explain how to get there.

About an hour later he calls me back to say that Ben had perked up a bit by the time they got to hospital, but that they're keeping him in to do a few tests. So now the poor sod has to leave Lindsey and his other little boy there and go home to get ready for the game. What a morning.

That's an unbelievable way to prepare for a match, yet somehow he manages to put all this to the back of his mind at Carrow Road a few hours later, plays really well and scores. He's back to his best. It's a beauty of a goal, too, a lovely curler of a shot from the edge of the 'D' after our passing and movement has dragged Crewe all over the shop. I'm really pleased for him. He hadn't scored in the previous eight games. He'd set loads up, but nobody bats an eye at who makes the goals and anyway, as a striker you want to be scoring.

Touch wood, something will be sorted this week. He'd love to sign, but we all know it's tricky – you don't want to bankrupt the club for one player. If you could guarantee promotion by signing Hucks then obviously the board would do it, but you can't. I'd love Crouchy to stay too – even though it would mean me keeping the bench warm until May – as long as we get promoted I don't care. Really.

We continue to play really well against Crewe but just can't get that second killer goal and we can feel the tension in the crowd at 1–0. They are so quiet you could hear a pin drop. I don't really understand that. We're second in the League, for God's sake! They've got high expectations of us now: they expect us to win every game and we've got to be able to handle that.

I'm still sitting on the bench, mulling all this over, when the final whistle goes. I'm delighted for the lads with our 1–0 win – it means we're still second as West Brom beat Forest – but I'm groaning inside. Oh no, I'm going to have to go and do a run with Dave Carolan. I hate that. It's cold, you're a bit down because you haven't played and don't really feel part of it, then you have to go and do a few laps of the pitch. But I didn't stop warming up all afternoon! And all the lads who've played are watching you sweat it out while they do their stretches to warm down. You feel like the kid with his nose pressed up against the sweet shop window. Then they're back in the dressing room celebrating way before you, using up all the soap!

Now I know how people like Easty feel. He's really down at the moment because he's been in and out of the side and the crowd have been booing him. I wish the fans would lay off him a bit. It doesn't help. Easty will never hide in a game. It doesn't matter what sort of game he's having, he'll always want the ball – and the more you want the ball the more mistakes you make, it's natural. As a fellow player, you'd rather have people like that alongside you in the team than people who don't want the ball just in case they make a mistake and the crowd gets on at them. I think sometimes one or two of the other players have been guilty of hiding behind Easty – 'They're going to pick on him today so at least they won't say anything about me.' Me, Squiz or Hucks can miss an open goal and the fans still sing our names. Easty gives the ball away near the halfway line and immediately gets booed. It's not fair.

Both of us are finding it hard to keep training at a high tempo all week, hoping for light at the end of the tunnel on a Saturday. Neither of us have got a chance of getting on at the moment, unless Hendo goes off the boil or Crouchy has an unfortunate accident with a grand piano being dropped on him from a great height. First things first: where can I get hold of a grand piano?

Not really, I'm not one for sulking. I'd never go in the dressing room after a game I haven't been involved in and mope around. I always go in, big grin on my face and have a good laugh with the gaffer and all the other staff and the boys. I think it's an important part of my role as club captain. But you do start to get paranoid. The gaffer keeps going on about how it's a squad game, but we've just had three games in a week and he made one change today, putting Mullers in for Damo, so where's the squad rotation? You have to be mentally strong.

These are testing times, especially for Molly. I try not

to take my worries home with me, but the poor dog certainly knows when I'm feeling frustrated – and she's getting walked to within an inch of her life right now!

Sunday 30th

A nice lazy day. Drive Ben over to Diss for his match. They're short of a linesman so yours truly volunteers. Twice I flag for offside, twice the ref ignores me standing there waving my flag in the air and twice Diss score. Our boys eventually lose 3–1. He over-ruled me twice and didn't over-rule their linesman once. I'm fuming but I calm down. I don't want everyone thinking 'Iwan Roberts what a knobhead' so I keep schtum. But it's got to come out somewhere . . . If it was the gaffer he'd have had him by the throat.

Nationwide League Division One

			HOME				AWAY						
Pos	Name	P	W	D	L	F	A	W	D	L	F	A	GD	PTS
1	West Bromwich Albion	20	6	2	2	13	6	6	2	2	18	11	+14	40
2	**Norwich City**	**21**	**9**	**1**	**1**	**20**	**9**	**2**	**5**	**3**	**10**	**11**	**+10**	**39**
3	Sheffield United	20	7	1	2	19	7	4	3	3	12	14	+10	37
4	Ipswich Town	20	6	2	2	24	12	4	2	4	16	18	+10	34
5	Wigan Athletic	20	6	4	0	16	6	3	3	4	12	14	+8	34
6	Reading	21	7	2	2	17	10	3	2	5	10	13	+4	34
7	West Ham United	20	4	5	1	17	9	4	4	2	10	7	+11	33
8	Sunderland	20	5	4	1	11	5	4	2	4	12	11	+7	33
9	Cardiff City	20	5	3	2	21	8	3	4	3	13	13	+13	31
10	Preston North End	20	6	2	2	17	9	2	2	6	9	14	+3	28
11	Millwall	21	6	3	1	13	5	1	4	6	11	18	+1	28
12	Crewe Alexandra	20	7	1	2	16	8	1	2	7	5	16	-3	27
13	Nottingham Forest	20	4	3	3	18	11	3	2	5	14	18	+3	26
14	Gillingham	21	5	1	5	15	16	2	4	4	12	18	-7	26
15	Coventry City	20	3	5	2	13	12	2	5	3	13	14	0	25
16	Burnley	21	4	3	3	16	12	2	4	5	13	22	-5	25
17	Walsall	20	5	3	2	17	10	1	3	6	6	13	0	24
18	Watford	21	3	5	2	11	9	3	1	7	11	17	-4	24
19	Crystal Palace	20	2	5	3	13	14	3	2	5	10	17	-8	22
20	Derby County	21	3	3	5	16	19	2	4	4	7	15	-11	22
21	Stoke City	20	4	4	2	13	10	1	1	8	9	19	-7	20
22	Rotherham United	20	4	3	3	10	10	0	5	5	6	18	-12	20
23	Bradford City	20	2	2	6	11	18	2	3	5	8	13	-12	17
24	Wimbledon	21	2	2	6	13	21	2	0	9	9	26	-25	14

DECEMBER

Monday 1st

Uh-oh. The dreaded Christmas month. Not only does Christmas mean that everyone else will be having fun without me, it also signals the start of our traditional slump – just as surely as indigestion follows Christmas dinner. The gaffer reminds us of this fact this morning. Our fans are always asking me why we suddenly turn rubbish over December and January and I can honestly say: 'I have no idea – now will you please stop talking about it to a superstitious footballer.'

We're even more determined than usual not to let it happen this season: our winter slump cost us a play-off place last year and at the moment we're sitting pretty in an automatic spot. At the moment.

I would love to win something with Norwich. After 18 years of hard slog, all I've got to show for my career in football is one play-off medal from when I was at Leicester and we beat Derby at Wembley. I remember the Derby players all had to sit there, on the turf, exhausted and mentally shattered and watch us go up the steps to the royal box to get our winners' medals. The play-off losers get nothing, as we discovered two years ago when we lost on penalties to Birmingham. Nobody really knew quite what to do. A few of the Norwich lads, because they hadn't been in a play-off final before, assumed we would go up before Birmingham and get a medal or something and then bugger off. Flem, Malky and I are chatting about it after training today. None of us really remember that much about the game but Malky says: 'Why did we wait around on the pitch while they had their fireworks and trophies?' It was agony, but I think we were too dazed to head to the tunnel.

It was awful. I scored in the 92nd minute and it will always be an 'if only'. If only I'd scored two minutes beforehand. Gutted. Absolutely gutted. What made it worse was that was the end of my international career. I was in the squad for a friendly the week after it but I pulled out because Mark Hughes wanted me to meet up with the Welsh squad straightaway. Not even go back with my family to the hotel for a few hugs. Just straight to the hotel the Welsh boys were at. To add insult to injury, it was the very same hotel the Birmingham lads were staying at.

I think Mark Hughes could have been more understanding. I'd just had the biggest disappointment of my entire career. I'd gone through the whole gamut of emotions during the game – from being elated to utterly deflated. I'd scored the most important goal of my career (two minutes too late – wish it had been golden goal rules!), lost the most important game of my career. Needless to say, I didn't want to go to the hotel Birmingham were at. Besides, there was a big party organised by Norwich and, although the atmosphere was depressing, I wanted to be there, to be with friends and team-mates.

In fact, I'm sorry, I didn't even want to see another football for eight weeks after we lost that game. I wasn't in the mood to train or play or go and put a brave face on it with anybody so I pulled out with a back injury and Sparky's not picked me since.

What particularly disappointed me is that this year Cardiff made the play-off final and the Cardiff boys who were in the Welsh squad, like Robert Page, pulled out of a friendly about a week after the play-offs and he's picked them since. Sparky's a great fellow and he's given me more caps than any other Welsh manager, so I've got a lot to thank him for and I always will, but I just think it was wrong. You've got to treat everybody the same.

To be fair, I was thinking of calling it a day with Wales anyway. I've never been a regular. Playing for your country involves a lot of travelling and, at best, all I'm going to be doing is sitting on the bench. I've had my time. We've got some great youngsters coming through now and really I'd be taking one of their places when they need the experience. I've never played well on the Saturday after coming back from international duty. I've always had a stinker. It catches up with you, especially the older you get. And I'd rather give my all to Norwich.

In the evening Ben and I go to cheer on the youth lads in their FA Youth Cup game against Bolton. It's great to see so many of my team-mates have had the same idea – a big up to Malky, Flem, Eddy, Briggsy, Adam, Easty, Crouch and Hucks. The lads play really, really well and I'm delighted that Ryan Jarvis scores the only goal of the game. Special mention, too, really must go to the gaffer's new beige mac. It's about two sizes too small for him and, I'm sorry gaffer, but we all agree it makes you look like a flasher.

Tuesday 2nd

Some of the lads have arranged to have a few drinks and a game of pool at the Garden House pub later, so obviously as club captain I am obliged to go. Well, somebody's got to try and force Easty to put something into the kitty, haven't they? For the record, Rivvo and Eddy are the pool sharks, Briggsy's just there to make up the numbers, and I'm somewhere in-between. It turns out to be a great night with lots of good-humoured teasing.

Wednesday 3rd

Hmm. What's that slight banging in my head? Good job we've got a day off. Julie's off Christmas shopping at the Bluewater Shopping Centre in Essex all day, so I'm in charge of getting the kids' tea. So that'll be a trip to Brewster's restaurant then with Eddy and his two children, as his wife Becky has gone shopping too.

Afterwards, I foolishly head for Greens, but the old 'sweat out the alcohol in the sauna' trick doesn't seem to work any more. After 15 minutes I'm feeling even worse than before so I give up and head for the city for some more Christmas shopping, before finally hitting the sack early.

Thursday 4th

The gaffer always wants to see us come through the Colney gates with a spring in our step after a day off and today we don't disappoint. We're really up for it and our crossing and shooting is, quite frankly, world class!

In the evening me and Julie head off to Ben's school for a parent-teachers meeting. The teachers all rave about him, how well he's doing and how much he's enjoying his schooling. Thank God. I joke that the kids all get it from Julie but they must have some of my genes too – my mum was a teacher and I quite enjoyed school – in fact, I was even made a prefect in my last year!

Friday 5th

Tomorrow's game at Millwall will be Crouchy's last for us as his three months are up and Villa want him back. I'll be genuinely sad to see him go. He's a nice lad and it feels like he's been here a lot longer than three months. He's fitted in so well, done brilliantly for us and I really hope that when he gets back to Villa he'll be given the chance to show their fans what a great player he is.

We're staying in a hotel in Greenwich. Room-mates are all decided at the start of the season, in consultation with the gaffer, but since my buddy Al retired from football, I either room on my own or with whoever makes up the numbers. Tonight I'm in with Briggsy so there'll be no need for any sleeping tablets. Actually, he's one of my closest friends at the club; that's why we slaughter each other all the time.

Ben calls before lights out: he can't wait to tell me that Wales have drawn England and Northern Ireland in the qualifying groups for the 2006 World Cup. We both sleep easy, knowing that's 12 points already in the bag.

Saturday 6th

Nationwide League Division One
Millwall 0   **Norwich City 0**
The New Den   Att: 9,850

The New Den is always an intimidating place to play, but it seems like the Millennium Stadium compared to their old place, Cold Blow Lane. Hot Blast Lane more like. As expected it's a tough game. Greeno is again outstanding, pulling off a string of great saves in the first half. One, in particular, is unbelievable. I'm sitting there on the bench, waiting for the net to bulge, but somehow he blocks the shot from three yards . . . with his face! Talented *and* hard as fuck.

We're under pressure throughout most of the second half, although they never look like scoring. The biggest cheer of the day comes from our fans when my old mate

Kevin Muscat gets sent off for a second bookable offence when he stupidly lashes out at Hucks.

I'm gutted not to get on. I'm sitting on the bench thinking: 'He's got to make a change soon – they're bombarding us, we're not even getting out of our own half.'

Crouchy's not having a great game, he's not holding the ball up and it's just pinging back into our half all the time. But the gaffer leaves him on. If it had been me having a 'mare out there, I think I'd have been off five minutes into the second half. Maybe he doesn't want to take Crouchy off because it's his last game . . . well, if that's the case there's no point in even putting me on the bench. I don't think there's any place for sentiment in football.

To be honest, I never thought this was Crouchy's sort of game. He's a great player, but he likes to have a few touches, whereas I'm very physical, I like to use my strength to get hold of the ball and lay it off quickly. The Millwall defenders are big, strong lads and I think Crouchy ended up being a bit bullied by them. I think I'd have caused them more problems, but it's not to be. The final whistle blows and the gaffer takes Crouchy over to the fans to take a bow. Sentimental sod. Good luck though, mate, you've done us proud.

Sunday 7th

Soft touch takes his two little girls shopping, caves in and buys them loads of stuff, and wins Dad of the Year award . . . then blows it in a moment of madness! The girls want a McDonalds, so I get them a Happy Meal with cakes, turn round to take the tray upstairs and one of the cakes goes flying everywhere – all over people's shoes. I'm so embarrassed, I can actually feel myself blushing. I mutter apologies to everyone splattered with cake (and a few others, just to be sure) and leg it upstairs to hide. I tell the girls and they're gutted to have missed seeing daddy make such a complete fool of himself.

In the afternoon we head over to Colney for the Christmas party organised by the club for the kids of all the staff. The kids have a great time playing games, dancing with Razz the clown and getting sweets from Splat the Cat. All the adults are crowded round the telly for the FA Cup Third Round draw. We're one of the last out the hat, away to Everton, which is very exciting. They're not having a great season, so we might be in with a chance of an upset. I hope so as half my family are Evertonians and they'll all want free tickets – it would be nice to make them pay for them somehow!

Monday 8th

It's our Christmas party tomorrow in London and, being a London lad, Damo has organised the hotel and a few places to indulge in a soft drink or three. My job is to pick up the train tickets.

Despite the prospect of a night on the tiles with yours truly and the rest of the lads, Hucks looks a bit down in training. Cardiff at home on Saturday could be his last game for us. If only there was some way we could hang on to him.

Tuesday 9th

Training, training, blah, blah, blah. We're off on the 1.40pm train, standard class of course, armed with a couple of crates of Stella, courtesy of Crichts. Cheers, mate!

The gaffer really does his homework on a player before he signs him and won't bring anyone to the club that he thinks is a bad apple – which is why he has no need to warn us to behave ourselves tonight. We're all conscious that when we're out we are representing Norwich City and in my six years here I've never seen any trouble involving any of the lads. They're a good bunch.

Damo's booked us a fantastic hotel in Covent Garden. I'm well impressed with the room, although obviously I'm not going to hang around admiring it. Freshly showered and glad rags on, I'm out of the door quicker than you can say 'we are almost top of the League!' We cut a bit of a dash if I do say so myself. The best-dressed, apart from yours truly, is Eddy, but the worst-dressed is definitely Squiz, who looks as if he's come straight from school.

We head for TGI Fridays for a bite to eat, before ending up in a club called Chinawhite. It's supposed to be one of the best clubs in London, but I can't really see what all the fuss is about. Maybe I am getting old. So, at about 2am, me and Hucks decide we've had enough and head back to the hotel. Hucks has the brilliant idea of avoiding all the black cabs and jumping on a red bus. See, no big-time Charlies here. We then sit on the bus for ten minutes until I point out that we have absolutely no idea where we're going. So we, um, get off and get a cab back to the hotel. Via McDonalds, of course.

Wednesday 10th

Rather foolishly, I'd decided to stay down in London and do – yes, my Christmas shopping. Well, having just charged Briggsy £50 for my last two paracetamol I can afford to splash out a bit. London's packed. I walk miles and miles and a lad in Selfridges tells me they've just sold out of my size in the pair of trainers I had my eye on.

Well, at least one of my sizes. Eventually struggle home with a ton of bags into the arms of my beautiful wife.

Thursday 11th

Ugh. I'm still very tired from Tuesday night, but I perk up when the gaffer names the team to face Cardiff on Saturday and I'm starting. No great surprise, I guess, now Crouchy's gone back, but I'm still delighted. I'm a bit worried about my match fitness though as I haven't played for a while and didn't even get on in the last two games. It's going to be a tough game: Cardiff are doing well in their first season back in this division for a while and have spent a lot of money. Their star striker, Robbie Earnshaw, is one of the hottest talents in English football. He's already past the 20-goal mark, which is tremendous at this stage of the season. I've known him a few years and am delighted Wales have got such a great prospect, but I really hope we can keep him quiet on Saturday.

Julie is out with Delia and the other players' wives and girlfriends for their Christmas party tonight, so I take the kids bowling so she can get ready in peace. I'm fairly rubbish at bowling, but it does have the added advantage that I can get out of cooking. Pizza and chips anyone?

Friday 12th

Julie is a bit 'tired' after her night out, so I take the kids to school. Apparently they all had a great time with a meal and 'a few' drinks in a bar called Optic and Delia was supposed to leave at 10pm, but didn't go until midnight – the dirty stop-out!

I arrive a bit later than usual for training. I'm still early though – I'm nearly as much of a stickler for time as the gaffer. It's a sad day today as it's Hucks' last day in training, so we all vote for him to wear the yellow jersey. Not really. He's been brilliant to have around the place – great fun and, as I've said before, a real player's player. I've really bonded with him and will definitely keep in touch. It's such a shame we couldn't afford to keep him. He'll go back to Man City on Monday and probably end up training with the youth team – what a waste of talent.

On the plus side, it looks like we've signed Leon McKenzie from Peterborough for an undisclosed fee. I don't know much about him (other than that he's another bloody striker!) as he's suffered a few bad injuries over the last couple of seasons. He has scored a few this season though and if his medical goes well today he will become a Norwich player on Monday. The gaffer tells us he still wants to strengthen the squad.

Finish doing my last Welsh radio interview previewing the game against Cardiff at 4pm and relax in front of the telly, before a very early night to make sure I'm right for tomorrow.

Saturday 13th

Nationwide League Division One

Norwich City 4   **Cardiff City 1**
Huckerby 34   Thorne 59
Roberts 54
Fleming 71
Vidmar (og) 79
Carrow Road   Att: 16,428

Oh yes! My sixth start of the season: my fourth goal. With form like that people should be knocking on the gaffer's door offering £20m for me. Maybe he's just not telling me . . .

But, funnily enough, my goal's not the main topic of conversation in the bars of Norwich after the game. A good friend of mine sees to that! It's a fantastic but sad day for everyone involved with the club. We thrash a good Cardiff side 4–1 and could have scored more, but it's Darren's last loan game and what a send-off he gives everybody. He is magnificent: scores two, makes mine and creates numerous chances.

It's quite emotional in the dressing room after the game. The gaffer says: 'I'd like to thank Hucks for his input over the last three months. He's been superb and it might not be over if we can try and do something with Man City.'

I look at Hucks and he's all choked up, so I shout to the gaffer: 'Leave it out! He's going to start crying in a minute!'

I wish he could have got his hat-trick today. He was superb. Every time he got the ball he looked like creating something; we could have won by six or seven goals. Right at the death he squared the ball to Squiz who blazed over when he should have scored, although the ball did bounce up a bit in front of him. But that's Hucks: he's such an unselfish player. There's no way I'd have passed: 4–1 up and on a hat-trick? No way.

He set me up beautifully for my goal. I chested a long ball down to him first time, turned and made a run and he slipped a great return pass through to me. I looked up and knew straight away where I was going to hit it, bottom corner. I knew I couldn't take a touch because the defenders were catching me, so I volleyed it, caught it quite nicely and just wellied it in.

What a feeling! I can't remember the last goal I scored in front of the Barclay End. The other two I've got at home this season have been down at the River End. It's great scoring in front of the Barclay because they go mad. As did I. I ran and got Hucks and was just hugging him, shouting 'Fucking hell!' As we ran back to the centre the Norwich fans were singing to the Cardiff fans:

'Fucked by a Welshman, you've just been fucked by a Welshman.'

I must admit it was particularly nice to score against them as I got quite a bit of stick off their fans. It's nice for me that the Welsh media are there to see that I can still play a bit. Julie's mum and dad are Cardiff fans, but I hope they're not too unhappy – I think they like to see their son-in-law do well! I came off with about ten minutes to go and got a great ovation from the Carrow Road faithful. I'm also delighted for Flem that he scored, although we were all trying to wind him up in the dressing room: 'Your goal Flem? Nah mate, it took a deflection, it'll definitely go down as an own goal!'

Hucks' wife, Lindsey, is down for the match so we all go out for a few drinks to say goodbye. It's really sad: it just feels as if they've been here for ever. Lindsey loves it here. And, over a few beers, Hucks tells me he much preferred playing up front with me than Crouchy.

'You're totally different players,' he says. 'You'll probably have two touches or even just one if you can, whereas Crouchy had to have a few, get it down, maybe do a trick. But by then my space is closed down and he's got two defenders on him. I feel you've just got more experience and we read each other's games well. Every time I've played with you I've really enjoyed it.'

I really appreciate him saying that. I've not really had an understanding with a fellow striker like that since Bellers left. I need someone like him or Hucks who can read my game, someone who I know exactly what he's going to do. I've thrived playing alongside Hucks. We've only actually played three games together: Wigan,

Watford and today. But in those three games I've scored two, he's scored two and we've won two games and lost one (but then everybody had a crap game against Watford). I'm sure if I'd had more games with Hucks I'd be on 96 or 97 goals by now, not 92. Oh well, I'm just pleased that today I've shown it's not the be all and end all if Crouchy's not here. I can still play a bit.

Anyway, it's a cracking night. Everybody turns up apart from Paul McVeigh, Greeno and Crichts. Greeno thought it had been cancelled, Crichts had to sort his house in Nottingham which he'd sold and Squiz – the little liar – told me he was delivering presents to Colchester, but told some of the lads he had another party in Southend. I don't mind if you don't come Squiz, but tell the truth!

Sunday 14th

Fantastic night but oh, how I'm paying for it this morning – and we've got no painkillers in the house. I'm still up at 8am to read about my goal in the papers though.

After a quick browse through the glowing reports (one even describes me as 'talisman' rather than 'veteran' – wahey! – although they do credit Hucks' second as an own goal by Tony Vidmar) I take the kids swimming at the Riverside pool, although I'm not that keen on swimming so I just watch them from the canteen. Loads of people come up to congratulate me on my goal and the team's performance.

The kids want a McDonalds. I don't eat one often, but it's a great hangover cure so I wolf down a chicken sandwich and large chips which does the job.

Mum and dad phone to tell me they saw the highlights on Welsh TV. And that they recorded it. And watched it over and over again. And they'd like a new video for Christmas please.

Monday 15th

The gaffer has given all the lads who played Saturday the day off today and boy do I need it. I'm aching all over. I head for a jacuzzi to ease my aching bones but realise I could sit here all day and it still wouldn't help.

It's the start of a very special week for everyone at the club. We've got the derby game against Ipswich on Sunday. The gaffer will try and play everything down by saying it's just another game, because he wants the lads to relax. But everyone knows what a huge match it is – the biggest of the season, especially this time around with it being just before Christmas. What were the fixture list people thinking? Don't they know that if we lose, Christmas will have to be cancelled?

In the afternoon all the lads play Santa: taking presents to kids in hospital and trying to cheer them up. It's horrible to have to be in hospital at Christmas, but it must be even worse for the kids and their families.

At the hospital I meet Leon McKenzie for the first time. His transfer has gone through. He seems a really nice lad, quite quiet (but they all are when they first join!) and I wish him well.

Tuesday 16th

Just before training the gaffer tells us the club has reached agreement with Man City over Hucks and now it's just up to Hucks to sort out a compensation package with them. Great news. Unfortunately, West Brom and Wigan have also agreed a fee with Man City for him, but luckily for us he wants to come here. With a bit of luck it could be sorted within a few days.

Another surprise: we've done a deal with Charlton for their Swedish international striker Matty Svensson and he's coming up to Norwich today to have a look around.

Blimey! All these strikers: good job I scored and played well on Saturday. Leon looks very good in training this morning: quick, strong and with a good left foot. I'm impressed, he looks a real handful. But I can't help thinking we should have used the money to make sure we get Darren here so I could play alongside him for the rest of the season. Very short-sighted!

As soon as training's over I ring Hucks to find out the score. He tells me that Sheffield United, Locomotiv Moscow and Rangers also want his signature, but he's desperate to come back to Norwich. Negotiations with Man City aren't going well though and he's gutted. As am I.

Wednesday 17th

As we're playing on Sunday rather than Saturday, we're in today and off tomorrow, for a change. We start by going through the way Ipswich will play and how we will combat their midfield diamond formation. Then we play against the reserves, lining up with the same team as we did against Cardiff but with Jarve up front alongside me, instead of Hucks. Could I be starting two games in a row? Surely not!

The game is intense with tackles flying in everywhere: we're all hyped up for Sunday. It's the closest call ever for the yellow jersey: Malky and Squiz both have seven votes, so it goes to a re-count. Still seven votes each. The gaffer asks for another vote and, over the other side of the pitch, we notice two young lads who've been watching training both stick their hands in the air for Malky. The gaffer decides they have the casting vote, and under duress Malky accepts it. Actually he takes it pretty well and we shout over to the lads that they can come again.

Thursday 18th

It's our day off, but I really wish I was training as Julie insists on dragging me round all the shops to get the kids' last things for Christmas. We start in Toys R Us and, as my wife starts filling up the trolley with gusto, I'm amazed to discover that we are, in fact, buying toys not just for our three, but seemingly for all the children in the village of Brundall. Thankfully (for me and for her) I'm distracted by loads of people telling me how well I played on Saturday so I get back into the festive spirit. It's great when the whole city is buzzing – it makes you feel really proud.

People also wish me all the best for Sunday and plead with me to make sure we beat Ipswich. It's at times like this you see just how much people care and you realise what a big effect you have on people's lives. The gaffer might play it cool by telling the press it's just another game, but believe me we all know it's anything but. There might be fewer people there than at a Manchester or Glasgow derby but we're no less passionate about it. It's exactly the same. Which makes it such a shit fixture to have just before Christmas. I would take a point right now: anything rather than lose and ruin everyone's holiday. Last year I got some right arsey messages off mates of mine when we lost to Ipswich at home. It did my head in. The gaffer's right that it's just another three points, but we do realise what's at stake and it means a lot to us too. I'm starting to feel the pressure . . . of shopping.

One hundred and eighty-seven shops later, we finally head to the local hypermarket, Macro, where I get ready for my big Christmas bender by stocking up on bottles and bottles of . . . Lucozade. Well, I don't want to run out on Christmas Day when everyone else is sitting there with a glass of wine, now do I?

Teletext informs me that Kevin Keegan says we are

favourites to sign Hucks. Let's hope so. There are rumours flying around all over the place. He rings me this evening to fill me in on the latest. He's told me he will take a 50 per cent pay cut to join us but he says Man City are not going to give him a penny of the £1.5m he's owed on his contract because they think Norwich are getting him on the cheap. He could take his pick of clubs but he wants to come here, so he's coming down tomorrow for talks and going to West Brom on Monday. He says he's not going to sign for them, but that he has to go out of respect to them. I agree. You can't just fob people off – you don't know when you might need them in the future.

I'd be surprised if he doesn't sign for us, but it won't be immediately: there's so much to sort out.

Friday 19th

The first person I bump into at training this morning (not literally) is Matty Svensson. He tells me he's signed, so I wish him all the best. I'm not sure if he understands it through my gritted false teeth, though!

At 9.55am, precisely, Webby comes into the dressing room and tells me the gaffer wants to see me. Boom. My heart hits the floor. I know exactly what he's going to say. Dougie and chief scout Alan Wood are also sitting in the gaffer's office. He starts by saying how well I'd done against Cardiff last Saturday, and then hits me with it. I know it's coming, but it still hurts. Leon and Matty are starting on Sunday. I'm gutted: I thought I'd done everything possible to keep my place. I'd played really well and scored, for God's sake.

He says Matty will have fresh legs, but I think that's a poor excuse and tell him so. There's nothing wrong with my legs or my fitness – it'll be eight days since the last game – and Matty's hardly played many games this season so he's not likely to be match-fit anyway. Leon's looked good in training and I know Matty's a good player, but to throw two brand new lads in up front when they don't know how we play, our strengths and weaknesses – well, I think it's a big risk. Again, I tell him I'm not going to sulk about it, he's the manager and he's paid to make decisions. But it's even harder for me to take because it's Ipswich. I've got a good goalscoring record against them and have never lost at Portman Road with Norwich. It's the derby for God's sake. I'm gutted. Malky, Flem, Eddy and Zema all come up and tell me they're shocked I'm not starting, which makes me feel slightly better.

It makes you wonder what you have to do. Has the gaffer got a problem with my age? Teddy Sheringham, Gary McAllister and Dennis Irwin can still do it at the highest level and I know I'm physically capable of doing it too. It did annoy me when the gaffer said he is planning for the future. I know I'm out of contract in the summer but, hey, I'm still part of the club now and I'm trying my best to get them promoted. It throws everything he says about taking your chance when you get it out the window. It's a load of shit really. God knows what the lads who are not in the side think: well if he can do it to Robbo . . .

So, on Wednesday I was playing in the team to combat Ipswich's formation: today I'm not even in the reserves. Me and Jarve are on the sidelines. I say to Jarve: 'Bloody hell mate, we've gone from starting the game to sitting on the bench again.'

Later, I have a chat with him and Hendo in the shower room. They are stressing about the number of appearances they've made this season.

'How many have you had this year, Jarve?'

'Nine.'

'So how many would you be happy with this season?'

'About 30.'

'All right, you're on course then,' I say. 'I bet you Wayne Rooney hasn't got nine appearances for Everton yet this year. Don't get disappointed, you're still really young mate.'

They cheer up a bit after that. Wish someone would bloody well cheer me up.

Anyway, I train well, even enjoying a bit of banter with the gaffer. I'm not one to sulk. He is on the opposite team and we both go into a tackle strongly – nothing malicious – and the gaffer goes down hard. We both laugh about it, but the lads give me hell, shouting: 'Ooh Robbo's beefed the gaffer!'

He's shouting to the lads: 'Don't let Robbo score, you mustn't let Robbo score.' I'm teasing him: 'Gaffer you know I always score in these games.'

And I do. And, I must admit, I do overdo the celebration, arm swirling round in the air, giving it the old Mick Channon number. Oh yes! I think that makes the score 7–1, which makes it even sweeter. We have a laugh and a joke and it's all forgotten about – I'm not one to hold grudges. I would, however, be lying if I said I was gutted when the gaffer got the yellow jersey!

Saturday 20th

It's really weird not having a game today. Saturday afternoons were made for playing football. The gaffer's in a good mood at training – until Squiz strolls in 25 minutes late. He didn't even ring. He doesn't say anything, just goes straight to his locker. I can tell by the gaffer's face he's furious.

'Squiz?'

'Oh, sorry, gaffer.'

The gaffer's just about controlling himself.

'And what about the lads? Good manners doesn't cost anything Squiz.'

So he apologises to us for being late. His excuse is the gates at the complex where he lives were playing up. Well, Jim and Mullers both got in on time and they live there too. It's only ten minutes away. The gaffer's not happy about it, but he's got the game to concentrate on, so it will be a fine and dealt with later.

Joe Royle's been mouthing off on the radio, saying that Ipswich have too much pace for us to cope with and that will be enough for them to go on and win the game tomorrow. The last thing the gaffer says to us is to go out there tomorrow and ram his words down his throat.

It's an early night for me: the noon kick-off tomorrow means I'll have to be up at 7.30am. So I'll have a grumble about that too – I hate changing my routine. What's more, it looks like it might snow so I'm going to have to drive my car up to the top of the hill where we live just in case it's too slippery to get up there tomorrow morning and I'm stranded. I don't want to risk anything going wrong tomorrow, it could be the day where I come off the bench and score my 93rd and 94th goals of the season as we win 2–1. Sweet dreams!

Sunday 21st

Nationwide League Division One
Ipswich Town 0　　　　**Norwich City 2**
　　　　　　　　　　　　　McKenzie 37, 76
Portman Road　　　　　Att: 30,152

'E-I-E-I-E-I-O! Up the Football League we go!' We are top of the League! Yes! Yes! Yes! Fucking yes!

Funny old game football: we had several chances before today to go top, but we wait until we're on our old rivals' patch to do it. So I find myself standing on the Portman Road pitch with the biggest grin ever, giving it loads. Our fans are going mental: we've won the game 2–0 with two goals from Leon on his debut and they're loving ramming it down the throats of the Ipswich fans, singing: 'Top of the League at Portman Road' over and over again.

We've all come out onto the pitch to applaud them: they've been magnificent, 2200 of them drowning out the home fans. Sensibly, Ipswich have kept them in for 20 minutes to avoid potential trouble, but I think they'd stay all afternoon if they could. I get a massive chant of 'Iwww-aannn, Iwww-aannn' which is nice, especially seeing as I only got on for 20 minutes and didn't really get any chances.

Delia and Michael and our chairman, Roger Munby, come out onto the pitch to applaud the fans who, if possible, go even wilder. We're all clapping each other. God, this is great. This is abso-fucking-lutely chuffing great. The only thing missing is a trophy. Everyone can have a decent Christmas now. Well, everyone except the groundsman heading towards me and Delia on his mower. Delia's got her back to him and he doesn't appear to have seen us, so I drag her out of the way and ask him for a smile. He bares his teeth – well, tooth, really, as most of his front ones are missing – so I shout to him: 'No, don't bother mate, just keep looking miserable.'

Funnily enough, when we get back to Norwich six or seven of the lads fancy a drink (well, it's not every day you go Top Of The League at Portman Road, is it?), so we head out to Delaney's. I walk in with Briggsy and a big crowd of people start giving it 'Iwaaaan Iwaaaaan!'. Briggsy looks at me in amazement: 'Bloody hell, you only got on for 15 minutes!' Normally I run straight for the corner in embarrassment, but I must admit tonight I'm loving it.

And so we stay and do what everyone else is doing and get well and truly rat-arsed. There are three reasons for this. One: with all the games over the Christmas period this is the boys' last chance for a night out. Two: if we'd lost we would have been stuck indoors, unable to show our faces until the summer, so the sense of relief is massive. Three: we've just gone top of the League – and at Ipswich, of all places. All night deliriously drunken fans come up to tell me what a good plan that was.

Monday 22nd

I'm still buzzing about yesterday. We've had a few chances to go top of the League before and not taken them. How ironic that we should finally do it at their place. Ask any Norwich supporter and they'd say we couldn't have done it better. We have played better, but we ground it out and defended superbly, although neither side had many chances.

It was pretty loud in the dressing room afterwards, a stark contrast to when we beat Ipswich at Portman Road a couple of years ago. That day remains one of my favourite footballing memories: well, I scored two! We were going mental in the dressing room after. But it was ex-Ipswich player Bryan Hamilton's first game in charge of Norwich and he told us all to shut-up, saying: 'Pipe down lads, you're a bit too loud. Show some restraint.' Incredible.

This time around the gaffer wasn't jumping around, that's not his style, but you could tell by his face he was well chuffed. Well chuffed! It's the biggest result of our season so far, and it looks like we might just have put that bloody Christmas jinx to bed.

My parents are coming down today and staying for the New Year, which is great because a) the kids absolutely love having them stay and b) I'm useless at wrapping presents so I can get my mum to give me a hand.

Tuesday 23rd

He's behind you! No, not Malky, the evil villain Abanzer. I'm in the Theatre Royal with the girls and Wishy Washy keeps mentioning the score on Sunday which gets a bigger cheer than anything else. The girls think the panto is great, apart from: 'There's too much singing in it.'

Gary and Lisa Holt are there with their son Luke too, and Darren and Kelly Eadie with their son Taylor and Neil Adams with . . . can't see Holly or Max, his kids. Maybe he's such a big panto fan he's come on his own.

Get in and switch on *Sky Sports News*: Hucks' move to us has apparently broken down. Must give him a call tomorrow to see how he is.

Wednesday 24th

The gaffer gives us a target of 50 points by the end of Sunday, which means a win and a draw from our next two games. He names the team for Forest on Boxing Day – unchanged from Sunday – and then he tells us the big news . . . Hucks won't be joining us.

Talks have broken down over money, apparently, and later on there is a big piece in the *Evening News* in which Hucks is reported saying that he had been willing to take a pay cut.

'However it became clear, first last night and again this morning, that Norwich were expecting more manoeuvra-bility from myself and Manchester City than they were prepared to do themselves. To the point where I have been forced to ask the question: 'Just how much did Norwich want me in the first place?''

That doesn't sound like Hucks to me. West Brom manager Gary Megson is also quoted in the article as saying that Norwich have made Hucks a very good offer and that 'it's one I wouldn't want to match.' God knows what's going on.

After training I foolishly take Ben to see *Lord of the Rings*, but it's not long before I'm wishing I'd waited for it to come out on DVD. Three-and-a-half hours! With my back. Are you sure? The people around us in the cinema must have thought I had ants in my pants, I was fidgeting so much. Ah well, at least I didn't fall asleep like the man sitting the other side of Ben. Ben thought it was hilarious when he started snoring.

While we were out, my mum and dad took the girls to the Christmas church service in Brundall as they really enjoyed it last year. I'm looking forward to this evening but dreading it too: they'll be so excited and it will be a nightmare to get them off to sleep. Mind you, I was worse as a kid: me and my brother used to wake up at 2am and wouldn't go back to sleep. At least they'll lie in until 7am – they have to, as we've told them we'll take away a present for every minute they're up before then!

Thursday 25th

Actually, I think the girls would have slept in until 9am, but for Ben. At 7.01am he's straight into the girls' bedroom to wake them up. Cheers, mate.

The girls are delighted to see Father Christmas has been. Ben, of course, being a man now, *knows*. I get some nice stuff, including a really lovely coat from Julie, a New York Giants football shirt from Ben and Prada trainers from the girls. I am quite hard to buy for because I've got everything I want (my lovely wife and three gorgeous kids, of course). But in the past my mum's got me some dodgy big fleeces which I call 'walking the dogs tops', which makes Ben laugh his head off. Sorry mum. Just to even it out, Julie's mum gets me the odd strange present too. This year she gets me a video called *Purple Helmets* – it's about motorbike stunt drivers in case you're wondering! In the past she's given me a football joke book, a nice corkscrew (but I don't like wine!) and one year I got an egg box with golf balls in – her old man's a greenkeeper and finds loads of balls.

Ben got a Miami Dolphins football shirt with 13 and Robbo on the back. I know it's unlucky but Dan Marino's number is 13. Actually it wouldn't bother me wearing 13 – although I'd still have to do my laces routine. After an hour or so, our living room looks like a bomb's hit it. Wrapping paper everywhere. I hate mess, so I head for the kitchen to make everyone bacon sarnies, well, everyone apart from yours truly – I'm saving myself for Christmas dinner. I've got training tonight, too.

Take the girls to the skate park so they can try out their new rollerblades, and play Ben at his new PlayStation games – and beat him at football, obviously. Then, at 2pm, we head up to the Hilton for Christmas dinner so that Julie and my mum can have a relaxing morning without worrying about burning the turkey. Our time together on Christmas Day is very precious, especially as I usually have to go off travelling or training. Some of the other guests there are seriously hungry: you could send out an expedition to conquer the mountain of food on their plates. I limit myself to a bit of turkey, a little pork, a few roast potatoes, some stuffing and some peas . . . and a lemonade and lime.

Then I head into training for 6pm to do a light jog to sweat off some of that turkey. I ring Easy at 5.55pm to see where he is. Playing Twister with his family is the answer: he thought we didn't have to be in until 6.15pm. Dozy sod! He makes it in record time.

The gaffer tells us the club is giving the fans the best Christmas present ever: Darren Huckerby. He'll be here tomorrow. The lads are all well pleased. But he warns us: 'Lads, the club aren't paying all of his wages, some of it is coming from other sources. I don't want people coming knocking at my door saying they want X amount of money, because it's just not there!'

We're like: 'Fucking hell gaffer, do we look silly?'

We haven't got a bee in our bonnet that Hucks is on more money than us, we're just delighted that he's signed. Good luck to him. You sign your own contract, you're happy to sign it and if someone else comes along and signs for more, good luck to them. I remember talking to board director Michael Foulger in Delaney's one night back when Hucks was on loan and he said: 'We're desperate to sign him but we don't want to cause any ructions in the squad.'

I told him then that that wouldn't be the case. Get Hucks and we've got a better chance of being promoted. And that's what we all want, simple as that. We all take into consideration the financial situation of the club. We know that if we get promoted we'll get rewarded, but we wouldn't expect to go up to what he's on. We don't want to end up like Ipswich, Leicester, Bradford or Derby where you could drive the club into administration. No way.

Friday 26th

Nationwide League Division One
Norwich City 1   **Nottingham Forest 0**
Svensson 14
Carrow Road   Att: 16,429

Tonight's game against Forest is live on Sky Sports, so we're not kicking off until the strange time of 5.35pm. Great: an extra couple of hours to wait around getting keyed up. The gaffer just tells us to go for a 20-minute walk this morning, which is fine by me and Molly. I get to the ground around 3.30pm and am delighted to see a friendly face having his medical. Hucks and his wife are chuffed to bits it's all sorted and can't wait to move down here with their two little boys.

The club's PR manager Joe Ferrari and brand marketing manager, Will Hoy, have had the brilliant idea of introducing him to the fans big-stylee, like a boxer, by taking him out on the pitch 15 minutes before kick-off. It has the desired effect: we can hear the roar in the dressing room, the whole ground just erupts. I knew he'd get that reaction but it's still great to hear. The fans are singing: 'On the fourth day of Christmas my Delia gave to me . . . Four Huckerbys, Three Huckerbys, Two Huckerbys and a Da-rren Huck-er-by.'

Oh no, he's going to start crying again!

West Brom only managed a draw against Derby earlier this afternoon, so we know if we win we can go three points clear at the top, which would be amazing. And we do. We win 1–0, with a quality finish from Matty Svensson, although Forest make it hard for us and we don't play particularly well. Me? I get my three minutes . . .

It is frustrating. Obviously, all the new boys need time to settle in, but neither of them held the ball up particularly well today and the longer the game went on the more Forest put pressure on us. I was itching to get on. I haven't told the gaffer that Hucks has said he'd prefer to play up front with me. If he can't see it on the pitch, even in training, the little bits that come off between me and him . . . maybe I should ask Hucks to put a word in for us.

Still, we get the three points, and that's the most important thing. In public the gaffer will defend us to the hilt, which is what you want from the manager, but he lets us know, in no uncertain terms, he's not happy with our performance.

But we're picking up wins even when we're not playing well. I wouldn't say it in public, but I would put a fiver on us to go up as champions. Right now. We're a better team than West Brom and we've got more games to play at home.

Saturday 27th

We don't have to be in training until midday today so I head for Greens and my sauna fix, which I've really missed lately thanks to the Christmas break. Then I pack my bags and head for Colney, where the gaffer announces there will be a few changes for the game at Derby tomorrow, due to tired legs. Hopefully that means I might get on!

The kids bought me *The Office* DVD for Christmas so I enjoy a bit of that on the three-hour journey north – and a bit of quiet time. I'm rooming with Easty tonight so I'll be lucky to get a word in edgeways but at least I'll be entertained – all bleeding night as it turns out. Easty loves talking so much he even does it in his sleep (when he's not snoring). The secret is not to answer him. I am pleased for Easty that he's made the squad, because he's not been involved for ages, but he tells me tonight he's not sure if he wants to get on because he's not sure what the crowd's reaction is going to be. I try to reassure him, but I'm not sure it works.

Sunday 28th

Nationwide League Division One

Derby County 0   **Norwich City 4**
                        Fleming 51
                        Mackay 78
                        McVeigh 81
                        McKenzie (pen) 88
Pride Park   Att: 23,783

I'm on the bloody bench again. The only change the gaffer has made is one that was forced upon him: Mullers has a bit of a hamstring strain so Damo's back in. Good for him: I thought he was a bit unlucky to be dropped in the first place.

Pride Park is a magnificent stadium and, once again, we have incredible support, despite it being a bitterly cold day. For once we start really well and we are unlucky not to go ahead, although Derby start to come back into it and Greeno makes a brilliant save to keep it 0–0 at half-time.

The second half is a totally different affair: we play some superb football and utterly dominate the half. It's quite a rough ground, Derby. I'm warming up in the corner between the Derby fans and ours and this Derby fan starts shouting 'Sheep-shagger' at me. He's got a nine-year-old boy with him as well. Anyway, he is a big fat bastard so, after the tenth time he's shouted this, I mime a fat tummy back to him. This sends him crazy and he comes steaming over to try and have a go at me, but the stewards stop him. Then they ask me to warm up somewhere else.

'Why?! I was just laughing at him.'

'You're antagonising our fans.'

'Bollocks! He's calling me all the names under the sun,

I pull a fat face back to him and I'm antagonising him. Why don't you stop him shouting at me?'

So I carry on stretching. The fat man keeps shouting.

'Roberts, Roberts! Hope you die!'

Nice. Great education for his kid. So I just signal the score with my fingers: 3–0 and shout:

'It's only a game, mate! Get over it.'

In the end, we win 4–0 with goals from Flem (yes, star striker Flem again – is he after my number 9 shirt too?), Malky, Squiz and Leon scoring from the penalty spot. I have to admit I'm a bit pissed off about this. I got on with five minutes to go, we won a penalty and the crowd was giving it 'Iwaaann! Iwaaannn!', but Leon picked up the ball, despite the fact he's only been here a couple of weeks. When you're at a new club you generally try to break yourself in gently. I could hear Holty shouting to him: 'Let Robbo take it.'

I was wondering what to do, so I started walking over, but realised he was going to take it whatever, so I went back and stood on the 'D', willing him to miss. Fair enough, he is confident and he scores – but afterwards he didn't even look at me. Not a split second thought of 'Hang on, I've only been here two minutes, who takes the penalties around here?'

Maybe he doesn't know about my 100. I don't want to be treated as a charity case but I think it's a little bit out of order, although I'm not going to make a song and dance about it. If he'd missed I probably would have said something. If it happens again I'll take the next one. Unless Rivvo's playing; he started the season as our pen-taker and scored two out of two, so I respect that.

Still, it's a great win and puts us six points clear at the top of the division. Let's hope we can keep it up. January hasn't traditionally been the best of months for us.

Monday 29th

Day off today but, as I only got five minutes yesterday, I head straight for a 40-minute run at Greens to keep my fitness levels up. At 10.30am I meet Julie and the kids in the city to get the girls some new school shoes and then take them swimming. Well, I should say, watch the girls swimming from the comfort of the canteen. They won't get me in there: it's too cold!

Call former Norwich manager Mike Walker for a chat. He left a message on Christmas Day and I feel terrible I haven't got back to him sooner. He's a lovely man, really sincere, and as the man who brought me to Norwich I have so much to thank him for.

My old team-mate Darren Kenton finally made his debut for Southampton this evening, as a sub, after struggling with injuries since his summer move from Norwich. Hopefully he's over all those now. Not only does he play well, he also manages to show off his upper body muscles live on Sky Sports. Well done, Kents mate!

Tuesday 30th

Yuck! It's cold and wet again. I just want to stay in bed, but I drag my body down to Colney to prepare for our FA Cup game away to Everton on Saturday. It's a massive game for us, but the way we are playing and with the confidence buzzing around this morning, I wouldn't bet against us getting a result. The lads who played on Sunday have a five-a-side with the gaffer, while the rest of us have a hard session with Webby and Steve Foley. I enjoy it, as it's mostly ball work, not just running, but I must admit, it is hard to get yourself going when you're in the reserves. I've been feeling a bit low and not starting against Ipswich still rankles. I'm normally a bubbly person around the training ground and I think people expect me to be up all the time, but today I just can't force a smile: sometimes you just can't help but show how you're feeling.

Still, I'm not as miserable as people like Briggsy and Rivvo who've not even got on the bench. It's hard. I don't know why Rivvo's not been playing. He doesn't go out drinking when he shouldn't. He's a family man, loves his fishing, hasn't got a bad bone in his body. People say maybe they've had an argument, but I can't see Rivvo upsetting anyone, let alone the gaffer. Rivvo is a bit pissed off that some people who aren't working as hard as he does in training are getting on the bench. Crewe came in for him to go on loan but the gaffer said no. We've not got a big squad so I can understand, but I hope he gets back in the side. I like him as a player and as a person.

Wednesday 31st

There will be no partying for us tonight. The gaffer has told us, in no uncertain terms, that he doesn't want anyone in training tomorrow reeking of alcohol. We're to have a couple of drinks and just be sensible, so I have a sensible couple of beers with little Al at lunchtime and head home. We've booked a table at our local pub, the Yare, for 5.30pm with my parents and Briggsy and his girlfriend Ann-Marie. The Yare's very child-friendly and we know all the locals so we're quickly having a really nice time. We finish eating and, having been on the lemonade and limes up until now, I decide to treat myself to a bottle of Bud. Of course, just as I put it to my lips some busy idiot walks past and shouts at me: 'Bloody hell, Iwan, you won't beat Everton drinking that, will you?'

Trust him just to see one of the two beers I have, not the six pints of lemonade and lime. I just shrug and say:

'I've got to have a life as well, mate,' and thankfully he buggers off, having 'made his point'. Good God, it's New Year's Eve and Iwan has two bottles of Bud. I should be shot.

I think my mum and dad make up for my lack of alcohol intake with a few whisky chasers – purely medicinal of course. Then we stroll back to mine at around 9.30pm, see the New Year in and half an hour later Briggsy and Ann-Marie head off home and we head off to bed. I bet that prat in the pub is pissed as a newt by now.

Nationwide League Division One

				HOME					AWAY					
Pos	Name	P	W	D	L	F	A	W	D	L	F	A	GD	PTS
1	**Norwich City**	**26**	**11**	**1**	**1**	**25**	**10**	**4**	**6**	**3**	**16**	**11**	**+20**	**52**
2	West Bromwich Albion	25	6	5	2	17	10	7	2	3	19	12	+14	46
3	Sheffield United	25	8	3	2	24	10	5	3	4	15	17	+12	45
4	Sunderland	26	7	5	1	17	7	5	3	5	17	15	+12	44
5	Ipswich Town	26	7	2	4	27	18	5	4	4	19	20	+8	42
6	Wigan Athletic	26	7	4	2	18	10	4	5	4	17	18	+7	42
7	West Ham United	26	5	5	3	21	14	5	6	2	14	9	+12	41
8	Preston North End	26	8	3	2	26	13	3	4	6	13	17	+9	40
9	Reading	26	7	2	4	17	16	4	3	6	13	17	-3	38
10	Millwall	26	6	5	2	14	7	3	4	6	15	19	+3	36
11	Crewe Alexandra	26	8	2	3	22	13	2	4	7	10	19	0	36
12	Cardiff City	26	5	4	4	24	14	4	4	5	18	21	+7	35
13	Walsall	26	6	5	2	20	12	3	3	7	8	15	+1	35
14	Stoke City	26	5	5	3	19	14	4	1	8	14	20	-1	33
15	Gillingham	25	6	1	6	16	17	3	5	4	15	20	-6	33
16	Rotherham United	26	5	4	4	12	12	3	5	5	12	20	-8	33
17	Coventry City	26	4	6	3	15	14	3	5	5	15	18	-2	32
18	Crystal Palace	26	3	5	5	15	18	5	2	6	17	22	-8	31
19	Watford	26	4	6	3	15	14	3	2	8	13	20	-6	29
20	Nottingham Forest	25	4	4	4	19	14	3	3	7	15	21	-1	28
21	Burnley	26	5	3	5	20	17	2	4	7	17	30	-10	28
22	Derby County	25	3	3	6	16	23	2	6	5	9	18	-16	24
23	Bradford City	26	3	2	8	12	21	2	3	8	8	18	-19	20
24	Wimbledon	25	2	2	8	14	24	3	0	10	13	28	-25	17

JANUARY

Thursday 1st

Wake up to discover there are loads of police cars in our village, and the centre seems to be all blocked off. Probably a bad car accident, I'm thinking as I drive to work this morning. Sadly not. Julie calls me straight after training to tell me the shocking news that a 17-year-old lad was murdered in Brundall last night. I can't believe it: it's such a nice, quiet village. Who would do something like that? Julie tells me they've arrested four youths in connection with the murder.

At the end of training I get some great news from the gaffer. I'm starting on Saturday alongside Hucks. I spend the rest of the day with a massive smile on my face, even when saying goodbye to my parents who are heading home to north Wales. Luckily, they don't take offence – anyway I'll see them on Saturday at the game.

Friday 2nd

We leave for Liverpool at 9am and finally arrive what feels like five days later, particularly in my lower back. In the afternoon we train at Bolton's training ground and I think it makes some of the lads realise how lucky they are to be at Norwich and what exceptional facilities we have. Bolton's aren't too bad, but the building is a bit like a Portakabin and the training pitches are a bit boggy with really long grass. I think it's a bit of an eye-opener for quite a few of the lads, some of whom maybe take what we've got for granted.

Afterwards, I have a quick chat with their assistant

manager, Phil Brown and striker coach, Frank Stapleton.
I played with Frank when I was at Huddersfield and we
got on really well. He's a real gentleman and Julie
completely fell in love with him. Frank was in the bar
once after a testimonial at Huddersfield and Julie was
like: 'Wow! Who's that over there? He's gorgeous!' Her
eyes were almost popping out of her head. Then he signed
for us about six weeks later. No, I wasn't worried at all!

Anyway, Phil and Frank have been watching us train and
they say they can tell we're top of the League and our
confidence is sky high from the amount of noise coming
from training. It's nice when you get compliments like
that. I must tell the gaffer: he loves people training with
as much passion and commitment as when they play.

I'm sorry for Matty that he's struggling with his knee
injury but delighted to finally be starting again and I feel
part of the team again after three frustrating weeks.
Especially because half my family are big Evertonians
and they'll all be at the game tomorrow. I think deep
down they'd like us to win, though.

I spend a quiet evening in the hotel reading. Shock,
horror! Footballer reads book and his name isn't Graeme
Le Saux! Actually I bought it for myself for Christmas:
it's the autobiography of Lance Armstrong, the American
Tour de France winner who's been battling cancer. It's
really inspiring and I would recommend it to anyone.

Saturday 3rd

FA Cup Third Round
Everton 3   **Norwich City 1**
Kilbane 15   *Brennan 27*
Ferguson (pens) 38, 70
Goodison Park   Att: 29,995

I have just got on the coach to go home from Everton and I'm really pissed off. Great game, fantastic atmosphere: nearly 6,000 of our fans there and they completely outsung the Evertonians. They were magnificent. I, on the other hand, had a game of two halves.

I played well, winning nearly all my headers and linking up well with Hucks. Then, in the 33rd minute I had a good goal disallowed for offside, when the replay clearly showed I was a yard onside. It would have put us 2–1 up and changed the game as we were all over them at that stage. And then I gave away two penalties.

I'm still seething about them now. They were both on Alan Stubbs at corners and in my opinion they were both poor decisions. Then there were two clear handballs by Everton players in the second half but the ref just waved play on.

We played really well, especially in the second half, when we pinned them back in their own half for about 25 minutes. In the first ten minutes we had about four corners and, before the fourth one, Nigel Martyn came up to me and said: 'Fucking hell Robbo, what do they put in your tea at half-time?'

That says it all really. Me and Nigel had a bit of a laugh. He's rolling the ball out so obviously I have to go and close him down so, just as I get close, he picks it up, kicks it and says: 'Robbo, I'm really sorry. I fucking hate doing that to strikers, I really, really do.'

'Well, if it makes you feel better, just leave it on the floor for me next time!'

Fitness coach Dave Carolan shows me my 'goal' on the bus on the way home. It's infuriating: if you're level you're onside and the ref's supposed to give the benefit of the doubt to the striker. But those are the sort of decisions that don't go your way when you're playing a Premiership side away from home.

It's the same with the two pens. I've just watched the second one on telly and I can see why he's given it – we interlocked arms, I've dragged him down. But I can't see for the life of me why he's given the first one. Someone's headed it back, it's gone through Flem's legs, bounced, I've caught Alan Stubbs' studs as I've gone to clear it and he's gone flying down as I fell over. I said to Holty, if you gave a pen every time something like that happened you'd be getting ten penalties a game.

Stubbs and I had another little tussle in the second half. They had a free-kick, I stood in front of him and he was pushing me so I slapped him in the face. To be fair to Stubbs he didn't go down and make a meal of it. The ref just pulled us both over and we shook hands.

Their manager, David Moyes, who I think is a top manager, was very complimentary about us afterwards. But we lost 3-1 and we're out of the cup yet again – that's six times in the last six years now that we've been dumped in the third round. If they'd scored three good goals, then fair enough, but two dubious pens?

Anyway, I'm gutted. Today was a big chance for me. Matty's out for few weeks and I wanted to make an impression, make the manager's decision that little bit harder. I scored a goal which should have stood but then conceded two penalties that were, at best, dubious. Whether it costs me my place remains to be seen.

It's a long journey home. We stop at some motorway services to get some crisps and drinks and all the Norwich fans' coaches are there. I decide not to get off. All the fans are lined up watching us eat. Malky has a massive Cornish pasty. The gaffer says we can eat what we want after a game as we have to replace all that spent energy – the boys would have been in the KFC but the queue was too long.

I ring Julie and she's been listening to Neil Adams' phone-in on Radio Norfolk. She is upset because a couple of fans have had a go at me, saying I am too slow and aggressive. Well, I've always been slow and football is an aggressive game. That's why I think I'm still playing at 35: I've never had the pace to lose so I'm not exactly going to miss it now. A couple of fans also had a pop at Greeno for not saving either of the pens. But you'll always get those people. That's why it's important the lads stick together. The gaffer says there'll be a time this season when things aren't going well for us and it's important we all stick together – players and fans!

Sunday 4th

Retail therapy: we head off early to Bluewater to do a bit of shopping in the sales. It's a nice family day out before the kids go back to school tomorrow. Hucks rings me while we're wandering round to see how I am; he's worried I'd be a bit down after conceding the two pens. I'm touched by that; it's very thoughtful.

On the way home we stop and get the kids a McDonalds for their tea. I open the window and the lad serving says: 'You played well yesterday. Shame about those two pens, what were you doing?'

Oh God. Is nowhere safe?

I finally get a chance to read last week's *Pink'Un*, which makes me smile. Their columnist, Man In The Stands – who I've always thought was quality by the way – says that I should be first choice to start up front with Hucks, as it's obvious we read each other's games well. In fact, he says it's a 'partnership made in footballing heaven'. Mmm, think I might photocopy the article and re-paper the gaffer's office with it.

Monday 5th

Hucks phones me early this morning – his flight back from Manchester has been delayed so he'll be late for training. I let the gaffer know and he's fine. Hucks' wife Lindsey and their kids are still living in Manchester so he stayed up after the game to see them.

We have a team meeting where the gaffer talks about his rotational system again. Sounds ominous for me. Again. I'll be very disappointed if I don't start against Bradford on Saturday: I think I played as well against Everton as I did in my previous start against Cardiff. I am feeling pretty stiff though. Thank God we just have a light morning – although unfortunately the warm-up with fitness coach Dave Carolan does absolutely nothing for my aching muscles. It seems no matter how much I stretch, my legs are still knackered, so I head off to Greens. Sitting in the jacuzzi for a couple of hours should do it.

Alan Stubbs is quoted in the *EDP* saying that Everton caused their own problems on Saturday, not Norwich, and he insists there's a massive gulf between us. Well, I wouldn't mind playing against him every week. I've always scored when I've come up against him.

He should remember the seasons he played for Bolton in the Second Division before he got his move to Celtic.

A bit further south West Brom are in turmoil. Their manager, Gary Megson, has been hammering his players in the press, something our gaffer would never do, which is just one of the many reasons why he'll never lose the dressing room. We respect him.

Tuesday 6th

Don't tell the gaffer, but I'm still knackered today. The Everton game took a lot out of me, but there's no way

I'm going to show it. I don't want him to have any excuse not to pick me for Saturday's game against Bradford. He did tell me at the start of the season that if I felt tired at any point just to tell him and he'd give me a couple of days off, which is very good of him. But I'm desperate to play so I battle through training, especially when I hear that Matty will need a minor operation on his knee and will be out for 4–6 weeks. I do genuinely feel for him, but I'm also desperate to stay in the team.

Wednesday 7th

Spend a lazy morning chatting with Flem in the sauna, before picking up the girls from school to take them ice-skating at the Forum's outside rink. Ben doesn't fancy it so he stands watching with his dad. I, of course, would love to have a go at a triple salco with a half-twist, but sadly I have signed a contract which forbids me from taking part in any high-risk activity such as ice-skating. Skiing, scuba-diving and fire-eating are also out, unfortunately. It's a shame, because I'm sure with balance and grace like mine I would have been a sensation on the ice. Afterwards we have a nice family tea at Mambo Jambos, before me and Ben crash out on the sofa to watch Chelsea v Liverpool.

Thursday 8th

Please, please let us be training inside today. Although the artificial surface kills my back, I would rather be anywhere than outside in the storm that's blowing around Colney this morning.

There's one brewing inside too. At 9.45am Steve Foley sticks his head round the dressing room door and says the gaffer wants to see me. You can probably guess what comes next. So I stick a big smile on my weary face and head for the gaffer's room. Before he can say a word, I say: 'I know you want to see me and I know why, but I don't want to speak to you!'

The gaffer has to laugh. He says he's starting with Hucks and Leon because he thinks their pace will cause Bradford problems. He also says that if it isn't working he will have no hesitation in putting me on. I'm disappointed. He keeps banging on about his rotational system, but it's the same players that keep getting rotated: me and Damo. Mullers will be back in for him on Saturday.

He also tells me that Walsall, Gillingham, QPR and Barnsley have come in for me to try and take me on loan, but that he's turned them all down. He says I still have a big part to play in his plans, he values my influence in the dressing room and he wants me around the place.

Fair enough. I respect him for being honest and I feel a bit more cheerful after our chat. To be honest, at this stage of my career I don't want to go anywhere else anyway.

To add injury to insult, we do start training outside – until it starts raining so hard that it's actually hurting our eyes.

Friday 9th

The gaffer's in a fantastic mood. He's really buzzing around this morning, humming to himself and smiling. When we have the team meeting at 10am, we're all sitting there expecting a new signing to walk through the door. Ronaldo, perhaps – well, it's bound to be a striker! But no. Finally he lets us in on the good news: Squiz has agreed to extend his contract for another two and a half years. We're all delighted with this news. It's a big boost to the team.

In the evening I watch our nearest rivals, West Brom,

take on Walsall on Sky, desperately hoping my old mate Neil Emblen and his side can do us a favour. Unfortunately for Neil and me, the Baggies win 2–0, despite the fact that they should have been 2–0 down in the first ten minutes.

Saturday 10th

Nationwide League Division One
Norwich City 0   **Bradford City 1**
                              Armstrong 45
Carrow Road   Att: 16,360

In the middle of a generally shit afternoon, one thing really gets my goat. Young Ian Henderson, our 18-year-old England whiz-kid, scorer of three goals in two fabulous games a couple of months ago, is not having the best of first halves and the odd pass is going astray. But instead of getting behind him, the crowd really start to get on his back. Some of our fans are even booing his every touch, and you can see him getting more and more demoralised, more tense and nervous with every ball that comes to him. I know fans want to see him taking people on and putting crosses in but that's not always on. Sometimes that option isn't there so you have to play a 'safety first' ball, back to the keeper or whatever.

I'm really disappointed with the crowd's reaction. In fact, I'm disgusted. If he'd cost the club £6m then fair enough, but he cost nothing and he's been playing pretty well – he's not even having a 'mare today. He's a local lad who loves the club. He's come through the ranks, he's only played a handful of games and he's still learning his trade. A bad crowd reaction can ruin a promising young footballer, absolutely shatter his confidence.

As he's walking off at half-time I run over to him, put my arm round his shoulder and tell him just to keep working hard, not to listen to the crowd. He's nearly in tears, the poor lad. Memories of my first season here come flooding back.

I feel even more sorry for him in the dressing room at half-time because we're all sitting there and the gaffer says: 'Right Hendo, you come off. Rivvo, you go on.'

I can see the poor lad's eyes filling up and for a second I think he might burst out crying. He's gone as white as a sheet. As soon as the gaffer finishes his speech I go over to him.

'You all right?'

He mumbles a 'yeah'. So I tell him: 'Fucking get your head up now! You've done all right. You've not given the ball away, just played it back. Now go and have a shower before you get pneumonia.'

'Yeah I will, Robbo,' he says.

He's very quiet, dejected even, on the bench in the second half, but he'll bounce back. I like him. He's usually got quite a cocky strut about him, but in a good way.

After 67 minutes the gaffer throws me into the fray. I get the ball and bring people into play a couple of times but there's nothing really on and the final whistle blows to signal our second home defeat of the season.

It's a bad day at the office. We haven't played well and, to rub salt into the wound, the only goal of the game is scored by Alun Armstrong – on loan to Bradford from a certain club just down the A140. In the dressing room afterwards the gaffer goes mad and questions the lads' bottle.

'Maybe I've got it wrong,' he screams. 'Maybe we're not good enough and we shouldn't be where we are. We didn't pass the ball and we got what we deserved from the game, which was nothing.'

He's quite right. Everyone expected us to win comfortably:

after all, Bradford are second from bottom. They've got some decent players, but we didn't help ourselves.

Earlier this week the gaffer had promised us the Friday, Saturday and Sunday of the FA Cup fourth round week-end off if things went well.

'You think you're having those days off?' he shouts now. 'Well, you can fuck off. You'll come in and work.'

It was a rubbish game to lose, and it really hits home when we see the other results and they've all gone for us apart from Ipswich winning. But, if we are going to have a bad patch, hopefully this is it . . . and hopefully it's over and done with now.

Bradford's Paul Heckingbottom is staying down after the game to go out with a few of the lads for a beer. He was a really popular lad during his short spell playing for us and we've all been looking forward to seeing him, so we risk the wrath of the City and go out as planned. Everyone apart from Greeno, Holty and, unsurprisingly, poor Hendo.

You have to stick together as a team even more when you've lost. I always thought we were a tight squad at Leicester but it's way better here. When I first came here, it was a bit cliquey, with players going off in twos and threes, but that's completely gone now: the manager worked really hard to get rid of all that. It happens at some clubs, but people here wouldn't dream of going into a little corner and saying 'It's not our fault, it's theirs.' Centre-forwards are usually the worst. If they score, but we lose the game, they can be like 'Well, I did my job.'

But there's none of that here. We believe in each other, there are no hidden agendas, we really are one big happy family. Which means that we have a nice night out and, thankfully, we don't get any bad reactions from fans. Crichts and Flem made New Year resolutions not to drink in January but, ahem, I think they might have broken them already.

Sunday 11th

I'm a bit fragile this morning, and I don't think it's because of the 23 minutes I had on the pitch yesterday, so it's straight out the door with Molly to clear the cobwebs away.

In the afternoon I take Ben to play against Drayton. I know it's going to be a tough fixture as Drayton are the best team in Ben's league and Thorpe Rovers haven't been having the best of times lately. Sure enough, Thorpe lose 15–0. It's not nice watching your son's team getting hammered like that.

Monday 12th

Knackered again, as I stayed up late watching American football last night. Well, it was the play-offs – and we all know how exciting and tense they can be. I'm gutted as my favourite team the Green Bay Packers lost to Philadelphia Eagles, but Eva has a Donovan McNabb shirt (Philadelphia's inspirational quarter-back) so she's chuffed when I tell her this morning and enjoys teasing daddy over breakfast.

Not a great start to the week then, and I'm dreading training this morning. The last time we lost, to Watford, it took the gaffer four days to get it out of his system. But, to his credit, he's fine this morning. It was a bad day at the office, now move on. He's calmed down since Saturday and tells us we can have next weekend off after all. He also asks me along to his staff lunch tomorrow to celebrate his manager of the month award for December.

The way the lads are talking about the Bradford game today, it seems they really missed having a target man up front. It's not why we lost, but it didn't help not having someone who could put himself about, hold the ball up and get it wide for the midfield to get crosses in. That's how you put teams under pressure. If there's no target man to hold the ball up it will keep pinging back at your defence, putting them under pressure and forcing them to drop deeper and deeper. I wonder if the gaffer will be able to think of anyone who can fill this role?

Tuesday 13th

There are only nine of us training today, as a few of the lads have got bugs and colds. We work on attack v defence and for once, the attackers come out on top. It doesn't happen very often against our back four, I can tell you. They're frustrating as hell to play against in training because they're as good during the week as they are on a Saturday.

When we've finished I have a few photos taken with a friend's nephew, Connor. His favourite player is Greeno, so I've arranged for him to meet him and take a few shots against him. I love doing stuff for kids: you can see how excited he is, and he has a fantastic morning getting all the players' autographs.

Then it's off for a very enjoyable lunch with the gaffer and all the staff. I have a very nice time chatting with Dave Carolan and Terry. On the way home Peter Grant rings me and says a friend of his wants to know if I'd consider playing for Dundee for six months. Thanks but no thanks, Granty. I'm happy here, even if I am only playing a bit part at the moment.

Wednesday 14th

We're supposed to be going out for dinner with Pam and Freddy from across the road tonight, but I don't feel too clever. I feel really queasy and don't dare eat anything as I'm sure I'd just bring it straight back up. I hope I haven't caught what the other lads have been going down with.

Thursday 15th

I'm not feeling sick when I wake up, thank God, but my neck is agony. I think I've pulled a muscle in my chest and it's making my neck and back sore. Every time I turn my head I get a shooting pain down my chest and back.

Shit. I have to be fit for Saturday as I'm starting up front with Leon. Hucks is playing on the left – well, actually, he's been given a licence to run anywhere he wants and wreak havoc.

Anyway, I manage to get through training okay, but I'm a bit worried. If it's still the same tomorrow I'm going to have to play on painkillers.

Friday 16th

Aargh. The neck and top of my back are still really painful, so I go in early to see Neal Reynolds. He has a good look at me for half an hour, clicking a few bits into place and getting his fingers deep into the painful tissue and it feels a lot, lot better. The test is whether it stands up to training.

As Neal's finishing off, Crichts walks in and his phone goes off. Like a speeding bullet, the gaffer comes dashing in from the waiting room.

'Did I just hear a phone?' he asks.

But Crichts has already scarpered and nobody says anything.

Later on the gaffer brings it up in court.

'Did I hear a phone go off?' he asks again.

Everyone looks at the floor.

'I just need someone to back me up,' he pleads, staring hard at the Fridge and Pete, his assistant. 'Any chance, lads?'

But, surprisingly, they keep schtum. My sources tell me Pete is keeping quiet because Crichts has something on him.

Next up is Webby. He got caught on the phone in the dressing room yesterday, but pleads that he was talking to another club's manager. An important work-related call.

'Sorry,' says Adam, '£10 fine.'

The Fridge jumps in to defend his fellow red coat.

'Oi, you can't do that, it's out of order. Going back to the phone the gaffer heard, well, it was Crichts's!'

But Adam's having none of it.

'No, no, mate, you can't be tried twice for the same crime. You had your chance to stitch him up but you're too late.'

When we finally start training I'm feeling under extra pressure as my friend Neil Featherby, who runs a sports shop in the city, has given me a pair of very, very flashy Kelme boots to try out. If I like them, he says they will sponsor me. Which would be nice. I was sponsored by Reebok for nearly ten years, but when I turned 30 for some reason they stopped calling. Their loss: I've played some of the best football of my career since then.

After a dodgy start (for both the neck and the boots) we all come good. I don't really like the look of the boots – but they're really comfortable and fit really well, which is something of a miracle in itself. Neal has done a great job on my ageing body and the neck and back feel fine. The yellow jersey has missed a great chance!

After training, the gaffer pulls me aside.

'Uh-oh!' I'm thinking. 'Come on, you only said I was in the bloody team yesterday!'

'Robbo,' he says, 'I just wanted to say that I made a mistake last Saturday not playing you. The two boys – Leon and Darren – are too similar and their game's not holding the ball up. Everyone can learn from their mistakes.'

Fair play to him that he had the bollocks to say that to me. Just proves again what an honest, decent manager he is.

After lunch we all pile onto the coach and leave Norwich at 1pm for the three and a half hour journey to Rotherham. No sitting back and taking it easy for me, though; I stand up for most of the journey, stretching my back and legs so they don't stiffen up again.

We're staying at a hotel in Sheffield tonight and I'm on my own again – all the other lads have got steady partners. So, after dinner I pop a couple of Voltarol and head up for an early night with Lance Armstrong's book – I'm on page 120 now!

Saturday 17th
Nationwide League Division One

Rotherham United 4	**Norwich City 4**
Butler 28, 42, 64	Roberts 29
Mullin 75	McKenzie 33
	Huckerby (pen) 45
	Francis 89
Millmoor	Att: 7,448

Cheers Neal. I wake up this morning feeling like I've got a brand new body. Well, okay, maybe not brand new, maybe not even the body of a 25-year-old, but I definitely feel a couple of years younger. Wish I looked it.

As usual, it's a cold, grey day in Yorkshire. The people are pretty welcoming though: I still keep in touch with lots of friends from my Huddersfield days. Well, they're mostly pretty friendly. When we go for our pre-match meal in the hotel we are ushered not into the dining room, but a meeting room. What's going on? It turns out that Sheffield United are at home to West Ham at 5.30pm and they're booked in for the afternoon too, so they get the dining room.

Now, I'm not saying the hotel staff were looking after their own first, but does it really take 20 minutes to make a piece of toast? All Hucks wants is a slice of plain bread for his traditional jam sandwich pre-match meal, but that takes just as long as the toast!

After the toast has finally arrived, Sheffield United's Rob Page comes out to see me and warns me our game today won't be easy. Rotherham lost to Northampton last week in the FA Cup and will be desperate to put that right. I tell Rob we'll be no pushovers either: we're desperate to put last week's defeat to Bradford behind us.

Rotherham has a great playing surface but the away dressing room is tiny. Earlier in the season West Ham were so unimpressed they actually got changed at their hotel. I think that's disrespectful to Rotherham but, honestly, there isn't room to swing a cat. So we have to get changed in shifts: us lads who are starting get changed first and go out to warm up, then the subs get changed. It's a bit of a walk to the pitch too, I think they're trying to knacker the opposition out before they even get there.

But they're not alone: Grimsby's dressing room isn't the best, Crewe's is old and decrepit. A lot of players won't drink tea at away grounds either, they're worried they might have put salt in it. Quite a lot of clubs turn the heating up to make you lethargic – most clubs in fact.

At least Rotherham have got a big bath, like we have – mind you, theirs does need a good clean. The standard varies wherever you go and it's not always dependent on the size of club. Some clubs put soap and other products out, but they're in the minority, so we tend to nick stuff from our hotel to use after the game. Palace have got Head and Shoulders shampoo and soap containers, but they're stuck to the wall. They obviously don't trust

visiting teams. If we do make it to the Premier I'm looking forward to seeing whether we suddenly get any spa
products. Man U and Chelsea have probably got their
own brand of soap, and we might even get monogrammed
dressing gowns to nick.

Anyway, for the first ten minutes of the match we're
under the cosh, and sure enough Rotherham take the
lead from a long throw. I try to clear it but my clearance
hits a few bodies and bounces to their striker Martin
Butler who scores. I don't know what I could have done
to avoid it. It's the first goal we've conceded away from
home in the First Division for more than seven hours.

A minute later I make amends: Squiz crosses the ball
to Holty who knows I always pull to the back post, so
instead of heading for goal, he glances a clever little
header into my path. The ball takes a lovely bounce and
sits up nicely, so I'm thinking 'Wow, just hit it.' So I do,
catching it sweetly, right on the laces of my brand new
boots. As soon as it leaves my foot I'm away. I know it's
in. It's such a relief to get back in the game straightaway
and I run straight over to Mullers who's warming up on
the touch-line for some high-fives before all the subs and
the rest of the lads pile in. Then I make sure I give the
thumbs-up to Terry – I always do that when I score. A
little lucky habit I started, but I really like Terry and feel
that little gesture sort of shows him how much he's
valued. I've never really been one for extravagant celebrations, I just go a bit mental in front of our fans. But
they're down the other end today, which is a bit far for
my aching legs.

Four minutes later Leon gets on the scoresheet to put
us 2–1 up. I hold the ball up, lay it off to him, he lays it
off to Hucks who takes his man on, pings a great ball in
and Leon heads it, the keeper saves it but he's there to
stick in the rebound.

Three minutes before the break Butler scores again to bring them level. This is turning into a cracker. At least the gaffer can't go any greyer! Just before half-time Hucks wins a penalty, picks himself up and puts it away; 3–2 to us when the ref blows his whistle . . . and then all hell breaks loose.

As we make our way to the tunnel their manager, Ronnie Moore, starts having a go at Hucks, screaming and shouting that he dived for the penalty. I'm still on the halfway line at this point, but the lads tell me that Ronnie really laid into Hucks, saying: 'Are you happy with yourself?'

So the ref sends him off. Apparently, Hucks did brilliantly to stay calm and just told him to watch the video. Ronnie's an experienced manager and should know better. If you've got something to say then say it, but there's a time and a place: that kind of reaction is ridiculous. I think they're still frustrated from Tuesday night as the prize for beating Northampton would have been Man U in the next round.

Did Hucks dive? All I can say is their fella's got his arms across Hucks, pulls him back and Hucks goes down. Why wouldn't he? Anyone with half a brain would do that if someone's dragging them all over the place in the box. If they think he went down easy they should take a look at the 'penalty' I conceded against Alan Stubbs at Everton the other week. Anyway, there was no way Hucks was giving me the ball for the penalty, so I'm never going out for a drink with him ever again.

By the time I get into the tunnel it's all going off. Everyone's pushing and shoving each other and one of their players is accusing Leon of spitting. I put my arm round him to get him out the way and ask what's happening. He says: 'Leon spat at me.' I look at his face and there's no spit on it whatsoever. 'Calm down mate, you're going to get yourself sent off and there's no need for it.'

The adrenaline is really pumping in the dressing room. We normally sit down, but everyone's on their feet, shouting at each other. We're a bit too fired up, if anything, and the gaffer tells everyone to calm down and keep their discipline. Nobody really says anything about the incident until the fourth official comes in and says Guy Branston has been sent off for violent conduct and Moore sent to the stands, but there is an allegation of spitting by our number 14. No-one seems to have seen it though, even though there were loads of stewards and other people around.

We've calmed down a lot by the time we come out for the second half. We're 3–2 up, kicking downhill, we've got the wind and I feel confident we'll go on and win the game quite comfortably. Unfortunately my legs disagree, and all through the second half they feel really heavy. Well, I'm not match fit, am I? I need to be playing regularly for that. I still have a few chances, though, and with a bit more luck I could have scored two or three.

In the end they score twice and it takes a last-minute goal from Damo to salvage a point for us.

We're still top of the League, but it feels like we really have dropped two points.

We're not down about it for long though. The good thing about this Norwich squad is that there's no blame culture: no-one is moaning that we've scored four goals away from home and only come away with a point. We're not like that: we attack together and we defend together. We're in this together. Sure, we all make mistakes and have our fallings out – like me and Malky. I disagree with Malky a lot about football, we're coming from opposite ends of the pitch, but I'm pretty close to him and would never let it affect our relationship off the pitch. It's the same with any of them.

I first met Malky when he was still at Celtic and I went

up to a game with Granty. I thought then what a nice lad he was. He's a diamond. But we argue like cat and dog. I've had some right ding-dongs with him in training; we're like a couple of schoolboys sometimes.

'Yeah, well you just do your job and I'll do mine!' we tell each other.

It's the same with all of them, but afterwards we always have a laugh about it. We all make little snidey comments in the heat of the moment because we're so passionate but it's all quickly forgotten.

Mullers is quite fiery too. He and Hendo had a little handbags at ten paces just before Christmas over something silly in training, a misplaced pass or a dodgy tackle. Mullers once got into a tussle with Zema in training, too, before he got injured. Zema brought him down from behind and Mullers turned round to have a go, looked up (a long look), realised it was Zema – who's built like the proverbial – and hastily went: 'Sorry mate.'

The good thing about today is that four different people scored. It was a bit of a gamble putting Hucks out on the left, but he does like playing wide and cutting in so he said it wasn't too alien for him. He's told me he doesn't want to make a career out there but he knows the team comes first. Obviously he doesn't give you as much as someone else would defensively but when you're as good going forward as Hucks is, when you can create that much havoc, it doesn't matter. You've got to give and take. You can't expect him to take on three or four defenders and then track all the way back.

It was my first time playing up-front with Leon and I thought the signs were good that we could get an understanding. I know he likes playing alongside someone big to feed him with knockdowns. I thought we linked up well, especially in the first half. He knows what he's doing and we played some nice little one-twos.

Hopefully, touch wood, I'll get a bit of a run in the team now. The way I look at it I've started eight games and scored in five of them, so I've proved I can do the job. OK, the Everton linesman said my goal was offside but it wasn't and I had that one wrongly disallowed at West Brom too. I'm enjoying my football and scoring goals, and that's what it's all about.

Get back home at 9.30pm to give the kids a cuddle, watch *The Premiership* and then hit the sack.

Sunday 18th

It's an early start for Ben and I this morning as he has a game against Bressingham, at Diss, about 40 miles away. They lose again but deserve something out of the game. Ben is captain for the first time today and plays very well.

Back home I decide to clean the car out, which inspires the girls to join me and clean their bikes and we have a lovely afternoon together in the winter sunshine.

Read the *Pink'Un* and am delighted to see that little Al came on for non-league local side King's Lynn for 35 minutes yesterday. He signed a contract with them during the week, but, unfortunately, he's not got his insurance payout for his professional career being ended by injury yet, so he's going to stop for now in case the insurers feel that he's back playing so they don't need to pay up. But he's not joined King's Lynn for the money: he's 23 and just desperate to play, see if his ankle holds up.

Monday 19th

Fitness tests! We each have to run on the treadmill for 18 minutes, with fitness coach Dave Carolan increasing the speed every three minutes. It hurts. After 18 minutes you stop and he takes a blood sample from your ear to measure the lactic acid that has built up: the less lactic acid, the quicker you recover from exercise. I'm pleased to say I'm pronounced one of the fittest at the club and my results are the same as they were at the start of the season. So, I'm fit as a fiddle and I've proved that, even at 35, I can still give some of these young lads a run for their money. Over a long distance, of course.

I have a session with Neal as I got kicked on the calf on Saturday and now it's swollen to twice its normal size. Neal has healing hands though, and after he's dug his fingers in it feels a lot better, although it's still very swollen and bruised.

Tuesday 20th

I feel really stiff after the tests yesterday: running on treadmills doesn't half give your joints a battering. To make matters worse, the ground out on the training pitch is really hard today. Just when I'm starting to get really paranoid that I'm showing my age, a few of the lads have a break and start moaning about how much their legs are aching too. Excellent!

In the evening Ben and I watch the youth team beat Sheffield United in the FA Youth Cup. Congratulations lads. They've got Man United in the next round. I over-hear someone say that United's youth team play at Accrington Stanley's ground, but I really hope they'll play this one at Old Trafford: it would be such a great experience for the young lads.

Wednesday 21st

The reserves are playing at Colchester this afternoon, so there are only nine of us in training today. I get in early to do my weights and get a rub on my calf. It's still very swollen but we've got those three days off this weekend, just as the gaffer promised, so it should be all right.

It will be a great chance for everyone to recharge their batteries. Some of the lads are going away for a few days – Phil and Squiz are off to Belfast to see family, Holty is going to Toronto to see his mum because she's had an operation, Jim's going to Milan with Sarah and Greeno's going to Majorca. Embo did call me to see if I wanted to go to Marbella, but it's hard to just take off for a few days when you've got kids at school.

So, tomorrow's the last day of training until next week, although we're all already dreading Monday morning's session when we know we'll be asked to run our bollocks off to compensate for our little break.

A nice relaxing Radox bath is in order this evening. The old legs are really feeling their age.

Thursday 22nd

The gaffer mentions the P-word for the first time today. · 'Well, I'm not too scared to say it,' he tells us. 'I'll talk about promotion because I think we're good enough to get it. I don't know if some of you are a bit wary, a bit anxious about this promotion, whether you might be in awe of going to places like Man U, but I'm not. Bring it on! Robbo, Malky, Flem, Holty, Eddy, it might be the last chance they get to play in the Premier. So if you're going to do it for anyone do it for them. I think we've got the best chance we'll ever have.'

I agree.

After the gaffer's psychology session, Adam announces he is resigning as judge: he'd been getting a bit of stick from the boys and the pressure was getting to him a bit. So we have a vote on who should take over and Webby just pips Squiz to the post. I'm a bit surprised by this, but I reckon it's because the lads know he'll be totally ruthless.

In the afternoon I head to Halfords to buy a bike. I've already got one, but it was made around the same time Noah was building his ark and my girls want to go out on long bike rides but my bike doesn't. So now I have a shiny new one made sometime this century.

Friday 23rd

Julie and I decide to spend our day off shopping in Cambridge. I think it's a beautiful city, some of the buildings are really impressive and they have a decent range of different shops. I manage to limit myself to a new pair of jeans and three T-shirts – pretty impressive, considering the sales are on.

In the evening I have arranged to meet up with Matty Svensson. I really like him, even though we're both fighting for the same place in the team. It's not a problem for either of us. I had the same situation at Wolves: Don Goodman and I were always fighting for the chance to partner Steve Bull up front, but we became very good friends.

Matty's dead quiet in the dressing room, but he's a mad bugger. Get a drink down him and he's Jekyll and Hyde. He does a great impression of Borak off *Ali G* that he just keeps doing over and over. It's funny the first few times but after a while you have to physically stop him: 'You're dying a death now, mate!'

I wonder what the city looks like on a Friday night?

Saturday 24th

Oh God! I am never, ever, ever, ever going out with Matty again. I feel absolutely shocking. I only drink lager and lime normally, but every time Matty went to the bar he bought us shots. Of course, I couldn't let the side down, so I had to drink them. I paid for it when I got in, though.

There's only one thing to be done: tracky bottoms on and take the girls out for the long bike ride I've promised them. The fresh air does me the world of good. When I get home an hour or so later I take some food up to the Memorial Hall in Brundall as they are holding a memorial service there later for Richard Barrington, the lad who died on New Year's Eve.

Then I head for Greens as the gaffer has asked us all to do a 30-minute run today, making sure I wear my heart monitor so he and Dave Carolan will be able to check I've done my homework.

The postman brings a letter from the club inviting me for an interview for the youth team coach's job on Wednesday. I'm surprised and delighted. I've never had an interview before so I'm not quite sure what to expect. Guess I'll have to wear a suit though. I'll have a chat with Webby and Steve Foley on Monday, although I feel a bit embarrassed now as I've just been quoted in the local paper as saying I'd like to play for another year.

In the evening we are out for dinner with a couple of friends. It won't be a late one though as I'm still feeling the after-effects of last night.

Sunday 25th

I feel fine this morning and make the kids bacon sarnies before taking Ben to his game against Dereham. Every Sunday morning I make the kids bacon rolls and I'm really tempted to indulge when the smell of bacon hits my nostrils, but I'm strong-willed.

Mind you, my best ever season for Huddersfield was fuelled by bacon sarnies. Every Saturday me and the rest of the lads would go to the George Hotel, where they'd have pasta and I'd have a bacon sandwich. I got 34 goals for them that season and won *Shoot!* magazine's Golden Boot, so it can't have been that bad for me, can it? We finished third, which meant the bloody play-offs again. We lost to Peterborough in the semis.

I still hold the record for most goals scored in a season at Leeds Road. Well, they moved to a new stadium after that, didn't they? That year, 1991/92 was amazing: I won everything, Top Scorer, Player of the Season you name it. Five trophies in all, I think. It was embarrassing.

I had some great times there – and yet, at first, I didn't really fancy it. I knew I was going nowhere with Watford after five years and Huddersfield's manager, Eoin Hand, offered £250,000 for me. But I didn't really fancy dropping from the First to the Second Division – or going up North – but I talked it over with Julie and my mum and dad and it was a good decision, with hindsight.

I had a bit of a dodgy first year: they'd bought me to replace Craig Maskell, aka God, who they'd sold to Bristol City. I was built up as 'the next big thing'. I got 15 goals in my first season there, but Craig used to get around 24 or 25 a season, so I don't think the fans were that impressed. I was their record signing, but at least I felt wanted, whereas at Watford, towards the end, I most definitely didn't.

I still remember the day I won the Huddersfield fans over. We were playing Bradford away – a local derby – and we were 2–0 down at half-time. I scored two goals in the second half to salvage a point.

Huddersfield is a good club – although I used to have to take my training kit home and wash it myself – and I made a lot of good friends up there. I still keep in touch with Chris Marsden, Simon Charlton and big Iffy Onura. Peter Jackson, who's now their manager, was my room-mate back then. We used to get into the odd scrape. I remember once going to Ireland and staying in a lovely hotel with a nightclub. The gaffer had told us we could have a few drinks, but he wanted us back in our rooms by midnight. Jacko had different ideas and suggested we sneak out into the nightclub. Stumbling the 100 yards back to our room after a few lemonade and limes, I somehow slipped off the kerb and went over on my left ankle – the one I always do. I was lucky not to break it. It swelled up like a balloon.

Jacko was as pissed as me and insisting I'd be fine, but I was really worried. 'How the hell am I going to explain I can't train tomorrow?' The next morning my ankle was black and blue and swollen to three times its normal size. I limped in to see the physio, Wayne Jones, who is now first team coach at Gillingham. Jonesy and I were pretty good mates.

'Well, you'll have to start training and then tell the gaffer you've tweaked your ankle,' he said.

Good plan. Otherwise I'd have been slapped with a fine. Of course, this was the one morning where the gaffer decided we should run to the training ground, about 15 minutes away, rather than take the minibus. Jonesy strapped up my ankle, but you should have seen me running. I was in agony. When we got there I managed to train for ten minutes, before crumpling to a heap under the slightest of challenges and limping off. Cheers, Jonesy. I still owe you one!

Anyway, today I'm keeping my fingers crossed for Thorpe Rovers: they have lost their last six games and not scored a goal for four. They really need a result today. All credit to them, their heads haven't dropped once during this losing streak. They've been working really hard, they're just not getting the results.

Unfortunately, with two minutes to go the boys are

3–2 down, despite having played quite well. Then, suddenly we equalise with a header from a corner and you'd have thought we'd won the League the way we all go mad on the touch-line, leaping about shouting and celebrating.

Monday 26th
I feel great after three days off, my legs and back feel brand new . . . until I read the local paper. It's full of how I want a new contract.

When I was out shopping on Friday Chris Wise of the *EDP* rang me up and said: 'Your contract's up at the end of the season, isn't it?'

'Yeah,' I said, 'but I'd love to carry on playing for another year because I still feel I have something to offer. I've started nine games and scored six this season, which makes me joint top scorer with Hucks, so who knows?'

Now I feel a bit embarrassed. It's got blown a bit out of proportion. I don't want the gaffer thinking I'm trying to put him under pressure. It was more a case of if someone asks you a question you answer it truthfully. The gaffer hasn't said a word to me about the article, but he doesn't need all this shit at the minute. He doesn't want any distractions, which I can fully understand. I hope he's not pissed off. I think he knows me better than that.

The *EDP* story can't be the reason he's in such a bad mood at training today, can it? He shouts at us that we're not working as hard as we should be. Maybe it's more of his mind games. Maybe Monday's the new Thursday. I certainly think we work harder in training than at any other club I've been at, and we're all absolutely determined to get promoted.

A few of the lads seem to get a bit nervous when he has a go like that, and become wary of making a mistake in case he shouts at them. But his mood lightens as the morning goes on. At the end of the session I score a few goals and he shouts: 'Fucking hell Robbo, you keep scoring like that, you'll be getting a new contract soon. You'll get that other year.'

He has a smile on his face.

I'm really enjoying my football these days, so I hope I do get a new contract. I know that next year Matty will be the gaffer's number one target man but if he gets injured or tired with 15–20 minutes to go, why not throw me on? What a finish to my career that would be, a season in the Premiership!

Tuesday 27th

Talk to the gaffer this morning about my interview on Thursday. He's very pleased for me and just tells me to go in there and be myself. The butterflies are already fluttering in the pit of my stomach. By the time 3pm Thursday comes they'll probably be worse than when I took the first penalty in the play-off final shoot-out. Well, I scored it, didn't I?

Even though it's very early in the week, we work on our formation for the match against Sheffield United on Saturday and how to counteract the way they will play. This is probably because it's such as big game for both teams: we both have ambitions of going straight up. During the session I play up front with Hucks. I'm not counting my chickens, but . . .

The gaffer's wife Sandra has organised a girls' get-together at Delia's Bar and Restaurant at Carrow Road this evening, so I have a nice quiet evening in, just me and the kids.

Wednesday 28th

Am woken very early by two very excited little girls, screaming that everything's covered in snow. I'd love to stay to be their snowball target all morning but I shoot into the city to get my car taxed. I say shoot, I mean crawl. The whole country's at a standstill. The sauna's never felt so good! Flem and Hucks are hibernating in here too, but Hucks has got a bad wisdom tooth so he nips off to the dentist.

I decide to walk to school to pick the girls up, as they would be gutted if I brought the car when there's a chance to snowball Dad on the way home. I hate walking, so it's a real labour of love.

Thursday 29th

It takes me 45 minutes to get to Colney this morning, three times as long as usual. It's been snowing again overnight and it's absolutely freezing. A couple of the lads are a few minutes late, but the gaffer's really pleased we just made it in okay and is merciful: we train in the indoor arena. Thank God.

After training I get all suited and booted for my interview and the butterflies are going ten to the dozen already. I've heard that 80 people sent in their CVs for the youth job but the club are only interviewing eight candidates, and I feel very proud and honoured to be one of them.

Except I'm not one of them – it's called off due to the interviewers being snowed in. So now I have until Monday at 3pm to be nervous. That's a whole lot of nervous.

Friday 30th

The back's surprisingly good today: it usually aches a bit after training on the artificial turf of the arena. We're in there again today, walking through the set pieces for tomorrow, followed by our usual old'uns v young'uns game. The young'uns have pulled the series back a bit and us oldies now have just the two game advantage. They're getting a bit cocky for my liking, especially Mullers. So we wipe the smiles off their faces. Today's game finishes 3–3 and goes to penalties, with yours truly scoring the winning penalty with my left foot. That's right, my left foot. This is not a misprint, it does happen. About as often as Easty buying a round, but it does happen.

I'm starting tomorrow and really looking forward to it. Sheffield United are one of the best teams in the division and if we beat them we will be seven points above them, having played the same number of games, which will put us in a fantastic position for claiming one of the automatic promotion places. The club are part-opening the new stand tomorrow, too, so there'll be an extra 3000 fans roaring us on, which should make for a cracking atmosphere.

Saturday 31st

Nationwide League Division One
Norwich City 1   **Sheffield United 0**
Roberts 59
Carrow Road   Att: 18,977

Wake up this morning to find all the snow has gone but it's been raining all night and is continuing to chuck it down. If it carries on like this the game could be in jeopardy.

Even Molly doesn't fancy it this morning. She looks at me like I'm mad when I suggest a walk. She soon realises that I am, quite possibly, mad: I need my Saturday morning walk to get some fresh air into my lungs and set me up for the day, so out we go.

Before kick-off I spend a few minutes catching up with old mates: Wayne Allison, who I played with at Watford, Mike Whitlow, who I was with at Leicester, and Rob Page and Carl Robinson who are former Welsh team-mates. Having been around as long as I have, I think I've probably got mates at pretty much every club.

The conditions are terrible – blustery, wet and the odd sleet shower – and it's such a big pressure game for both sides that it's no surprise when the first 15–20 minutes are fast and furious. There's not much football being played and it's pretty even between us. I win most of my headers but we never really create any chances and at half-time it's 0–0.

But the crowd are magnificent, really up for it and the extra 3,000 fans really add to the noise levels. We're talking about it at half-time.

'They're singing in the South Stand!'

'Are you sure?'

The old stand was always really quiet. The new one looks as though it's going to be completely different. I hope so. It really lifts the players.

The gaffer is pleased we've started at a good pace and that it's still 0–0 with everything to play for. He doesn't have to say much – he knows how important the game is to us so he just tells us to pen them in and use the advantage that we'll be kicking downhill in the second half.

People may be shocked to know there are hills in Norfolk, but there's a feeling among the lads that the pitch slopes down – ever so slightly – from the Barclay towards the River End.

We go back out, fired up and determined to win. I'm really enjoying myself and we're passing the ball around nicely.

My old mate Pagey is marking me and I can tell I've got him worried. He's getting more and more agitated and keeps having a go at the ref. I'm getting hold of the ball really well and he can't get near me, can't get a look-in.

In the 59th minute I win the ball near the halfway line and flick it on for Hucks who makes one of his by now traditional blistering runs down the left and cuts the ball across the six-yard box. Pagey half-clears it, but only as far as me, thundering in from the half-way line. To be honest I would normally have bust a gut and sprinted to get into the six-yard box, but my legs were getting a bit heavy and I realised there was no way I was going to get there. So I've three-quarters paced it from the half-way line which is lucky for me because when Pagey clears it to the edge of the box it drops right in front of me. Thanks mate! The ball takes a nice bounce so I don't even have to break stride before I hit it first time on the half-volley. Hard! I don't catch it quite as sweetly as I'd have liked, but it drives down into the ground and inside the post. Carrow Road erupts.

I'm already off: as soon as it's hit the ground, I know. I'm excited: the first goal in games like this is vital. I'm so excited in fact that I do a Klinsmann, diving to the floor, arms spread, as all the lads pile in on top of me. Ouch! Now I remember why I don't do that very often, it kills my back!

Five minutes later I miss a golden opportunity to make it 2–0. The ball comes at me really quickly, but I still manage to get decent contact on the header. Unfortunately not decent direction. No time to think. Just head it. Either side and it's a goal, but it goes straight into the keeper's arms. Shit! I should have just let the ball come to me, rather than throwing my head at it. That would have been number 95, only five to go. I should have scored and I'm gutted.

But I talk myself back into the game.

'Okay, come on! Pick yourself up. Remember all the best strikers in the world miss chances. Can't let it affect you, otherwise you'll snatch at the next chance you have. Forget it. Move on.'

My confidence is still sky high. The gaffer always urges us to enjoy the game and play with smiles on our faces and I am. The final whistle blows and we've done it. It's a massive, massive win. We're now seven points clear of Sheffield United. I think it's probably one of the most important goals I've ever scored for this club. This result could be crucial to our season and it was a great game to play in; I enjoyed it as much as the Cardiff game before Christmas.

As I'm walking back in to the tunnel, I see a furious Neil Warnock. Neil could have an argument in an empty room, but he was my manager at Huddersfield for three and a half months and I got on really well with him. We had quite a nice chat before the game. No chance now. I shake hands with his assistant, David Kelly and Neil turns round and says: 'Oh well done Robbo, I see you took my tactics on today, playing the long ball game!'

Cheeky sod.

'At the end of the day you've just got to play to the conditions, haven't you Neil?' I say and walk off.

You can tell the gaffer is buzzing. He doesn't have to say well done, he just praises our hard work and tells us not to underestimate what a big result this is. He shakes everyone's hands as usual and kisses his favourite son Adam on the cheek: 'You can have a lie-in tomorrow, Ad,' he says. 'You don't have to tidy your room!'

He showers while we go back out onto the pitch to do our usual warm-down, and by the time we get in he's ready to face the press, putting on his tie and doing his wig. He does his interviews and then goes to his room with his assistant Dougie and their families for a drink.

I finally turn my phone on (in silent mode as there's a £50 fine for mobiles going off in the dressing room). Embo's is the first text.

'Well done, mate, you've given the gaffer something to think about.'

'You're on fire,' says little Al.

Two lads I met on holiday in America, Everton and Forest supporters, text: 'You boys are flying.'

There's a fairly random, unrepeatable one from a mad woman who sits in the lower Barclay and another from my 'mate' Chris.

'Thought you miss-hit it mate, but good result.'

You what? Two minutes later he's at it again.

'Bullshit! Fucking great strike mate! You're back to your best!'

Why, you . . .

Out in the tunnel, Neil Warnock is being interviewed by TV and is hammering the ref, saying they should have had a penalty just before I scored. Well, we should have had two in the first half! Hucks' wasn't clear-cut but I've seen them given. I thought United's Michael Tonge went down quite easily for their 'pen', but Warnock (apparently also known as Colin W . . . according to some fans I was talking to yesterday, as it's a perfect anagram of his name – have a think about it) is having none of it. Midway through the interview, he spots the ref and breaks off to go and give him hell.

I'm buzzing. We've got a table for ten booked at Ha-Ha's bar and restaurant but in the end about 20 of us go out. Someone sends over a bottle of champagne for me. It's a brilliant gesture, but I don't like the stuff and the lads aren't bothered about it either (surely it's just for spraying?). So I have a quick peek to make sure the lad who sent it isn't watching and offer it to the woman at the next table celebrating her birthday.

We have a great night. It was Jimmy Brennan's first game today and I thought he did really well. I think there's a lot more to come from him. He's a left-back and was playing out of position on the left wing, but he's got one of the best left feet I've ever seen – a right great left foot. He worked his socks off today. All night people are coming over to congratulate us and tell me it's the best they've seen me play for a while. A lot of people say they thought I should have got 'Man of the Match', but things like that don't bother me. I know I played well and did my job. That's enough for me. I thought Damo, who did get it, was outstanding. Anyway, not only do I not like champagne and but the 'Man of the Match' has to go into the Gunn Club and do a post-match interview and all sorts of presentations and photos with sponsors and I wanted to shoot off to get ready for my night out!

A few vodka and red bulls later and I'm ready for my taxi when it arrives at 1am.

Nationwide League Division One

			HOME					AWAY					
Pos	Name	P	W	D	L	F	A	W	D	L	F	A	GD	PTS
1	**Norwich City**	**29**	**12**	**1**	**2**	**26**	**11**	**4**	**7**	**3**	**20**	**15**	**+20**	**56**
2	West Bromwich Albion	29	8	5	2	22	11	7	4	3	20	13	+18	54
3	Sheffield United	29	8	4	2	27	13	6	3	6	18	20	+12	49
4	Sunderland	28	8	5	1	18	7	5	3	6	18	17	+12	47
5	Ipswich Town	29	8	2	4	33	22	5	6	4	21	22	+10	47
6	Wigan Athletic	29	7	6	2	18	10	5	5	4	21	20	+9	47
7	West Ham United	29	6	5	4	24	17	5	7	2	17	12	+12	45
8	Reading	29	8	3	4	21	18	5	3	6	14	17	0	45
9	Preston North End	28	8	3	3	28	17	4	4	6	15	18	+8	43
10	Millwall	29	7	5	2	16	8	4	5	6	17	20	+5	43
11	Cardiff City	29	6	5	4	27	16	5	4	5	19	21	+9	42
12	Stoke City	29	7	5	3	24	17	5	1	8	15	20	+2	42
13	Crystal Palace	30	4	6	5	18	19	7	2	6	24	24	-1	41
14	Crewe Alexandra	29	9	2	4	24	15	2	4	8	14	25	-2	39
15	Coventry City	29	4	8	3	16	15	4	5	5	21	19	+3	37
16	Gillingham	28	7	1	7	17	20	3	5	5	16	22	-9	36
17	Walsall	29	6	5	3	21	18	3	3	9	10	20	-7	35
18	Rotherham United	29	5	5	4	16	16	3	5	7	15	25	-10	34
19	Burnley	29	5	4	5	21	18	2	6	7	17	30	-10	31
20	Watford	29	4	6	4	16	19	3	3	9	14	23	-12	30
21	Derby County	29	5	3	6	20	24	2	6	7	11	23	-16	30
22	Nottingham Forest	28	4	4	5	19	15	3	4	8	15	22	-3	29
23	Bradford City	30	3	2	10	13	24	3	3	9	9	19	-21	23
24	Wimbledon	29	2	3	9	14	25	3	0	12	14	32	-29	18

FEBRUARY

Sunday 1st

I'm too excited to sleep and wake up at 4am and 6am before eventually getting up at 7.30am. Disaster! The papers are late so I can't read about myself. When they do eventually arrive they've forgotten the *Pink'Un*, so I have to wait until Julie drops Eva at a party and brings it back for me. Bizarrely, there's a pic of Hucks on the front page. Hello? Didn't I score yesterday? Aren't you bored with having his ugly mug on the cover?

Neil Adams, who also writes a column in the *Pink'Un*, texts me saying:

'People have been writing you off for 18 months now and I've been sticking up for you and I'm just glad that at long last you've proved me right!'

Cheeky sod.

I watch *Sky Sports News* and see Crouchy scored a couple for Aston Villa yesterday. I'm really pleased for him: he took his goals well. What's nice is that he thanks Norwich for playing a part in his goals by restoring his confidence. Aah!

Then I watch Ian Walker man-handling the supporter who ran onto the pitch at the Walkers Stadium and started having a go at him yesterday. Ian pushed him away and the fan deserved it, he's got no right to get on the pitch. He's lucky Ian didn't smack him one; I would have. As soon as someone crosses that white line and comes on the pitch I think that gives you every right. You don't know what they're carrying. Hopefully that fan will get a life ban. People are asking whether the FA should charge Ian, but why should they? He's not the one in the wrong. What's he supposed to do? Just stand there and take all the abuse and risk getting hit or stabbed even? You just don't know. Where were the police and stewards? They've got an obligation to protect the players, too.

Eva's at a party and Ben's playing with his friend Mark, so Chase gives her daddy a hand cleaning out his car. She really is a good little helper.

Try to stay awake to watch the Super Bowl at 10pm but wake up on the sofa at midnight so I head off to bed.

Monday 2nd

We're all really tired this morning: it was a tough game on Saturday and on a pitch made very heavy by the weather. I actually thought the game might have been under threat because of all that snow from the previous night but the Carrow Road groundsman Gary and his team did a great job and it wasn't too bad.

The gaffer tells us that Neil Warnock went in his office for a drink after the game on Saturday and, as he was leaving, said: 'We'll see you again this season.'

The gaffer's like: 'Well, he might be in the play-offs but we won't be!'

He tells us that this Saturday's game away to Wimbledon, sorry the MK Dons, sorry Franchise FC, is a must-win.

In the afternoon I finally have my interview for the youth team job, the one I should have had last Thursday. I'd only hired my suit for two days so I had to go back and get it out again! It is my first ever interview, so I've no idea how these things are supposed to work, but I think it goes well. It's with club secretary Kevan Platt, academy director Sammy Morgan and director Michael

Foulger – all of whom I get on really well with, so I relax a little and we talk for 45 minutes.

It's a strange situation: I don't feel under any pressure because ideally I'd love to play for another year, so if they give the job to someone else so be it. They ask what I think I can bring to the job. I say I know I'm not as experienced as 99 per cent of the people applying because I'm still playing, but I think my enthusiasm and passion for the club speaks volumes. I've been here nearly seven years now. I know everyone who works here and how they work. I know all the young lads really well and I think I've got their respect.

There are encouraging vibes, but they're not giving too much away. It's a big job. I might have misread it, but I get the vibe that if I were to finish playing now I might get the job. Platty intimates that there will be something for me one day. I've got my Uefa B licence and I will do the A badge, but I don't need that to get the job, so I could do it as on the job training.

But maybe, just maybe, I'll get a new contract. I'm still thinking about my goal on Saturday – and my missed chance. I've got six goals to go to get my 100 and it does seem an awful long way away still. But we've got 17 games left and if I play all of them . . . In my career I've averaged a goal every two and a half games so if I can keep that up I should get them. I just don't know whether I'm going to play all the games. I'm due a double though. Next time we get a pen I *am* taking it.

Can you imagine if it came down to the last day of the season? We're away to Crewe and we need to win the game to guarantee promotion. It's 1–1 and there's one minute left, I'm on 99 goals and we get a penalty. I don't think I could take it. I'd say, 'Gaffer, you've got to give me another year because I just can't take that to get my 100. I'm a nervous wreck. I'll take a pen next year when we're 5–0 down against Man United.'

It was easier to take that first penalty of the play-off shoot-out against Birmingham because my confidence was sky-high after I'd already scored. In a funny kind of way, the pressure was off. I'd done what was asked of me. I really don't think I could take the pen if it was the last game of the season. But I hope it won't come to that. We're still top of the League and all we're bothered about is putting a gap between the top two and the four play-off positions. No, I don't know the date of the play-off final. We're not going back there. It was agony. That's why we're all determined to do it automatically.

Tuesday 3rd

Today's one of those days when training really drags for some reason. We split into two groups as the reserves are playing tomorrow night at Carrow Road and the youth team join in working on team shape for the Wimbledon game with the lads who played Saturday. It's good experience for the young lads as they have to work harder on their touch and passing, but some of them are so eager to impress they get a bit too stuck in for our liking!

A friend rings me to tell me that on the fans' website, the *Wrath Of The Barclay*, one poster gave me 187/10 for my performance on Saturday. Cheers, whoever you are!

At 6.30pm, Squiz and I are off to Nando's restaurant to present a couple of shirts to someone. I'm wondering why Squiz is so up for it – he's quite shy normally, but he volunteered to do this one – when he tells me they've offered us a free meal. Ah, that'll be it.

Poor old Eva's in tears when I get home. She's been really sick this evening and she's supposed to be doing a modelling shoot for *Pop Idol* magazine tomorrow in London. It breaks her little heart when we tell her gently we think she's too ill to go – she's been so excited and has told all her friends about it.

Wednesday 4th

In the morning Eva insists she's fine. We're not convinced but she hasn't been sick for eight hours so Julie says she'll take her on the train to London and see how it goes. Then at 8am Ben comes back into the house. Apparently, there were no other kids at the bus stop and the school's closed today due to burst pipes. So Chase is absolutely gutted. Everyone's getting a day off except her. We tell her that Ben will be going to school in the afternoon, but she's still not happy.

Ben and I have a lovely day in the city, looking at trainers. I usually wear a cap when I'm out as my hair tends to get me recognised, but when things are going well I can risk going out without one. A few people stop me and ask for autographs and some take my photo with their phones. I don't mind when people want to be in the picture with you because then you've got something to do – put your arm around them or something. But I feel a right lemon standing there on my own, posing. Luckily, Ben doesn't get embarrassed, unlike his dad. One lad takes about five minutes to get the shot and I'm begging him to hurry up.

'Mate, people are looking. I feel a right twat.'

In the afternoon we pick Chase up from school. When she sees Ben she knows she's been conned and is furious. I'm not sure if it's revenge, but she picks this moment to utter the words every father dreads hearing.

'Daddy, I've got a boyfriend.'

At eight years old! I had to wait until I was 14 before I had my first girlfriend.

The three of us go ten-pin bowling down by the Riverside.

I'm pants at it and Ben wins both games – although he has those barriers that go down the sides to help him. I'd ask for some but I look stupid enough playing the game already. There are a couple of young lads next to us, spinning the ball wide like Beckham, getting strike after strike. I want to ask them for advice, but I settle for saying, 'Not bad boys, you watch me now . . .' I get three! I remember one afternoon a couple of years ago a few of the lads came down and our former winger Chris Llewellyn threw his ball down and did a Klinsmann dive all the way down the alley after it. He still didn't get all the pins down! I can see people looking at me, wondering if I really am a sportsman. Hello. Yes, it's me. This just isn't my game, all right?

I'm not bad at snooker and pool – my highest snooker break's 46 and I once won a pool tournament against the rest of the lads. It's the result of a misspent youth: as a teenager in Wales I used to work in a pub, collecting glasses and cleaning windows. I was too young to drink, but I played a lot of pool.

Thursday 5th

I did an interview for the matchday programme last Saturday and, flicking through the pages before training, I realise there's not one good picture of me. In one of them I look like I've swallowed the ball, in another one I look like the Devil. The only one I quite like is one where you can see the definition on my thighs. People, preferably women, might think, 'cor, he's a bit meaty.' But I just don't take good photos. I'll have to ask my supermodel daughters for some advice.

I knew after the Sheff U game that I'd be starting this Saturday, and before training today the gaffer says to me 'Look after yourself, take it easy.'

But I feel really fresh and I need to train as hard as everyone else, so I do.

Friday 6th

Webby is flexing his muscle. As newly appointed judge and Drury, he's decided to come down hard – on us players at least. We now know that unless there is concrete evidence against his fellow red coats they won't get fined at all. I don't think it says anything in the rule book about bringing video cameras to training, so maybe that's what we'll have to do.

Only a two-hour journey today to our hotel in Milton Keynes so my back's delighted. The gaffer tells us that, amazingly, we have sold 3,500 tickets for tomorrow's game so that means half the crowd will be our fans. At the risk of sounding like an anorak, it's another new ground for me to chalk off. There are only a handful of grounds in all four divisions I haven't played at – Lincoln, Carlisle, Kidderminster, the new Man City one, Wycombe, Boston, Chesterfield . . . oh and Northampton – I was gutted to be injured when we played them in the Carling Cup at the start of the season.

Saturday 7th

Nationwide League Division One
Wimbledon 0   Norwich City 1
                                    Huckerby 16
National Hockey Stadium Att: 7,368

Wake at 7.15am, even earlier than normal, and I can't get back to sleep, so I lie in bed reading *The Sun* for a while. It's a glorious day and I feel very fresh.

The hockey stadium that Wimbledon now play at is better than I expected: good dressing rooms and a decent-ish pitch. The stands are a bit open though, so I'm glad for our fans that it's not raining.

It is, however, blowing a gale, which doesn't make for a great game of football. We have the wind in the first half and take the lead on 16 minutes with a wonder goal by Hucks: a superb first-time volley after a magnificent 40-yard cross-field pass from Squiz. I only really get one chance: I turn defender Mark Williams and have a clear sight of goal, but he makes a brilliant tackle to clear the ball away.

Four minutes later, on 75 minutes, the gaffer takes me off so Matty can have a run-out after his month out with his knee injury. Eight minutes from time Hucks is clean through on goal but Steve Banks comes out of his area and handles the ball, so he's sent off, followed by Williams for disputing the decision. It doesn't matter: we're in control and just grinding out the result by then.

Then we get the great news that West Brom and Sheffield United have both lost and Sunderland only drew, which means we are now five points clear of West Brom and ten points clear of third-placed Sheffield United.

I think in the last three or four games we've started to show we can mix it up a little. If we need to be direct rather than play nicey-nice football then we can do it. Radio Norfolk's Roy Waller pissed a few of the boys off the other week, saying he doesn't think we're playing well enough to be in the top two. We know we're not playing as well as we can, but we're picking up results and at this stage of the season that's what's important. Now we're getting slagged off because we're not playing silky football all the time? Sometimes you can't win.

Sunday 8th

Oh my legs are stiff today. Fingers crossed they'll be okay for training tomorrow. I go through my usual quiet Sunday routine of walking Molly, sauna and jacuzzi and then take Ben and his friend to the cinema to see *Rock School*, which is hilarious, before settling down for the latest episode of *Dream Team*.

Monday 9th

I think the media thought our bubble had burst when we lost to Bradford and drew 4–4 at Rotherham, but we've won our last two games and Saturday's victory was especially pleasing as it could have been a real banana skin. So we're back. In training this morning someone says we've only lost five of the last 30 games, which is an amazing run by anyone's standards – except possibly Arsenal's.

We're all feeling very stiff and sore after Saturday, so are delighted to just do a 20-minute base run – which means maintaining a good, steady, pace – with the gaffer this morning, before heading for Greens and our usual sauna and jacuzzi session. I am bumping into more and more team-mates down here as the season progresses.

Tuesday 10th

The gaffer totally shocks me and the rest of the lads this morning. We're top of the League, we've won our last two games, things are going really well, but you'd think we are in the bottom two the way he goes on. We're just chatting about how Coventry will play on Saturday and what we'll have to do to counteract them when he starts having a right go at us. Suddenly he tears into us, screaming that we're not working hard enough, we're not focussed and we don't want it like he does.

You what? Is he saying that in jest? There's no humour in his voice, so I look again at his face. Not even a hint of a smile. He's serious. What a thing to say. It really pisses the lads off. Cheers, gaffer. There's a difference between keeping us on our toes and totally shooting us down in flames.

He follows this up with a long, tedious training session focussing on how we will play against Coventry which involves lots of stopping and starting – not really what the doctor ordered when we're all so stiff and it's freezing cold.

In the evening I watch Leicester take on Bolton, hoping for a Leicester win.

I had two-and-a-half great years at Leicester: I was top scorer there both full seasons. In my first half season I scored 13 goals in 28 games and we snuck into the play-offs. But I bloody broke my ribs with just six games to go, didn't I? I didn't play in the two play-off semi-finals; I only got the all-clear to train three days before the final itself. It's so frustrating when you break your ribs: you can't do anything. The day before the final, the gaffer came up to me and asked me how my ribs were. I said they were fine, that obviously I wasn't match-fit, but if he started me I would give him my all until I conked out.

The final against Derby was an amazing day: the first time I'd ever played at Wembley and it was just a sea of blue and white. There must have been 80,000 fans there. Walking out of the tunnel was surreal: it's that moment you've dreamt of ever since you were a kid. The noise was awesome. The day passed by in a flash, a blur. I couldn't enjoy it because I didn't know what the result was going to be. It always makes me laugh when you hear people say that. Just enjoy the day. Bollocks. You want to win.

It was boiling hot and I was breathing out of my arse, but despite that, and the ribs, I managed to last 60 minutes before being taken off. We went 1–0 down, then big Stevie Walsh scored two, the last one with five minutes to go. And we were promoted. And it was fantastic. Unreal. We drove straight back to Leicester that night, to a civic reception, with Oasis blaring out on the stereo and the beers being handed round. We had a really good squad, nearly as tight a bunch of lads as we have here. And that was the biggest factor in our promotion.

Of course, my first full season was hard. We were everyone's favourites to go straight back down. And we did. That was a hard old season. That was the year that Leicester, Ipswich and ourselves all got relegated. And where are we all now? Leicester are in the Premiership (although probably not for very much longer), we're just about there and Ipswich . . . well, let's just say they're a wee way off.

Leicester and I bounced back the following year. Again, I finished top scorer with 20 goals, again we finished in the play-offs and again, I broke my ribs six weeks before the play-off final. Well, it was getting to be a lucky habit. Except I didn't play in this final. Martin O'Neill told me a couple of days beforehand that he'd really like to put me on the bench. I said 'Yeah I'd love to.'

He said: 'But I don't want to put you on the bench if I'm not convinced that, if someone has to come off after five minutes, you will be able to last 85 minutes.'

I appreciated his honesty and had to be honest in return. I told him I didn't think I could last that long, as I hadn't trained, but if he wanted to throw me on with 15–20 minutes to go I didn't think that would be a problem. In the end, he went with Mark Robins on the bench, which

I had no problem with, and we beat Crystal Palace: Steve Claridge scored a great goal with the last kick of the game.

I was quite gutted to leave Leicester in the end. But I had a bit of a run-in with the then chairman, Martin George. Before that last play-off final Julie was in one of the boxes with Alan Birchenall. Birchy asked her: 'Is the Big Man on the bench? Does he have a chance of playing?' And Martin went past and said: 'Well, he doesn't deserve to play, does he? The players that deserve to play are the ones that got us here.' I was only top scorer! I think I'd got 20 in 30 games.

It really pissed me off. He wasn't even in the conversation. We had a do at a hotel in Leicester that night and I pulled him aside and said: 'So I didn't deserve to play today then?' He just said: 'No, no, I didn't say that. Your wife's got selective hearing.'

I just walked away. His behaviour really, really hurt me. I was out of contract at the end of that season and I had a phone call from Mark McGhee, asking me to join him at Wolves. And that made up my mind. I might have been cutting off my nose to spite my face, but I wasn't going to let people, especially the chairman, treat me like that. Anyway, at the time, I thought Wolves were a bigger club, even though they were still in the First Division and Leicester had just got promoted – and I was going to be closer to home. Ah well. Leicester went on and did really well, winning the League Cup. I wish I'd stayed. Martin O'Neill told me later that he would never have signed Ian Marshall if I'd stayed, that I'd have always been his first choice, along with Stevie Claridge. But I don't like to dwell on what might have been . . . and, anyway, I'll always be grateful for the Wolves move, because otherwise I'd probably not have ended up at Norwich.

Leicester haven't had the best of times in recent weeks, and tonight's game ends 2–2.

Wednesday 11th

Poor old Ben. His foot has been sore since he hurt it playing basketball at school last week and this morning the doctor tells him his metatarsal and cuboid bones are badly bruised. So he's not allowed to do any kind of sports activities until the pain and swelling have gone, which could take up to six weeks.

In the evening Julie and I have dinner with Pam and Freddy from across the road. They're great fun; possibly too much fun sometimes – we had a barbecue last summer and they were the last to leave. At 6am. We have a great night out at the Reedham Ferry Boat and I'm starving, so I pig out on the 20oz T-bone with fat chips. Sauna for Mr Roberts!

Thursday 12th

Mr Jekyll is back. Or is it Mr Hyde? It's the nice one anyway, the one who thinks we're half-decent players and knows we try our socks off. Welcome back gaffer. It's good to see the guys relax a bit.

We're just finishing the warm-up when I come over all dizzy and start seeing little stars in front of my eyes. I feel really light-headed, like I'm about to black out. I get this every now and then, probably because I don't eat breakfast. I know I should, but I just don't feel hungry first thing in the morning. I ask the gaffer for permission to go and get some jaffa cakes to get some glucose into my body and, after a few of those and a swig of Lucozade, I'm feeling as right as rain again.

Drop the girls off at the school disco. They look more like 18 than eight and are busy acting all grown-up, so I make myself scarce. They make it quite clear that I'm cramping their style and that having your dad hanging around is not cool – even if he does play for Norwich City.

Friday 13th

I think I might have given the impression that I'm the most superstitious footballer in Norwich – all right then, Britain. But, for some reason, Friday 13th doesn't bother me at all. Not one little bit. It bothers the other lads though – the first thing Holty says when he puts his head into the dressing room this morning is: 'I can't believe we're travelling on Friday the 13th!'

Crichts was fined last week for something trivial and has to pay up this morning. Of course, being the practical joker he is, he's stayed up half the night counting out all the one pence pieces he had in his big whisky bottle and putting them in a bag to give to Steve Foley.

'There you go Steve, £20 fine!' he says as he tips the entire contents of his rucksack onto the table, pennies flying everywhere. I don't dare ask Steve whether he found them all . . .

Crichts is again in good form once we've checked into our hotel for the evening, the Hilton in Coventry. It's a normal Friday night stopover, apart from the fact that the lads are gutted that the hotel doesn't have Sky Sports. Oh, and the fact that it is opposite Toys R Us. Being the big kid that he is, that's obviously Crichts's first stop. And what does he buy? A water pistol, of course.

At dinner there are two separate tables, so some of the lads are sitting with their backs to him and he keeps squirting them, to everyone's amusement. Then the gaffer comes in to check the food's all right. Crichts is desperate to get him too, but the gaffer's quite shrewd and spots Crichts's hand under the table.

'What have you got there?'

'Nothing, gaffer.'

'Yes you have. Come on, what is it?'

So the gaffer takes the water pistol off Crichts, turns and squirts Leon's back. Leon turns round and has a go

at Crichts, who holds his hands up to say 'It's not me.'
Leon turns back and carries on eating and the gaffer gets
him again. And again. It's hilarious. Leon's not going to
accuse the gaffer now, is he?

Once the gaffer has drenched poor Leon and made sure
everyone is sorted, he goes off for a chat with the rest of
the red coats. We'll be up in our rooms like good little
boys by the time they sit down to eat, about 8pm I think.
Of course, they wouldn't have shepherd's pie with us, they
can have the good gear, eat off the a la carte, enjoy a
couple of glasses of wine. Maybe it won't be so bad when
I retire from playing after all.

As players we get to stay in all these nice hotels but we
don't see anything of them – just the four walls of our
rooms. We don't sit in the bar, we don't use the gym, we
don't eat in the fancy restaurant. If there's a health club
I'll shoot down for a jacuzzi, but we wouldn't have a swim
or anything – it's all about conserving energy for the next
day. A few of the lads might have a game of cards or
snooker if there's a table, or a cup of tea and a chat, but
we're all upstairs by 7.30pm.

Saturday 14th

Nationwide League Division One
Coventry City 0   **Norwich City 2**
                             Holt 38
                             Brennan 85
Highfield Road   Att: 15,757

It's Valentine's Day, and after a long lie-in, breakfast in
bed, a massage from Julie, cards and presents . . . I eventually wake up. Alone. Oh, the romance. Actually, I slept
really well last night in the world's largest bed and I'm

raring to go. The conditions are perfect for playing football: no wind, rain or sun and it's cold.

There was a big Valentine's disco in the hotel last night
and I think the Fridge and Jimmy, the goalkeeping coach,
were hovering around it by the looks of them this morning. God, how the other half lives.

Ben is coming to the game and Julie is off to Leicester
to see friends and do a bit of shopping, then she'll meet
me after for a romantic dinner – with a load of our
friends.

Once again, we don't play as well as we can, but we work
really hard and fight for every single ball, limiting them
to the odd long-range effort. Holty gets our first goal on
38 minutes. I'm really pleased for him as it's been quite
a while since he last scored – over two years I think –
and I think it's been playing on his mind a bit.

The goal comes from their corner: Squiz clears the ball
into the channel, Hucks tears up the wing with it and
smashes it into the six-yard box where Holty bundles it
in from close range. I don't know what he was doing that
far forward – perhaps someone dropped a pound coin in
the box. He looks ecstatic and runs straight over to our
fans giving it loads. It's almost as if he doesn't know what
to do, so he does a bit of everything. I've never seen him
move so quick – we're all chasing him to try and celebrate with him and eventually catch up with him. We
congratulate him and he says: 'Yeah, I'm lethal from two
and a half yards out!'

I nearly add a second just before half-time after Hucks
slips a lovely ball through to me, and I try to dink the
keeper, but he just gets his shoulder in the way, a really
good instinctive save. Then, a few minutes later, he clat-
ters into me, not maliciously, and catches me in the top
of the thigh with his knee. It really hurts and stiffens up
quickly but I don't want to come off and I'm sure I can

run it off. I'm developing an interesting-looking bruise, though.

The leg stiffens up more during half-time – all that sitting about getting cold – and I really start to feel it in the second half. We're playing well and looking comfortable, but I'm not getting hold of the ball as well as I usually do and it's becoming a bit of a battle. Just on the hour mark I have a great chance to put us 2–0 up. Squiz swings in a long corner to me at the far post and I get up well to meet the ball with my head. But instead of heading it back across the keeper I try to squeeze it in the gap between him and the upright and it goes into the side netting. Damn, it was a tighter angle than I thought.

Nine minutes later the gaffer brings Matty on for me, which I'm quite relieved about as my dead leg is becoming zombie leg. Wish I'd bloody scored though. Sitting on the bench, I can't see them scoring, but we really need another goal just to make sure. Finally, five minutes from time, Hucks – God, he's amazing, he's as quick in the last minute as the first – sets up Jimmy B who cracks a superb left-footed drive into the top corner of the net. Goodnight Vienna.

Special mention must go to the back five, who are magnificent – that's our third straight win and clean sheet – and our 12th man, the fans, who once again turned up in their thousands and never stopped singing. They're going mad at the final whistle. This is the sort of result we never used to pick up. We've always been pants away from home, but now we haven't lost on the road since October 18th!

It's a great record, but all the press want to talk about afterwards is Jimmy B's hair. He's had it cut: a sort of spiky mohican Becks thing with a small blond streak in it. It's not that bad, in fact I think it looks all right. But as I walk out to get on the coach about twenty past five, this journo collars me and the first thing he asks is: 'What's Jim trying to do with his hair?'

'Erm,' I say, 'I think he's just dyed it.'

'What do you think of it?'

I can't believe he's asking me about his bloody haircut, so I go for the tongue-in-cheek, 'It's minging to be honest,' thinking he won't write anything. Holty obviously thinks so too, because he goes right to town, saying he thinks it makes him look like a gremlin, that it's all Hucks's fault because Jim hangs on everything Hucks says and copies everything he does, like he's Hucks's puppet . . .

I've never really experimented with my hair. I thought about having a few blond bits on the tips a couple of years ago and asked Julie what she thought of the idea. She just looked me slowly up and down and said: 'How old are you?' Which put me off. It's not fair, I don't go on at her having highlights. The worst I've done was when the Wolves team went to La Manga once. We got drunk one night, got back into one of the lads' rooms and Keith Curle had some clippers so we all had a Steve Bull and shaved our heads. Me, Embo, Simon Obsorn, Steve Froggatt, Steve Corica, Geoff Thomas – we all did it. Julie went mad. Quite rightly: it did look horrible. Good idea at the time . . .

But that's my limit. We had a lad here a few years ago, Jamie Cureton, who dyed his hair green for a derby game at Portman Road. I've never been tempted to do that – mind you, he did score. We might do something a bit different if, touch wood, we're promoted, maybe for the last home game of season. Jimmy B said yesterday it would be good to all do something stupid with our hair. Maybe we could all have 'NCFC' shaved into our hair. Or each have a different letter, spelling out 'Thank you fans.' On second thoughts, that's a bad idea. Knowing us and how excited everyone would be, we'd line up wrongly and it would end up reading 'Fuck you fans' or something daft.

The gaffer very kindly lets Ben get a lift with us on the team bus back to the Hilton. He's absolutely loving it, jumping around on his seat, beaming. Julie picks us both up and we go to see one of my former Leicester teammates, Richard Smith, his wife Kate and son Callum.

Sunday 15th

Very good news. Geoff Thomas's wife phones to tell us he's just come out of hospital after his bone marrow transplant and it seems it was a success. I'm so relieved and pleased. He's fought leukaemia all the way, been so strong, and thankfully now seems on the way to recovery. Geoff is a fighter and he will fight this until he wins. I'm thinking of you, buddy. Still happy to remind you of when you were clean through for England against France and you went to chip the goalie and it ended up going for a throw-in, though. Shocking, mate, absolutely shocking!

Monday 16th

The Sun is full of quotes from Holty and others going on about the state of Jimmy B's hair. Dave Carolan has photocopied the article about ten times and stuck it all over the dressing room, paying special attention to Jim's locker door. He isn't happy. All morning his phone's been going with mates texting him about the article. There have also been quotes from his hairdresser in the local paper. Everyone's gone mad. I don't know what the fuss is all about. It's just a little blond streak, you can hardly see it and he's a good-looking boy who can carry it off.

The gaffer says that West Ham manager Alan Pardew was on telly on Saturday saying how his side are the best in the division. That's a little bit premature, if you ask me. They're a good side, fair enough, but you could say any of the top ten teams are. The best team in the division will win the title and we won't know who that is until May. So, now we have an extra incentive for Saturday – not that we needed one.

The next four games will be key to our season: we've got West Ham at home on Saturday, then we've got the long trip up to Sunderland the following Saturday, West Brom at our place the Tuesday after and Ipswich at home the Sunday after that. If we can stay unbeaten for those four games then, dare I say it, we will have one foot in the promised land.

Training today consists of 40 laps walking in the pool at Greens as there's a lot of stiffness flying around the changing rooms this morning. It's quite hard work with Dave Carolan ensuring we keep up a good pace so afterwards we all flop into the jacuzzi.

I've promised to take the kids bowling this afternoon but when we get there there is a two-hour queue so we head off to spend daddy's win bonus in the arcade instead. I'm very embarrassed as we are leaving as Chase gets frustrated with one of those infuriating penny waterfall machines and gives it a right whack to try to get the coins to fall. I manage to drag her out before the alarm goes and we get arrested.

Tuesday 17th

The passing in the keep-ball session at training today is excellent – quick and accurate – and the gaffer is well pleased, as we haven't passed the ball as well as we can in the last three games. The legs still feel very heavy though – not helped by all the rain we've had lately, which has made the ground really tough going.

In the afternoon I take the kids to the cinema to see *Haunted Mansion* with Eddie Murphy. They love it, and I'm probably laughing more at their reactions than anything. Afterwards, I'm desperate to go to Pizza Hut but Chase doesn't like pizza, so we head for Old Orleans for a family tea.

Jimmy B's arranged for a few of us to go out for a quiet drink this evening in the Walnut Tree Shades, hidden down an alleyway in the city centre. He's only been here five minutes and he's still found a pub I've never been in before. It's a decent pub and we don't get bothered, so we enjoy a quiet couple of drinks before a reasonably early night.

Wednesday 18th

Doh! I phone up to book a lane at Hollywood Bowl and they're fully booked until tonight. Anyone would think it was half-term or something. So we end up going swimming. Well, the girls do. They love it, but Ben and I aren't keen so we sit and watch them while Ben plays Top Trumps. Then the last of my pay cheque disappears on more goes on the racing cars in the arcade . . .

My phone's constantly buzzing this afternoon with mates asking for tickets for the West Ham game. Normally the boys will have a few spare but demand's so high there are none going at all. We each get a couple of comps. Julie sits inside and watches on the telly with the girls – which you don't need tickets for – so my tickets go to Ben, my mate Dave and his son Ben. But I do try to get the odd ticket for mates, like Tom from the night-club Optic – he looks after us when we go there, so I try to scratch his back a little.

Easty normally gives me his tickets. In return, I have to buy him a bottle of Lucozade every morning and leave it in the fridge for after training. Most of the players' tickets are in the Upper Barclay, but his are in the Lower, noisier section, because his dad's got some kind of bad leg. Our guests don't really get any hassle in the Upper Barclay, although Matt Jackson's dad was the world's worst and used to slag the players off something rotten. Apparently Holty's had a couple of people in his seats hammer the players too. The good thing about Jacko's dad was he'd hammer Jacko as much as the rest of us. You don't mind that. But generally, I think if you get given a comp, you've given up the right to hammer people.

I think my dad gets a buzz from people shouting 'IWAAAN, IWAAAAN.' I'd love to get a camera in there when I score to see Ben's reaction. People tell me 'Oh you should have seen Ben, he looked so proud' but I've never seen what he does, whether he jumps up and down and gets all excited. He might look a bit embarrassed next time I score though. Chase has told me I've got to do a cartwheel. She does them all the time and I did one in the bedroom the other day and she said 'Cor dad, you're really good.' I've promised her that next time I score I'll do one for her. But I know what I'm like, I'll forget and just run straight up to the Barclay.

Thursday 19th

Find out that the fans have voted me their 'Player of the Month' for January. I'll be getting the award on the pitch before the match on Saturday and I'm well pleased. I'm especially chuffed as there have been some good performances from the rest of the lads as well – Hucks, Greeno, Flem and Malky have been outstanding. They've been magnificent. So thanks a lot. I'm very touched.

The press are out in force at Colney this morning. Ah, that's right: we're playing glamour team and title favourites West Ham on Saturday. We haven't shouted our mouths off and we never will. But apparently their striker Bobby Zamora was the latest to go on about how wonderful they are yesterday and their defender Tomas Repka has been mouthing off about how he's going to rough up Hucks and stop him playing. Hmm, I know Hucks can look after himself, but I'll be watching his back.

It's Malky's birthday today. No-one ever knows it's anyone's birthday until they turn up with a tray of cream cakes. I have to say, it's a very good selection. I thoroughly approve and select a chocolate eclair. Now, either it cost him a fair few bob or he got his wife, Pam, to stay up all night making the cakes, then went and nicked a few boxes from Sainsbury's to put them in and make it look like he'd splashed out . . . Either way, happy birthday mate, although you should really stop pretending to be young by blow-drying your hair over your bald patch – Rab C Nesbitt is not a good look!

Jarve gets the yellow jersey this morning. We're going through the team shape when he turns straight into Damo's shoulder and immediately crumples to the floor. For a minute we're all worried he's broken his jaw, he goes down that hard, but he's all right, although it's very tender. So, when we vote for the worst trainer afterwards, I vote for Shacks because I feel sorry for Jarve. Unfortunately the vote's split evenly between Jarve and Damo so the gaffer makes us do the old Mike Reid *Runaround* routine and stand behind the player we think has been worst to decide (sadly, the gaffer doesn't actually shout 'Runaround!' in a gruff voice). I'm offered the chance to switch but I stay with Jarve in the end, otherwise I would have been lying to myself and Damo. Sorry Jarve.

Friday 20th

Bad day for me today. First off, I get fined for walking into the dining room to pick up my mail whilst wearing my hat. I'd totally forgotten about that rule, until I looked up and saw all the red coats sitting there with big grins all over their faces. It's a fair cop, so I hand over the tenner, but they should have to pay me for wearing such a stylish Prada hat in the first place.

Now to the worst bit: I have finally won the dreaded yellow jersey. I must admit I didn't train to my usual high standards and I did miss a couple of chances in the young v old game, but I did score my penalty in the shoot-out at the end, so I thought that might have saved me. Oh well, it's a laugh. No it isn't: Rivvo was worse than me and he missed his pen, which cost us the game, so he should have had it. I'm absolutely gutted. I thought I'd never win it, although Hucks and a couple of other lads have won it three or four times.

I thought Hucks was going to get it last Tuesday. He was having a shocker. So, of course, I wound him up about the jersey, which made him try even harder and get worse and worse. Then in the very last game he hit a volley into the top corner which got him out of jail, turned to me and shouted: 'Fucking hell Robbo, I've only got you 25 goals this season, all right?!'

Oh, I suppose so. People keep going on about us relying on Hucks, but if you've got someone of his quality then why not? He would be an asset to anybody. He can have all the plaudits: he's the difference between finishing in the top two or the play-offs. He puts bums on seats, then gets people on the edge of them and wins you games. Not many players can do that.

Saturday 21st

Nationwide League Division One
Norwich City 1   **West Ham United 1**
Huckerby 76   *Harewood 61*
Carrow Road   Att: 23,940

The new South Stand (to be known simply as the New Stand until they decide on a sponsor) is officially opened today and it looks fantastic completely full. Former manager Ken Brown is celebrating his 70th birthday and cuts the ribbon to declare it open and our fans raise the roof. It's a perfect start to this top of the table clash.

The game starts at a furious pace, with chances for either side. I almost score on 11 minutes from a great lob from Squiz, but my header from 12 yards out goes just wide. But things aren't going that well for me this afternoon – I've got trampoline touch and balls are bouncing off my shin left, right and centre.

Both sides go close, but it's still 0–0 until West Ham finally take the lead on 61 minutes with a very good goal from Marlon Harewood from 25 yards.

After that it's end to end stuff and must be great to watch, but it's very tiring and I'm shattered when I come off with 25 minutes to go. We equalise 15 minutes later when Hucks races onto a weak headed backpass from Repka, rounds the goalie and slots it into the back of the net. The place just erupts: the New Stand certainly adding to the carnival atmosphere.

Repka and Hucks have been having a ding-dong battle all afternoon so for his mistake to let Hucks in is a sweet moment. Repka squared up to the ref earlier, disputing a decision right in his face, and I think he should have been sent off then. Most of our boys don't think he's the world's greatest player; I certainly don't find it too tough playing against him. It really pissed us off when we played down there and we saw him get into a Ferrari Maranello. We couldn't believe it. We're sat on the coach and he's got a £120,000 motor. Where have we gone wrong? Jesus!

The game's heading for a draw which is probably a fair result for both sides. West Ham are definitely the best team we've played, although we do finish the stronger team – another ten minutes please, so we can win! – and we deserve a penalty five minutes from time when Christian Dailly is all over Hucks. Dailly's ripping his shirt off and it's a definite pen. That could have won us the game and with those extra two points we'd have been on 64 and they would have been out of the running for a place in the top two.

Right at the death there's a comedy moment when their winger, Matthew Etherington, gets sent off. He's about to take a corner but the ball isn't inside the arc. So our fans in the Snakepit, who sit just behind that corner spot, rear up and are giving it loads to the ref. The ref warns Etherington three or four times but he just moves the ball a smidge. So in the end the ref books him and, as it's his second yellow, sends him off, much to the delight of all our fans. It's probably a bit harsh but, to be fair, he was warned. He was wasting time and that's a bookable offence, but I think our fans had a lot to do with it. Well done!

When the final whistle blows a few minutes later, Alan Pardew starts having a go at the ref and, for some reason, then decides to start having a go at Hucks. That's just stupid. There's a time and a place, as I've said before. Don't do it in front of the fans. So then Marlon Harewood starts having a go at Hucks. I'm not having that, so I shout back at him.

'What are YOU having a go at him for?'

So he shouts back at me – and this is brilliant this: 'Sort your teeth out anyway!'

Haven't heard that one before. Mind you, my return shot isn't that much cleverer.

'You sort your breath out! It's minging.'

Yeah, all right, we do sound like a couple of schoolkids!

Later on, me and most of the boys head off to the Sport Village complex to watch a few of the local boxers in action. It's nice to support them, as quite a few are Norwich fans: Graham Everett, Jackson Williams and Earl Ling. Neil Featherby had got us the tickets and he asks me and Hucks if we would walk with Jackson to the ring. We're both really nervous about this, especially when we find out Herbie Hide is also walking with us. But we seem to do the job: Jackson looks really sharp and wins his fight in six. Malky is asked to walk Earl in and, of course, absolutely loves it.

I'm having a brilliant night until Squiz turns up with ten mates who've come over from Ireland, so I have to try to get them all in, too. People say to me 'You never answer your phone.' That's because when it rings on a night out, it's usually trouble. 'Ah, Robbo'll sort it.' I'm not going to take it with me any more.

Mike Milligan's out tonight. He and his missus, Emma, had a baby boy, Oliver George, last week. Milly likes the odd beer or three, so I've started the rumour that Milly named his son after a couple of alcoholics: Oliver Reed and George Best. Julie fell for it: she asked Emma the other day if it's true. I told Julie they've taken gullible out of the dictionary too.

Anyway, the lads put on a great show and we all have a brilliant time, especially Leon McKenzie who comes from a long line of boxers – Duke McKenzie is his uncle.

Sunday 22nd

We meet up with Lorraine Grant and her two little boys, Peter Jnr and Raymond, for breakfast. They came up to watch the game as Peter is now West Ham's first team coach but he had to go back with the lads last night as they're training this morning for their FA Cup replay on Tuesday.

It's great to see them all again – we've been friends for seven years now – and I'm delighted Peter's doing so well at West Ham. He's really good at his job and always had something constructive to say when he was here. He's a smashing fella, although he would talk the hind legs off a donkey. But he's very well-spoken – unlike his son. We're sat in the Castle Mall shopping centre, having breakfast, when Ben comes over.

'Dad, you should have heard what Raymond just said.'

'What?'

'He said 'That Darren Huckerby's a twat!''

I don't know where to look. Or how to stiffle my giggles. Raymond looks like an angel and he's only six or seven – a bit young for sour grapes, even if Hucks did score yesterday!

Monday 23rd

The gaffer's delighted with the point and the performance on Saturday and we have a light morning, basically just warming down and stretching the stiffness out of our limbs.

I have to say, the gaffer and his team do get it spot-on when it comes to knowing when to rest the lads. We always work especially hard on Tuesdays, have a steady day's training on Thursdays and a lighter session on Fridays. But, and I know I've said it before, I do feel we work harder as a unit than at any other club I – and quite a few of the boys – have been at. I think it's that combination of really intense training, together with rests when the lads need them to recover, that gives us the edge and why we finish so many games the stronger team. I honestly believe we are the fittest side in the division. Not sure my legs agree with me today, though!

After training, the gaffer tells us that we are flying up to Sunderland on Friday afternoon, as the game kicks off at 12.30pm on Saturday and we will be flying back after. That's great news for me and my back, as both of us had been dreading the six-hour coach trip up there. On the other hand, it's shite news for me and my brain, as neither of us like flying. We had a bad experience a few years ago when we flew up to Blackpool to play them in the cup. It was blowing a gale up there and the plane was one of those little prop things where the pilot is right in front of you and you can watch what he's doing. There was a lot of turbulence and quite a few of the lads were spewing up; Dougie Livermore's face went completely grey. It really put me off flying. But if it's a choice between 45 minutes on a plane or six hours on a coach I'll go through the worry and nerves and just sweat it out.

We received forms from the PFA this morning to vote for the Division One Team of the Year, Player of the Season and Young Player of the Season. So we all sit in the canteen filling them in and comparing who's voting for whom. You can't vote for your team-mates so I'm going for an all-Welsh XI; the other lads all have their own mates they vote for. It's very much like being back at school copying each other's homework as the air is thick with shouts of 'Oi, how d'you spell Gabbidon?' and 'Who have you got for left-back?' Gabbidon is about the only one I'm sure I've spelled correctly: I know it's definitely a double B, because he's Welsh.

As soon as I go to mark my first choice on the team-sheet

I realise I'm stuffed for a Welsh XI. So I've gone for Forest's Darren Ward in goal, my right-back is Crewe's David Wright (Adam says he's good!), left-back is Paul Heckingbottom of Bradford, who's a good mate after he was here last season and he played well when we played them. They are all English lads but the central spine of my team is Welsh: centre-halves are Cardiff's Danny Gabbidon and my Sheffield United mate Robert Page. My midfield consists of Welsh internationals John Oster of Sunderland, Andy Johnson from Forest and West Brom's Jason Koumas, along with Andy Reid from Forest (he's a fellow Celt, so he's in). Up-front I've got Cardiff's Robbie Earnshaw and the other Andy Johnson, from Palace, because he's a nice lad.

So that's my team, although my loyalty to Wales and my mates means there is no room for the strongest opponent I've faced this season who has to be Forest's Michael Dawson. He's strong in the air and the tackle, but not dirty and won't be far from the England squad, although he's had injury problems this season.

My Player of the Year has to be Thierry Henry – he's just got everything – and my young player is Scotty Parker. I got on well with him when he was on loan here a few years ago. Shit! I've just realised, he's 23. I think. He might be too old to be the Young Player of the Year. Oh well, I can't think of anyone else.

Tuesday 24th

I'm supposed to have a minor operation this morning, but the club doctor's double-booked. I showed him a mole on my forearm yesterday that I have been a little bit worried about as it's changed shape and colour a bit and he wants to do a biopsy just to make sure it's all okay. He says he'll do it after the game next Tuesday instead.

I've had it ages – it's like a freckle but black and a bit rough and raised. The doctor is going to remove half of it under local anaesthetic, so it'll be just like going to the dentist really. It's not playing on my mind at all – I'm just not sleeping at night. I cheer up when I go to get my post and there's a letter from Delia telling me she wants to name one of the fast-food outlets in the new stand after me. Obviously, it will be the one selling chips and bottles of Bud!

An hour later I'm feeling down again as I have to do something I never, ever thought I would. That's right, I'm wearing the dreaded yellow jersey I won last week. Oh the shame. To be honest, I'm well-pleased to have another layer of clothing on as it's even more Siberia-like up at Colney today. Anyway, I train really well and am confident of being able to pass it on to some other poor schmuck. Like Hendo. He's having a shocker. Excellent. Bye-bye jersey.

Actually, training's quite a laugh at the minute. Hucks is a completely different character to Craig Bellamy, but he does come out with the odd comment that puts you in mind of him.

'Any distance, I'll be the best runner,' he says today.

So me and Flem are like: 'Fucking hell it's Bellers – Best In Club.'

That was his nickname here. He would say stuff like 'I'm the best passer at this club, you'd be sunk without me' all the time. Bellers was always saying 'I've got the best snooker cue in the club, best tennis racket' – even though he was no good, he'd still buy the best gear available.

Hucks gets a bit upset.

'Don't call me that. I'm nothing like that.'

To be fair, he isn't, he's nothing like Bellers. But he's so competitive and sometimes goes on about how he's got the quickest car at the club or whatever. So that's why we call him 'Best In Club'. If it wasn't for Bellers we wouldn't think anything of it, but Hucks is right: he's not at all full of himself, but we do like to wind him up about it.

His kids are in today. They're very cute but too young to wander round on their own, so they have a kick of the ball for ten minutes before heading home. All the lads have brought their kids in at some point – the gaffer's kids come up quite a bit in the holidays. One of his sons is a really good runner so he just does constant laps of the training pitch and we just watch him until we feel dizzy. Another one is a really good rugby player. But the gaffer's youngest one – I think he's about six – really makes me laugh: he's like a little old man. He's got a little clipboard with tactics on and he sits in the gaffer's chair, writing notes. He's like a mini-me gaffer. Maybe he'll give me a new contract! He gets on really well with Eva and Chase, too, especially Eva – I'm sure he fancies her.

After training I shoot up to the city to present a trophy to the winners of the annual *Evening News* Pancake Race. Did I toss a pancake myself? With TV cameras around? You must be flipping joking.

Wednesday 25th

It's Julie's birthday on Monday and, as I don't have a clue what to get her and she hasn't given me any hints, I traipse round every single ladies' clothes and shoe shop in the city. And it's a surprisingly big city when you're wandering aimlessly around it. First stop, however, is WH Smith, where I buy every single copy of the *Disney Club* magazine and get a right funny look from the woman behind the till. Chase is on the front cover and has a few photo spreads inside. I'm so proud.

Sunderland beat Birmingham 2–0 in the FA Cup tonight, after extra time. Excellent. I'm really looking forward to Saturday's game now. They won't get back until the early hours of tomorrow and they'll all be knackered and on a high and, as they say, it's always after the Lord Mayor's Show that you're vulnerable . . .

It will be weird kicking off at 12.35pm. Three o'clock on a Saturday is when you should play. But we're live on telly and it will give us a chance to show people why we're top of the League and have been for two months now.

I'd better get an early night to make sure I'm right for Saturday. I'm a bit sneezy at the moment and feel like I've got a cold coming on. I'm not eating properly. I suppose I should eat more vegetables, but I just love meat.

Thursday 26th

God! The ground's frozen rock solid this morning and the lads are sliding around all over the place, ideal conditions for pulling muscles. Matty tries to cover up against the cold – and the fact that he's having a 'mare – by playing in Ronaldo-style tights. It does him no good whatsoever, we all rip the piss out of him and give him the yellow jersey to boot. I'm taking Ben training tonight, although, for once, I think I'll watch from the warmth of the car.

Friday 27th

It's been snowing overnight so we're allowed to train inside the dome. Not for long though. A short session to loosen the muscles and we're off to Norwich airport to board the plane the club has chartered especially for us. My fear of flying gets worse when I see that it's a little thing with propellers. Oh God. Thankfully, the 45 minutes to Sunderland pass without too many lumps and bumps and I'm in my hotel room by 3.30pm. Dinner is normally at 5.30–6pm, but it's late tonight, much to the lads' delight. Neal Reynolds is supposed to organise meal-times so that will mean a fine for him and more money in our end-of-season knees-up fund.

Saturday 28th

I didn't think the signs were good when I woke up at 3am to go to the loo. Outside, everywhere was white and it was still snowing heavily. Five hours later, I look out of the same window and I'm pretty sure the game's going to be called off, despite Sunderland having undersoil heating. I shower and run downstairs for breakfast at 9am. Dougie and the gaffer look at me and Dougie gives me the news I've been dreading. The game's off.

We're all really disappointed as we are all psyched up to play and it would have been a great time to play them, as they would have been tired after their midweek game. Plus, we'll have to go up there in midweek now. As will our fans: I'm really gutted for them as many set off at 4.30am and will be nearly in Sunderland now. One guy and his young son come over to ask us if the game's still on. He left at two this morning to get here in plenty of time and I hate having to tell him it's off. It's a kick in the teeth for everyone who's spent their hard-earned getting here. They deserve medals.

Luckily for us, Newcastle airport is still open so we jump on a plane back to Norwich around 1pm and mooch around for the rest of the day.

Sunday 29th

Good long training session today as we are playing West Brom on Tuesday night. My parents are staying the night as they are flying from Stansted to Rome tomorrow, so Dad brings Ben down to watch training. Afterwards, we all go out for a meal at my favourite Norwich restaurant, the Recruiting Sergeant – the food is fantastic and the portions are huge!

Nationwide League Division One

Pos	Name	P	HOME					AWAY					GD	PTS
			W	D	L	F	A	W	D	L	F	A		
1	**Norwich City**	32	12	2	2	27	12	6	7	3	23	15	+23	63
2	West Bromwich Albion	32	9	5	2	24	12	8	4	4	22	17	+17	60
3	Wigan Athletic	32	8	6	2	20	10	6	6	4	25	22	+13	54
4	Ipswich Town	32	9	2	5	37	26	5	6	5	23	26	+8	50
5	West Ham United	31	6	5	4	24	17	6	8	2	20	14	+13	49
6	Sheffield United	31	8	4	4	28	18	6	3	6	18	20	+8	49
7	Sunderland	30	8	5	1	18	7	5	4	7	20	23	+8	48
8	Reading	31	8	3	4	21	18	6	3	7	16	22	-3	48
9	Millwall	31	7	6	2	17	9	5	5	6	19	21	+6	47
10	Crystal Palace	33	5	6	5	24	22	8	2	7	28	26	+4	47
11	Cardiff City	32	7	5	4	31	16	5	5	6	22	25	+12	46
12	Preston North End	31	9	3	4	32	19	4	4	7	15	20	+8	46
13	Stoke City	32	7	6	3	25	18	5	2	9	19	27	-1	44
14	Coventry City	32	4	8	4	16	17	6	5	5	25	19	+5	43
15	Crewe Alexandra	31	9	2	4	24	15	2	5	9	16	28	-3	40
16	Rotherham United	31	6	6	4	22	18	3	5	7	15	25	-6	38
17	Burnley	31	7	4	5	26	20	2	6	7	17	30	-7	37
18	Walsall	32	6	6	4	22	20	3	4	9	13	23	-8	37
19	Watford	32	5	7	4	20	21	4	3	9	15	23	-9	37
20	Gillingham	30	7	1	8	17	21	3	5	6	16	23	-11	36
21	Derby County	32	6	4	6	24	27	2	6	8	11	25	-17	34
22	Nottingham Forest	31	4	5	6	22	19	3	5	8	16	23	-4	31
23	Bradford City	33	4	2	11	16	27	3	3	10	10	22	-23	26
24	Wimbledon	31	2	3	11	14	29	3	0	12	14	32	-33	18

MARCH

Monday 1st

It's St David's Day and Julie's birthday today, although I'm not allowed to say how old she is! We're all up early to give her her cards and presents. I'd asked her last week if there was anything she really wanted and she said no (ah, cheers, love). But of course when I got back in from going shopping she said, 'Oh I know what you should have got me. Some Issey Miyake perfume. I've run out. But don't worry I've got some Boots vouchers, so I'll get it next week.' But that's what I'd bought. Ha! You should see the look on her face when I give her the perfume. I also give her some clothes from trendy shop, Catfish, and a diamond eternity ring because she's always wanted one. So that's me in the good books – at least until tomorrow!

Tuesday 2nd

Nationwide League Division One
Norwich City 0   **West Bromwich Albion 0**
Carrow Road   Att: 23, 223

Tonight is probably the biggest game of the season – although they're all pretty massive games at this stage – as we're live on Sky against West Brom. The gaffer calls us in for a light jog and stretch just to get our legs moving and, on the way home, I drop off some tickets for tonight's game for little Al.

After my usual pasta, walk the dog, sleep, preparation, I'm raring to go. We know that West Brom are an aggressive, physical side and we will have to scrap for every ball. I'm hoping to put in a really good performance: I've not scored for three games now and was a bit disappointed with myself on Saturday; I just felt I could have been a bit brighter.

I'm happier with myself tonight. The game's no classic – more aggressive than anything – but I get quite a few more touches than I did on Saturday and get hold of the ball much better than I have recently before coming off for Matty after 70 minutes. He has a loud shout for a penalty turned down, and then gets booked for having a pop at the ref. In fact, we could have had four penalties: James Chambers clearly hauled down Hucks in the first half. I'm worried about Adam Drury; he limped off after 58 minutes after one tough challenge too many. Hope he's going to be all right for Sunday.

After the game, I have my biopsy. It's painless and takes a matter of minutes. I lie awake thinking and finally fall asleep around 2.30am.

Wednesday 3rd

I am absolutely shattered after just five hours' sleep. We're in for a warm-down today then off tomorrow as our game against Ipswich is on Sunday.

After the warm-down I head for the sauna with Hucks and he tells me he might be charged by the FA for remarks he made about the ref last night – basically, he said that if the ref didn't see Chambers pull him down he needs shooting. He's dead right, but unfortunately these days, you can't have an opinion on anything without being asked to go and see the officials at Lancaster Gate. Shit, I hope they're not reading this!

Thursday 4th

A nice lazy day taking the girls to school and my wife shopping in Cambridge is followed by an equally lovely, relaxing two-hour drive to Stansted to pick up Mum and Dad, back from their holiday in Rome. It's great to see them all buzzy and happy. My mum was really nervous about the trip as she had never flown before, but now she can't wait to get back on a plane. I don't think she looked out of the window, though. Despite thick fog on the way home we make it back for 1am.

Friday 5th

Colney is chaotic this morning with hordes of journalists and photographers all wanting the story of our preparations for the Ipswich game on Sunday. I'm sat in the dressing room when Jim the goalkeeping coach comes up and says the gaffer wants to see me. Here we go again.

Matty and his fresh legs are in the team for Sunday, me and my ageing ones are out. If I'm totally honest I thought Matty would probably start. I haven't scored in four games and he did really well on Tuesday night when he came on for me. At the end of the day it's a squad game and as long as we win on Sunday and eventually get promotion it doesn't really matter who plays. So I say 'fair enough, gaffer', although, obviously I'm always disappointed not to play against Ipswich. He tells me I've done really well over the last few weeks and we shake hands.

By the evening I'm limping like mad. Damien and I went in for a hard tackle this morning and at the time I didn't feel anything but as the day has gone on it's got really painful down the side and ball of my foot. I don't think I've broken anything, though, and hopefully it will be a lot better in the morning.

Saturday 6th

The foot's still very tender, so I hop in early to see the Fridge. He has a look and says it's just very badly bruised but if I don't train on it or aggravate it, with a bit of luck I might still be able to make the sub's bench tomorrow.

Alongside me, Adam Drury is having treatment on the hip he badly bruised on Tuesday night, but has no chance of making an appearance tomorrow. Now I'm not saying West Brom are an overly physical side – my injury happened in training – but out of 24 pros, 18 of us are in the treatment room at some stage this morning.

I spend a quiet afternoon with my foot up and on ice watching the Six Nations rugby, followed by a very early night. As tomorrow's game kicks off at noon, we will have to have our pre-match meal at 8.30am. God, these weird kick-off times play havoc with your routine.

Sunday 7th

Nationwide League Division One
Norwich City 3   **Ipswich Town 1**
Mackay 50, 59   *Miller 87 (pen)*
Huckerby 88
Carrow Road   Att: 23,942

All the icing I did yesterday has paid off. The swelling's come down a lot and the bruising is coming out which is always a good sign that it's healing.

There's a fantastic atmosphere at Carrow Road, too, but once again we don't start well. In fact, during the first half we probably play the worst we have all season and could easily be two or three goals down by half-time, although somehow we manage to keep it goalless. Luck? No, woodwork! The gaffer doesn't lose his cool too often, but I've never seen him lose it in quite the spectacular way he does at half-time. He gives us the full hairdryer treatment, goes absolutely mad and has every right to.

It works. We are a completely different side in the second half. Malky scores twice from free-kicks won by Hendo – the first with his head, the second with his foot, to put us 2–0 up. I come on for Matty about 15 minutes from time. With three minutes to go, they are awarded a very dodgy penalty. The nerves are jangling now. No they're not. From kick-off the ball is played up to me, I flick it on for Hucks and he does what he does best. The crowd go berserk. We've done the double over Ipswich for the first time in years. We're now three points ahead of West Brom and ten ahead of Wigan in third place, with 12 games to go. What a chance we've got now!

Monday 8th
The boys are all off today, but not me. As I only got 15 minutes yesterday I go in to join the reserves and a few of the youth team for a session of keep-ball, crossing and shooting with Webby. We don't do too much as there's a reserve game at Colchester tomorrow afternoon, but it's good for my fitness levels.

Tuesday 9th
The gaffer has a good chat with us about Sunday's game and brings up what that world-class player, Fabian Wilnis, said about us in the press yesterday after we beat them 3–1. He really spat his dummy out: 'They are not good enough to be top of the League. I know what it takes to be in the Premiership. They will not stay up. If they did go up, they would need about 15 new players.' It seems they all drink wine made from sour grapes over at

Portman Road now, not just Joe Royle! The gaffer tells us to stick his words right where the sun don't shine. Anyway, that's more than enough about that sore loser.

My girls have been picked to play football for their school. I'm so proud. Ben comes along too to give his support. Their little legs must be absolutely freezing; it feels like minus 10 degrees. They lose 5–1 but both say they really enjoyed it. Ben never stops shouting advice and encouragement to his sisters' team. I think he might make a good manager in years to come.

Wednesday 10th

I'm walking back to the car after a fruitless morning's shopping in the city centre when my phone goes. It's a voicemail from the doc. He says he's got the results of my biopsy and that it's imperative I call him at his surgery as soon as I get this message. My heart starts thudding. I can tell by the sound of his voice that it's not good news.

I ring him back straightaway and wait for what seems like hours while the receptionist goes to get him. The doc comes on the phone and says that we have to get the mole on my arm removed as quickly as possible as it is a malignant melanoma. In other words, I have skin cancer. I shit myself. All sorts of things race through my mind and I can't really take in what he's saying. He tells me he's booked me in to see Dr O'Neill at the Bupa hospital at 10.30am tomorrow and then I'm booked in to have it removed on Friday, which means I won't be able to travel to Cardiff for the game.

I'm stunned. I'm fit as a fiddle, don't smoke and there's no history of cancer in my family. I walk slowly into our house and tell Julie who bursts out crying. We decide not to tell anyone until we know more about the cancer, how we're going to get rid of it and whether there will be any after-effects.

The gaffer is brilliant: he rings me and tells me to have as much time off as I need. He says: 'I don't want to see you until you're right – take ten days off if you want.' I say thanks but I'd rather just get on with my normal life. He tells me he understands that but urges me to at least have the weekend off.

Every time I look at the kids this evening I nearly start crying. Will I see them grow up? Get married? In the worst case scenario I might not. It's only a little malignant mole but it might develop into something else. I keep thinking about Embo's mum, who died of cancer. What if it's too late for me too? The doctor told me to just keep checking under my arms to make sure my glands aren't swelling up, but as footballers, our glands in our groin and underarms are often swollen: we get little cuts on our legs which get infected with the chemicals they put on the pitch. My mind starts playing tricks on me: every little part of my body is itchy now. That little mole on my back is itching. Could it be . . . ?

No. I've got quite a few moles and freckles, but nothing that looks nasty. You won't get me, I tell you. I'll bloody fight you!

Thursday 11th

Not the best night's sleep ever: I just lie awake most of the night thinking about stuff.

Get up and get to training early and have a chat with the Fridge, who reckons I should just tell the rest of the lads that my wisdom tooth is playing up. I'd rather tell them the truth about why I'm not training, but if that's what he thinks best . . . The gaffer says he'll tell the media that I've got a slight calf strain, which is why I won't be travelling to Wales.

I head off to the Bupa hospital, two miles down the road from Colney. Dr O'Neill is a real gentleman. He's very kind and we sit talking about football for a while before he explains what a melanoma is and what the procedure is for getting rid of it. He thinks, from looking at it, that they've caught it early, which is excellent news. He says there's no chemo or radio they can give me – all they can do is keep cutting out the melanoma. I'm not sure why. Maybe if it was to spread to another part of my body, they would give me extra treatment.

He asks me if I can wait an hour, as he can fit me in for surgery today. As that means I can travel to Cardiff tomorrow, I have no problem with hanging around the waiting room for a bit.

I call the Fridge to let him know the score and ask him to let the gaffer know I'd love to travel tomorrow if that's okay with him. I'd rather travel than sit at home, watching telly with my mind whirring.

After half an hour a lovely nurse called Karen takes me into the operating room. I only have a local anaesthetic so I'm wide awake during the operation, but I don't feel a thing and it's all over and done with in about five minutes. They take out maybe an inch of tissue, although the mole itself was only the size of a small fingernail. There's a bit of a dent in my arm as they took quite a lot out in the end, but it should be okay now. I'm left with a nice scar with eight blue stitches in and a big dent in my arm, where the tissue was. I feel so relieved it's out, but I have to go back next week for the test results and then we'll know for sure what's going to happen. It will be a very, very long week waiting, but I feel so much better now I know it's not inside me any more.

Back home the girls think Frankenstein has walked in

when they see me and my stitches and start screaming, 'Oooh, daddy, get away!'

The only thing I am a bit worried about is that after a few tests, the doc is going to draw up a graph showing me the percentage chance of the cancer coming back. It's all relative to your age. I think that's a bit morbid: if he tells me next week there's a 90 per cent chance, he'll effectively be saying it's definitely coming back.

Friday 12th

My arm feels fine this morning, although it's a bit swollen. I've been told to let it heal naturally, so when I walk into training the lads spot it immediately.

'Fucking hell, Robbo, what have you done?'

I tell them I had to go and have the mole removed yesterday as it was cancerous. And they're like: 'Fucking hell.' Pause. 'So, how's the tooth?'

Daft bastards.

Actually they're all really shocked. Footballers don't often show how much they really care, but they all come up to me and offer a 'welcome back' or a 'good luck mate'. Malky tries to reassure me by telling me one of his wife Pamela's relatives gets these moles on his head all the time and they just cut them off.

Rivvo immediately says: 'That's it. I'm never going on a sunbed again.'

I'm not sure it will put Hucks and Jimmy B off; they are dedicated sunbed worshippers. I haven't done sunbeds for six months or so now. I don't think they caused it, but they definitely didn't help.

The worst time for me is pre-season when it's boiling hot. I always sun cream my face, but I'd never thought of creaming my arms: I thought I wouldn't burn there as they are down by my side most of the time when I'm running. Now, though, I know that it's no good me slathering myself in factor eight; I'm going to have to cover up completely. I'll be the same with the kids. 'You're not going out unless you've got emulsion paint on!'

Neal straps up the arm really well in case someone accidentally knocks it in training, and in fact I train well without any problems with the arm and we leave at 1.15pm for the flight to Cardiff.

It feels odd to be going back: I haven't been there since that fateful day two years ago. Our coach driver, Ray, meets us there – he drove down yesterday with all the kit – and we drive through the city centre to our hotel. Unfortunately, our route takes us past the Millennium Stadium and I start to well up. I still get a lump in my throat every time I see it on telly.

I'm rooming with Easty tonight as he's back in the squad. He sits watching *The Weakest Link* on telly and takes my mind off things by telling me that he's thinking about going on the programme. Now that I would love to see: he'd put Anne Robinson right in her place. I might have to join him after what she said about the Welsh!

Saturday 13th

Nationwide League Division One

Cardiff City 2	**Norwich City 1**
Parry 17	*McKenzie 55*
Earnshaw 20	
Ninian Park	Att: 16,370

Easty spends the whole night talking in his sleep, trying to chat up some bird by the sound of it. I spare him the embarrassment of asking whether he did eventually pull. It's a glorious morning, just perfect for football.

The gaffer had said he'd have a chat with me to see if I was mentally right to take my place on the bench, but he doesn't have to ask. He just walks past, sticks his thumb up and I return the gesture. It's been a long couple of days, but now I just want to get on with life, get back to normal.

We start the game well, but are rocked by two strange goals in quick succession, on 17 and 20 minutes. The first is a cross-shot that eludes Robbie Earnshaw and bounces oddly over him and Greeno and into the net, surprising them both. The second comes from an unlucky slip by Marc Edworthy, who just lost his footing on the slippery surface, to let Parry in to cross for an Earnshaw tap-in.

We pull one back through an excellent finish from Leon McKenzie, a half-time sub, then completely dominate the second half, but the equaliser just won't come. I come on for Matty with 15 minutes left and, with four minutes to go, slip the ball into the back of the net from Leon's cross. Bastard, it's offside.

It's the first time we have been beaten away from home since October 18th and I really thought we deserved something from the game. The lads are all really disappointed, but the gaffer's fairly upbeat and says we just have to bounce back against Gillingham on Tuesday night, as we always have done in the past.

Sunday 14th

Even though we lost yesterday, there's a great atmosphere around the training ground. The gaffer tells us he wants to see us walking around with smiles on our faces: we're still top of the League and we played well yesterday, particularly in the second half.

The thing about us is we never panic if we lose, we just get on with the job and start putting another unbeaten run together. I think it's because we all believe in each other so much; we know there'll be the odd blip, but we also know we can do it.

Ben plays his first game in about six weeks this afternoon: he couldn't play for five of them because of that bone in his foot and, of course, last week we were too busy kicking Fabian Wilnis' and Ipswich's arses. Thorpe play very well, especially Ben, but lose 5–3 to Bressingham.

Later I meet Eddy and Hucks at Greens for a sauna, jacuzzi and chat. Eddy accepts my invite to Sunday dinner as Becky and the boys are away, but Hucks declines as he doesn't like roast dinners. Ah well, more for me!

Monday 15th

Am woken by the phone at 6.15am. This had better be good . . . it is. Our friend Sue has gone into labour and we had said we'd look after their two young lads for her and her husband David. Actually, her contractions started at 2am, but she didn't want to wake us up then so she waited until now, bless her, to phone. So they drop off the boys at 6.30am before heading off to the hospital.

I drop the boys off at school for 8am, so I'm in training super early. It looks like a hospital in here as well. Leon is struggling with his hamstring, Hucks has damaged his ribs, Adam's done his hip again and is very doubtful for tomorrow night, Matty broke his nose on Saturday. As a result, we don't do very much in training: the gaffer's too worried about losing anyone else.

In the afternoon I get a call and a text message: Sue had 9lb 5oz baby Jacob at about midday and my ex-Norwich team-mate Keith O'Neill has popped the big question to his girlfriend Zoe. Thankfully, she said yes, although I'm not sure she knows what she's letting herself in for!

Congratulations to Sue and Keith – and, Shaq – I hate to mention it, but I would make a fantastic best man . . .

Tuesday 16th

Nationwide League Division One
Norwich City 3   Gillingham 0
Pouton (og) 63
Mulryne 65
McVeigh 67
Carrow Road   Att: 23,198

I'm really annoyed with the Fridge. I go in to see him just before the game and ask what he wants me to do on Thursday.

'What do you mean?' he says.

'Well, I'm seeing the specialist and getting my results, aren't I?'

'Oh, well, there's no point in you going training. Come and see me after you've spoken to the specialist and if you do need to do a bit of work, go and do a session with Dave Carolan.'

'What? I'm not being funny but if he tells me there's a 50 per cent chance of it coming back I'm going to be in no state of mind to train.'

'Yeah yeah, we'll worry about that when it happens.'

I bite my tongue, but I'm incredulous at his reaction. He sounded really cold about what's going to be a huge day for me, but thinking about it I'm sure it was just thoughtless. I do get on well with him and I know he wouldn't have meant to upset me. But I am upset. I know he's had a lot on his mind with all the injury worries we've got, but still.

The crowd are really anxious tonight. We're not playing

badly, but we are a bit edgy and I think their tension is adding to ours. I'm on the bench, as usual, but I'm in the dressing room at half-time to hear the gaffer tell the lads just to go out and enjoy playing football. He puts Mullers on in place of Damo and – fantastic though I think Damo has been for us – it seems to do the trick. We always pass well when Mullers is playing.

In the second half the fans decide to put their worries to one side and really get behind us which seems to lift the lads. Everyone now seems to be working as one and, in a five-minute spell, we completely destroy Gillingham: an own goal, followed minutes later by a Mullers special and finally a curler from just outside the area from Squiz.

With five minutes to go the gaffer brings me on for Hucks. Ah, so he doesn't have a problem with my age after all; he obviously thinks I'm the only one with pace to match Darren's!

Nothing's really on and after the game I have to go back out and run my testicles off with the rest of the lads who didn't play. But we're all delighted with the three points. We're on 70 points for the season now and I'd like to think that another 15 points will see us through to the Premiership.

Wednesday 17th

Day off today – even for me – and I've got to see the dentist. Really! I'm dreading it, but not half as much as I'm dreading seeing the doctor again tomorrow.

I suppose I should be used to dentists by now – all the work I've had done – but I still get nervous, probably because of the amount of work I've had done. Obviously I can't feel the top of my palate, so I sometimes find it difficult speaking and I lisp a little bit. I used to live in Broseley, near Telford, and Embo would hammer me. 'Here's Wobbo from Bwosley!'

So I've promised myself that when I finish playing I will get crowns on my teeth instead of this plate. Most of the time I don't notice it, but I take my teeth out to eat if I'm not in company: I enjoy my dinner more because I can really chew it without bits of food getting stuck behind my plate. The family don't mind – even when I plonk my teeth on the table right next to their dinner. The girls love trying them on! When they first lost their front teeth, they'd ask to try them all the time. Once I was watching TV, eating a sandwich, and I'd put them on the arm of the chair. I was engrossed in the programme, but suddenly distracted by this 'slurp slurp' noise. I turned round to see Molly licking merrily away at my falsies as if they were a bone!

Thursday 18th

I've not been eating or sleeping right all this week, and I've had headaches almost every night which is very unusual for me and has had me worrying if it's a sign of something bad, so in a way I'm relieved to be finally getting this over and done with.

Julie comes with me to the hospital this time and we see the nurse, Karen, at 10.50am. She takes my stitches out and then we go in to see Dr O'Neill. He says that because the melanoma was 0.8mm deep, they want to do further tests. They're not too worried if melanomas are less than 0.76mm deep, but mine's just a little bit deeper than they would have liked.

He thinks they got most of the cancer cells the last time, but that I should come in on April 7th to have another chunk taken out and sent for analysis, just to be sure. He says he's 80 per cent convinced that it won't come back, but they're going to keep an eye on me and that I should keep an eye on myself and come straight back if I'm at all unsure about anything – which all sounds reassuring and scary all at the same time.

I'm not really bothered about having to go back again. He asks me if I'll want a local or general anaesthetic for that one. I say local. I want to walk out of that hospital as quickly as I can. Unfortunately, it looks like I'll probably miss the Wigan game, as there is a danger the wound could open up during the game.

I've got two or three moles on my back so I get him to check those out and get the all-clear on them, thank God. Then I give him one of my shirts, signed by all the lads, because he's got a six-year-old son who's a big Norwich fan and I want to say thanks because he's been brilliant.

Back at Colney I tell the gaffer what the doctor said. I watch his face cloud over as I tell him there's a 20 per cent chance of the cancer returning and I can see he doesn't know quite what to say. He's good as gold though and offers me ten days off. I say I'd rather train. He understands and says something about keeping working hard and getting on with my life. Well, you have to, don't you?

The only time it really gets to me is when I'm thinking about my kids. If I died when they were nine or ten . . . fucking hell, how much am I going to miss? It's not worth thinking about, so I try to take my mind off it. Thinking about that too much would kill me.

In the afternoon Julie and I go over to see David, Sue and baby Jacob. I've still got the knack: I give him his feed and talk him to sleep!

Friday 19th

We've signed Kevin Cooper on loan from Wolves until the end of the season and he comes in this morning to meet the lads. I'm delighted; he's a nice bloke and a very good player. Most Norwich fans will remember him from the fantastic 30-yard screamer he scored against us in the second leg of the play-off semi-final at Molineux. It had to be a special strike to beat Greeno that night as he was outstanding. It set up a very anxious last 15 minutes for everyone. But we won. Ha-ha!

The gaffer says he's looking to bring in at least one, maybe two, more signings. No idea who . . . just as long as it's not another bloody striker . . .

Saturday 20th

Nationwide League Division One
Crystal Palace 1   **Norwich City 0**
Routledge 41
Selhurst Park   Att: 23,798

Ah the joys of trying to get to Selhurst Park. Anyone who's been will tell you it's a nightmare – and we're only travelling from Croydon where we stayed last night. It's pissing with rain and I'm not in the best of moods. Still, at least I got a good night's sleep without Easty gabbing on all night!

Despite having signed Coops, the gaffer's not playing him today. As he says, it's a squad game and, while we haven't got the biggest, I think we now have one of the best in the division. Mullers is in for Damo, but that's the only change.

The conditions are hell: swirling wind, bordering on a hurricane, and torrential rain. We don't have a good record at their place, but we do have more than 8,000 fans down for the occasion and they're doing their best to make a carnival atmosphere out of a soggy day.

It's one of those games where it's very difficult for either side to try and play football: at one point we take a throw-in and it blows straight back out. Palace are a good side and I wouldn't be surprised if they make the play-offs: they've really done well under Iain Dowie in the short time he's been in charge.

They are probably the better team in the first half and take the lead just before the break through Wayne Routledge. At half-time the gaffer makes the switch we all knew was coming: Coops is on for Hendo. I knew he'd be first sub on today, but Hendo's not happy about being taken off. To be fair, he's done all right. So I go over to him.

'Keep going mate, keep your head up.' He's fuming.

'Fucking hell, Robbo, if he wanted to play him he should have played him from the start, not bring him on at half-time.'

'Yeah all right mate, don't go ranting and raving. There's a time and a place for everything and this isn't it.'

Another youngster having a bit of a torrid time is Jason Shackell. He's used to playing at centre-half, but has done a fantastic job for us this season when asked to play at left-back to cover for Adam. Defensively, he's having a really good game, nobody is getting past him, it's just going forward. The wind has blown quite a few of his passes out of play, bless him. He's taking quite a bit of stick from the home fans for it, but seems to be handling it pretty well.

We have the wind to our backs in the second half so we manage to pin them in their half for long periods and Nico Vaesen makes two great saves from Matty and Leon. I get on for Shacks for the last 15 minutes and suddenly realise what hell it is out there. Sitting on the bench, I could see crisp packets flying high in the sky and other rubbish swirling around and raindrops as big as golf balls – but I didn't realise how ridiculous conditions were until I actually set foot on the pitch. It's horrible. I don't get a chance and the game ends 1–0 to Palace.

That's the second away game we've lost on the trot so people will probably start panicking now. Not us. We know if we stay focussed and keep working hard, we'll get the results.

Sunday 21st
It's Mother's Day so me and the kids take Julie breakfast in bed, cards and presents. After she's had a long lie-in, of course. Then, because I'm extra-specially nice, I sweep the kitchen floor, hoover the house and take the girls swimming. I actually join them in the pool, for once, and am surprised to say, I really enjoy it, chasing them around and having a laugh. Ben doesn't come: like the true pro that he is, he's conserving his energy for Thorpe Rovers' game this afternoon against Old Catton.

I really feel for all the lads in Ben's team at the moment: they are working so hard and playing so well without getting any reward for it. They play really well again this afternoon, but lose 4–2. Zac the goalkeeper had to come off after spraining his wrist and they didn't have a sub to put on, so that didn't help. But they're still enjoying their football, which is all credit to them – and, after all, what it's supposed to be all about.

Monday 22nd
The gaffer tells us he was filling up his car at the garage yesterday and kept getting people interrupting him.

'Are we going to make it?'

'Can we do it?'

'Why the sudden loss in form?'

Okay, so we've lost our last two away games, but they were very tough games. We are still eight points clear of third place. If you could get all 25,000 of them in the dressing room at Colney then our fans would relax, they'd see how confident we are. The lads get it wherever we go.

'Are we going to do it? Are we going to do it?'

I've got no doubts whatsoever that we'll get promoted. We can almost touch it. We're eight points clear of Sunderland. They've got a tough run-in. Okay, we've still got to go and play them up at their place, but with the points we've got in the bag we can go up there without needing to win the game. Hopefully we'll already be up by then, anyway.

We could be promoted by the time we entertain Walsall on April 17th. I make no apologies if that sounds arrogant. We have to be confident. As Hucks says: 'If we were bottom of the League and we needed to win five games out of nine to make sure we stayed up we'd be confident of doing it.' Hucks is confident enough to say, 'Boys, we're the best team in the League. We shouldn't have to worry about anybody'.

I do sometimes wonder whether some people actually want us to get promoted, there's so much doom and gloom out there. Believe me, we're fucking determined to show everyone. Having said that, we don't start training too well today and the gaffer makes us do one of those horrible fast laps of the pitch – everybody round in less than 60 seconds or we all do it again. It's a real leg and lung-burner. We all make sure we make it and training continues at a much higher pace.

Afterwards the gaffer introduces us to Martin Hunter from the FA who takes us for a couple of sessions. It's good to have something different. You can get a bit bored doing pretty much the same stuff day in, day out, and even having someone new to take a session – maybe it's just a different voice shouting at us – gives everyone a lift.

Back down to reality this evening: I take Ben and Chase ten-pin bowling and . . . well, let's just say that they're a little bit better than me!

Tuesday 23rd

An early start at training as we are having our body fat measured. This happens about once every six weeks or so, just to sort out any potential problems before they get too big, if you'll pardon the pun. Mine is 12.4 per cent – which isn't too bad.

After training I gather together a few of the lads to go for the *Soccer AM* 'Halfway Line Challenge'. Funnily enough, it involves trying to hit the crossbar from . . . you get the picture. I'm first up and have a shocker: I don't get anywhere near the crossbar, in fact the ball was last seen heading down the A47 towards King's Lynn. I can't wait to see myself making a fool of myself on telly on Saturday morning. My only consolation is that we all fail – Mullers, Greeno, Matty, Jimmy B, Crichts – even the gaffer, whose effort is, if anything, worse than mine.

Wednesday 24th

Day off. I consider spending it in the company of two blondes, drinking champagne, snorting coke and driving around in my Lotus at 120mph. But then I think 'Nah. I'll have my usual sauna at Greens, walk Molly and sit down with my son to watch Chelsea take on Arsenal in the Champions League.' You want scandal? Don't tell my Man United-loving son, but I love watching the Gunners play; I think they're currently the best side in Europe. Sorry, Ben, but it's true and I want this book to be honest.

Thursday 25th

The gaffer calls us in for a 'Big Meeting'. He tells us he's just told all the press boys that we will get promoted, that we only need five wins from our remaining nine games and that 85 points should see us safely up. All the time he's talking he looks deadly serious; no little grins or hints that he's happy, just a determination to make sure we do it.

There have never ever been any doubts in our minds. I'm really pleased he's come out and said it categorically. 'We will get promoted.' So us players can say that now. We've been wanting to say it since January. We are that confident. All right, so we lost two away games on the spin, two tough away games, but it's all about the way you bounce back from that. We bounced back against Gillingham and beat them 3–0. Okay, it wasn't the best performance at Palace but we will bounce back against Stoke on Saturday.

We're not feeling any pressure. As the fans keep singing, we're 'top of the League and having a laugh', for crying out loud. I guess I'm not really feeling any anyway, as I'm not so closely involved at the moment: if I was starting every game I'd probably feel it more. Even though I still prepare the same way, I do subconsciously relax a bit more. It's not until you know you're coming on that the butterflies start going.

But the lads who are playing every week, the likes of Flem, Malky, Adam, they don't show it in their personalities. That's why I'm quite confident that we will be okay, because other people have panicked when we've lost games, but we haven't. I see it every day in training. They look relaxed and I know them so well by now that I know what they're thinking, how determined they are. The bottom line is that the lads trust each other. And that's priceless, especially when you're up against it.

We've not really been hammered by anyone this season and we don't concede that many goals very often. I think every player has got the utmost faith in who he's playing with – whoever that might be at the time.

I've got so much faith in the team. I look at the side and think 'Fucking hell, that's not a bad team.' I expect us to win every time. Even the games where we've not played well in the first half, I've not doubted we'll go on and win the game. Heads don't drop even when we go a goal behind.

A big part of this is obviously down to the gaffer; he's a great motivator and praises the lads a lot. He tells us to believe in ourselves and enjoy our football. He's also had Steve Foley put up posters everywhere at Colney. Slogans like: 'Live promotion, Eat promotion, Sleep promotion' are dotted all over the place. My favourite is 'Don't blame the mirror for your looks.' They remind us how we got here and what a big improvement there's been in the three years since the gaffer's been here.

The gaffer names the team for Saturday's game against Stoke City and, once again, I'm very disappointed not to be starting. I must admit I really thought I had a chance. Matty had been giving it loads in the papers about how much he wants to play up front with Hucks. Well, since he's been in the side, we've lost two out of the last four. When I was in the side prior to that, we were unbeaten in six. No disrespect to Matty – and I'll probably get hammered for saying this – but I don't think he's set the world on fire. And I don't think you should go to the papers, you should let your football do the talking. Maybe I'm just being bitter and twisted.

I take the rest of the lads who aren't going to play on Saturday for a little session, away from the first team lads who are doing formation work. We all seem to really enjoy it and I think they respond well to me as the quality's first class.

In the afternoon I watch the girls play football for their
school. Chase is in goal for the first half and concedes
two and they eventually go down 4–0, bless them. Eva
is going to be the next Vinnie Jones: she kicked anything
that moved – girls, boys – she didn't discriminate. She
even gave away a penalty and in a normal game she would
have been sent off for a professional foul. They missed
the penalty by the way.

Friday 26th

The young'uns win the weekly young v old game on penalties today, which means our lead is now down to two
games. The lads are almost as focussed on who will win
the series as we are on getting promotion.

Delia and Michael come up to watch the last bit of training and have lunch with us. It's always lovely to see them.
There's no speech, or anything like that, they tend to just
stay in the background. I will be so chuffed for them when
we get promoted. They're genuine people, they love the
club and you can't beat people like that. They've put
everything into it. They love the players as well. And we
love them too. They're spot on.

Saturday 27th

Nationwide League Division One
Norwich City 1   **Stoke City 0**
Svensson 45
Carrow Road   Att: 23,565

Nerves? What nerves? We start well this afternoon, quick
out of the traps, having listened hard to the gaffer's
ear-bashing about not falling asleep in the first half.

It might also have something to do with the gaffer's pre-match entertainment. Back in 2001/2002, the season we got into the play-offs, at ten to three every Saturday he would play us a snippet of the American football movie, *Any Given Sunday*. Al Pacino's the coach and he gives this three-minute long team talk which is fucking wicked.

'Inches become yards . . . look at the man next to you, he'd die for you. We're all in this together.'

It really gets you going, makes the hairs on the back of your neck stand up. This afternoon is the first time he's played it since the play-off final. I look round at the boys and they're really concentrating on Pacino's inspiring words. It definitely touches something deep inside you.

So, we're playing really well, although Matty's having a bit of a 'mare and the crowd are really getting on his back. Both me and the gaffer have told Matty we think he spends too much time out of the box. He wants to get involved in the play so much he forgets what he's in the team for and that's to score goals. You always want to be involved, but, as a striker, when the ball's out wide you need to be in the box getting on the end of it. Matty is a genuine lad but I think he sometimes works too hard in the wrong areas, running into the channels and wanting to link play up and get touches from Eddy and Adam, when, most of the time, he should leave that to people like Hucks. I try and stay within the channel that runs between the two 18-yard boxes: that's where I'm going to score from, not out on the wing.

I'm aware that if it carries on like this I might get on early in the second half, might even get 35–40 minutes. But I'm cringing for Matty. Behind the dug-out, fans are shouting 'Get him off! Bring Robbo on.' I don't like that and I really feel for him. I know what that's like: you can't relax and play well because you're worried about the crowd's reaction every time you even get near the ball. I don't want to hear people shouting for me like that. He might have family out there who hear it. Even Julie says she cringes when she hears people shouting for me to come on instead of him.

Then, just before half-time, Matty shuts up the boo-boys. What's more, he does it in some style with his second for the club. It's a great strike from about ten yards out into the top right corner. I'm really pleased for him – genuinely – he's a good lad and I get on well with him. I've got to have a word with him about his goal celebration, though. He's obviously heard some of the abuse and runs to the Barclay End with a finger pressed up against his lips, as if to silence his critics. Fair play to him. But then he does some strange little dance, which I can only assume is a Swedish jig. Sorry, Matty, mate, you can't dance to save your life. Do a cartwheel next time. I'll have to take him under my wing. It was as bad as Malky pointing to the name on the back of his shirt after he scored against Ipswich the other week. He's been here five years – everyone knows who he is, don't they?

There are a couple more chances in the second half, including a penalty won by Gary Holt, taken by Hucks and saved by Ed De Goey. He looks massive in the goalmouth. I'm watching Hucks take his run-up and thinking: 'Bloody hell, where's Hucks going to be able to put that?' It's as if he'd filled every inch of space. On 64 minutes Stoke finally have a second shot on target. We're in control and looking good.

Leon looks really good this afternoon. His touch is improving every game. He'd be the first to admit that, when he first joined us, holding the ball up wasn't one of his strengths. He looked a bit raw. But he's really improved: he's a strong little bugger, he can hold people off, he twists and turns well, gets himself into good positions, and has been unlucky not to play more games. He always looks like getting us a goal and is very lively today.

Then, 11 minutes from the end, just as the nerves are beginning to jangle a bit, Greeno shows why he's a world-class keeper: palming away a point blank Gerry Taggart header and then somehow clearing the rebound with his right foot. It's an amazing double save, absolutely incredible.

In the showers afterwards I overhear a couple of the lads saying that Greeno's been called up.

'Greeno, are you in the England squad?' I ask him.

'Yeah.'

'You kept that quiet!' I say and walk over to shake his hand.

'Yeah, yeah. Cheers.'

He's so laid-back it's scary. He's a very quiet lad. The only time I've seen him mad was when we were in Marbella a couple of years ago – the club promised us a holiday if we got into the play-offs. Greeno had a few beers one night and he was hilarious. I've never seen him like that before or since. Because he's been at Norwich such a long time, he's got his own mates in the city who don't really know us so he goes out with them and does his own thing.

He's a smashing fella, a bright lad and nothing fazes him. The only time I've ever seen him fazed was when we lost to Chelsea in the FA Cup. He was at fault for one, maybe two, of the four goals we conceded at their place (having held them to a 0–0 draw at ours) but he really took it personally. I could tell in the dressing room afterwards that he was really filling up. I went up to him and said: 'Listen don't worry about it. Everybody makes mistakes. I can make a mistake and miss an open goal but it doesn't really matter if they haven't scored. You make a mistake and it's a goal, there's nothing you can do about it.'

He looked like a rabbit caught in headlights. After that Crichts got in the team for a couple of games, but Greeno got back in and has never looked back. He's very focussed on what he wants and he knows he's going to be a top keeper. He's dedicated, a model pro. You can tell by the way he trains, works his bollocks off, and the good thing is he's come out and said he wants to do it with Norwich, he wants to play in the Premier League with Norwich, which is fantastic. He's saved us so many times, so I'm delighted he's been called into the England squad. For him, because he deserves it, and for me, because now I won't have to stand naked in Jarrold's shop window.

I got on for Matty for ten minutes and just failed to connect with a cross from Kevin Cooper, but by that stage, the game was all over. I'm glad we've got such a good win under our belts, as we're all out tonight with David Pett to wet baby Jake's head. Rusty (Stoke's Darel Russell) stayed down to come out with us. He was at Norwich until last summer, when they couldn't agree a new contract and he thought it was time to move on. I don't think there were any hard feelings.

He got a good cheer from the Norwich fans when his name was announced today – and I thought it was a nice touch by his manager that he was made captain for the day. Stoke's other ex-Norwich player, Ade Akinbiyi, didn't get quite the same friendly reception. Mind you, I didn't hear any of our lads who remember him from his time here sticking up for him – in fact you should have heard what Malky has to say about him! Ade's an all right lad, but he didn't have the best of times at Carrow Road and, while he's quick and strong and puts himself about a bit, I don't think he's got the best touch, he's not the world's most natural goalscorer. But I guess he must have earned a few bob from the moves he's had, so good luck to him.

Sunday 28th

Ouch! Bit of a hangover this morning so I take Molly for a long walk. The clocks went forward last night as well so, after *Dream Team*, it's bed for me, as I'm still a bit tired from losing that hour!

Monday 29th

Greeno's gone off with England, Jarve and Hendo have gone with their England age groups, Mullers is off with Northern Ireland and Jimmy B has gone to a training camp in Manchester with Canada. So what the hell are Gary Holt and Malky Mackay still doing here? Has Berti Vogts discovered Roy Keane and Jaap Stam are in fact Scottish or something? I can't believe those two aren't getting a game, the form they've been in.

Ben plays centre-forward this afternoon for his school. They win 2–0 and he sets up one of the goals. Halfway through he has to come off with a sore knee after a clash with the goalkeeper, but you can't keep a Roberts down for long and he's back on within minutes. Hard as nails!

Tuesday 30th

Spring is probably my favourite time of year, especially once the clocks have gone forward and we start getting the long evenings. Everything feels fresh again and a bright sunshiny morning gives you that extra push to get out of bed and into training. I love days like this. After a great session – us strikers had shooting practice with Steve Foley, which I love as you are constantly hitting the back of the net – I head off to Zizzi's to book a table for 12 tonight as the lads fancy pasta. I turn down the offer of nine holes at the Sprowston Manor Hotel with the rest of the lads in favour of going home to see my gorgeous kids.

Ben is so funny: the kids are watching telly this afternoon when Busted appear on screen. Every time he sees
them on telly he gives it large: 'Scum! Scum!' as Busted
are supposed to be Ipswich fans (The Darkness are apparently Norwich fans). Of course, being eight years old, Eva
and Chase love Busted, so he winds them up saying: 'That
must mean you love Ipswich then!' They're horrified. 'No
we don't!' He's learning well . . .

Most of the lads make it out this evening. Easty, Damo
and Matty are off to London, Coops is off to Stafford to
see his parents and Holty tells me he can't make it as
he's got to go to the dentist.

'What time?'

'6pm.'

'Well, we're not meeting until 7pm, so come along after.'

'Yeah, but I'm having my tooth out. And I'll have the
wee man with me as he's having a check-up.'

Oh, all right, whatever. He's not very sociable, our Holty.
He's always first away from training. Maybe that's just
as well. He's all right, but he doesn't have very good
manners. We'll be sitting listening to the gaffer in the
team meeting and he'll fart. But really obviously, as if
he's trying to squeeze one out. And then he belches really
loudly, too. I look at Malky and we're both just shaking
our heads in disgust.

He used to be a chef in the Army and he's always the
first to complain about the food. We were in a hotel somewhere last year and the gaffer came in and asked me what
the food was like, as he always does. I said it was good.
Malky said it was good. The rest of the lads in the queue
said it was good. And then he asked Holty, who said 'It's
average.' The gaffer went mad: 'Fucking hell, I've got six
goods and an average!' Holty changed his mind then:
'Nah, it's all right – although it could have done with an
extra bit of sauce.'

But he's been fantastic for us this season. He's been back to his best, harrying, closing people down, getting tackles in and giving the ball nice and easy to people who can play. He works his socks off and covers the ground really well. He's one of the best in the division at what he does.

I know I have a moan about him but he can be a really funny bloke. He's out of contract like me in June, and he comes in every morning, giving us a running update.

'93 days to go.'

'What's that then?'

'Till I'm out of contract.'

Next day, it's '92 days to go.' The gaffer still hasn't spoken to me, Holty or Crichts. To be fair, I don't expect him to until we know what's happening with the club.

Wednesday 31st

Up bright and early to do a Welsh radio interview at 7.30am. Well, up early anyway . . . not too sure about the bright. Speaking Welsh: the best cure for a hangover. Maybe. Ha! Talking of which, I bump into Hucks at Greens and his face looks like it's being sponsored by them.

I leave the queasy one alone and head for the football club. Me and Greeno are quite involved in a charity called the Matthew Project, set up to help teenagers with drug and alcohol problems. They're launching a new website today which will offer help to parents with worries and give them more information, videos and DVDs on the subject or just friendly advice. If by doing this, I could help a teenager with a problem by talking or listening to them, I would be very proud. Ben's at high school now and you know that drugs do get into schools. I've got no doubts whatsoever that Ben would never try them, but you can't be with them all the time. Greeno obviously can't make it but his girlfriend, Sarah Thomas, is here. She's gorgeous and a really nice girl. No wonder Greeno never has time to shave and his hair always looks a mess.

In the evening Ben and I settle in to watch the Sweden v England game. Well, we're interested now Greeno's out there, aren't we? We've even been watching the training sessions on Sky, for God's sake, just to catch a glimpse of him. I hope he gets on. Ben says: 'I hope Sweden score but only when Greeno's not playing.' Spoken like a true Welshman. I'm proud of you, son!

But Ben and I end up gutted: the Top Man didn't get on. I don't understand why Eriksson didn't put him on. He knows what James can do, he knows he's his number one keeper. Robinson's hurt his hand, it's a friendly in Sweden – for Chrissakes, give him his first cap. One day soon, mate.

Nationwide League Division One

Pos	Name	P	HOME					AWAY					GD	PTS
			W	D	L	F	A	W	D	L	F	A		
1	**Norwich City**	**38**	**15**	**3**	**2**	**34**	**13**	**6**	**7**	**5**	**24**	**18**	**+27**	**73**
2	West Bromwich Albion	38	12	5	3	31	14	9	5	4	24	18	+23	73
3	Sunderland	37	11	7	1	28	13	7	4	7	25	24	+16	65
4	West Ham United	39	10	6	4	36	20	6	9	4	22	21	+17	63
5	Millwall	38	10	6	2	25	11	7	6	7	25	25	+14	63
6	Sheffield United	39	10	5	4	33	20	8	4	8	24	25	+12	63
7	Wigan Athletic	38	10	6	3	25	14	6	8	5	27	25	+13	62
8	Ipswich Town	39	11	2	6	44	30	7	6	7	29	33	+10	62
9	Reading	39	9	5	5	25	23	8	4	8	24	29	-3	60
10	Cardiff City	38	9	5	6	37	22	6	5	7	23	26	+12	55
11	Coventry City	39	7	8	5	27	20	7	5	7	27	24	+10	55
12	Crystal Palace	38	7	7	5	28	24	8	2	9	30	31	+3	54
13	Preston North End	39	10	4	5	35	22	4	6	10	20	31	+2	52
14	Stoke City	38	9	6	3	30	19	5	4	11	20	31	0	52
15	Crewe Alexandra	39	10	2	7	27	19	3	6	11	21	36	-7	47
16	Nottingham Forest	39	7	7	6	30	23	4	5	10	20	29	-2	45
17	Rotherham United	38	7	7	5	25	21	4	5	10	17	30	-9	45
18	Walsall	39	7	7	6	26	27	4	5	10	15	25	-11	45
19	Burnley	38	7	6	5	28	22	3	8	9	22	40	-12	44
20	Watford	39	7	8	5	27	25	4	3	12	17	32	-13	44
21	Gillingham	38	9	1	8	21	22	3	7	10	18	31	-14	44
22	Derby County	39	8	5	6	29	29	2	7	11	14	32	-18	42
23	Bradford City	39	5	3	12	19	29	4	3	12	13	27	-24	33
24	Wimbledon	37	2	3	14	15	33	3	0	15	14	42	-46	18

APRIL

Thursday 1st

Eva and Chase are trying all sorts of tricks this morning and every time they do anything they shout 'April Fool!' I tell them they should have got up way earlier if they wanted to catch their old man out.

Thursdays are press days at Colney and for some unknown reason, all the press want to talk to me this morning. Rick Waghorn from the *Evening News* is in reception with a shirt with 300 on the back. I ask him what's going on.

'If you play or get on on Saturday it will be your 300th appearance for the club,' he explains.

Doh! I knew I was close but I didn't realise it was that close. I'm delighted: it will be a massive honour to have played 300 games for such a fantastic club.

It makes me feel old though (I thought for a second he was holding up a shirt with my age on it). Thinking about it, it is a massive milestone: in these days of freedom of contract there aren't that many players who'll play that number of games for one club. So I do feel proud. I don't know whether I'll get on or not yet though, as the gaffer isn't in today: he's attending the funeral of a close friend in Blackpool.

Rick lets me keep the shirt so I give it to Terry. He's a bit down at the minute as he's got so much work to do. Some of the lads take advantage of him a bit. If there are balls to be signed they will go straight to Terry and ask him to organise them, without thinking that we're travelling away tomorrow and he's got to get 15 lots of kit, training kit, boots, drinks etc organised. It's a tough job and he does it all on his own, although he has a lady to wash the kit. But he does a good job and I like him a lot, so I always try to help him out if I can.

It's nice to be in demand this morning because if you're not starting you don't do many interviews, but they were all after me today – BBC, ITV, Sky Sports, all the radio and paper boys. It made me feel wanted again. I wish I'd known in advance though: they all wanted pictures and I was having a particularly bad hair day so I had to plonk a cap on it.

Friday 2nd

Welcome back, Greeno! We all shake his hand in training this morning and tell him exactly what we think of Sven Goran Eriksson's ridiculous decision not to even give him five minutes! He says it was fantastic, he really enjoyed it and that there were no prima donnas: all the other lads in the squad were really down to earth and friendly.

The papers are full of rumours that we're interested in Teddy Sheringham. Well, if that's the case, the gaffer can't have a bee in his bonnet about age, so I'm not sure if that's good news for me or bad. I really want to get my 100 goals for the club, but there are only eight games left this season for me to score six goals. So I don't think it's do-able . . . Unless I get another year . . .

I still haven't heard anything about that or about the youth team job. I know they've not given the youth team job to anyone. They're going to wait a bit longer. But I do want to play for at least another year and I wouldn't be able to combine playing with the youth team job, so maybe it wouldn't be right for me anyway.

We run through the usual set-pieces before heading for Norwich airport at 2pm to catch our plane to Burnley. Well, Blackpool, actually. No chance of a go on the amusements though: our bus is waiting to whisk us straight to the hotel for another wild night of pasta, cards, telly and lights out at 10pm.

Saturday 3rd

Nationwide League Division One

Burnley 3	**Norwich City 5**
Wood 7	Svensson 14, 62
May 29	Huckerby 30, 88
Blake 37	McKenzie 51
Turf Moor	Att: 12,484

No wonder managers have heart problems: watching games like this one can't be good for you. At least the gaffer can't get any greyer. What a game. I'm breathing hard – and I'm on the bench! We go 1–0 down, then equalise, then 2–1 down, then equalise, then 3–2 down. Still with me? It's half-time. The gaffer goes ballistic at the back four.

'We're defending too deep – where's the communication?' he asks. 'We're throwing points away here and the daft thing is we can still win it.'

It does the trick. Second half: we equalise, then score again. And then score again. 5–3, with five minutes to go. Brilliant!

Then I come on with three minutes to go for my 300th appearance and I'm also agonisingly close to getting my 95th goal. Hucks makes a trademark run down the left wing, squares the ball to me and I throw my whole body towards it, but I'm still inches from getting a touch on it as it arcs over my head. I could have scored it if I had been 6ft 5! I'm gutted. I'd have loved to have marked my 300th appearance with a goal.

Back in the dressing room, in between taking on extra oxygen, we discover all the teams immediately below us have lost. Fan-fucking-tastic. All we need now is for our near-neighbours to beat West Brom tomorrow. I never thought I would say this but 'Come on you Blues!' Ouch. That hurt.

Sunday 4th

Have a great chat about football with some fans in the sauna at Greens first thing in the morning (they're always great chats when you're winning!), followed by lunch at the football club for all the players and their families. It's a present from Delia and Michael. Back in December they promised us they'd buy us lunch if we beat Ipswich. Think we should get extra pudding for having gone 'Top Of The League At Portman Road' on that day too! They are fantastic people and we're so lucky to have them.

As soon as we arrive Ben makes a bee-line for a prime seat in front of the big screen showing the Millwall v Sunderland FA Cup semi-final. So he's happy, if not very talkative! Most people (especially an overexcited Delia!) are very happy that Millwall win and I'm delighted for Andy Roberts.

A few of the lads haven't turned up, which I think is pathetic. Delia and Michael have taken the time out to organise and flipping pay for today themselves and I think when someone's gone to the trouble of doing some-thing nice like that for you, the least you can do is be arsed to turn up. Shame on you, you know who you are. I know it was a family lunch, but Matty and Malky came even though their wives couldn't make it. I think the gaffer should have made it compulsory.

I have every intention of having a couple of pints, espe-cially while watching the football, but I walk in and see the lads are all drinking orange and lemonade. I don't think anyone would mind if we had a pint, but I don't want to be the only one.

It's a fabulous meal, as usual (I believe our major share-holder knows a thing or three about food). I queue up to get my carvery main course and the gaffer's wife Sandra is standing in front of me. She doesn't like her meat too rare so she points to a bit on the side that looks quite well-done and asks the chef:

'Oh, do you mind if I have that bit there?'

'Well, actually I'm saving that bit for Delia,' he says.

'Oh,' she says and accepts another piece without a fuss.

'You should have told him who you are!' I tell her as we walk back to our seats. 'You should have said: 'Look, mate, I'm the manager's wife and I want that bit. Now give it to me or I'll get you the sack!'

But she's not like that. Actually, I'm only like that on behalf of other people. But it was funny . . .

After lunch we head off for Leon's baby Mariah's chris-tening party. Most of the lads turn up, which is nice to see and a few of his old team-mates have really gone out of their way to be here: West Ham's Hayden Mullins is here, as is George Ndah and his two brothers. They've laid on a magician and a disco for the kids, so I finally get to have a bottle of Bud in peace! Oh and Mariah? She's gorgeous, mate.

Monday 5th

Spend the morning watching a video nasty: a tape of the three goals we conceded on Saturday. They were sloppy goals and that's not like us: our back four has been outstanding all season and we're the tightest defensive unit in the League. They won't let that happen too often.

The video has a happy ending though: all five of our

goals were of the highest quality. Matty's header came from a great cross from Adam. It's the sort of ball that, as a centre-forward, you're thinking 'Jeez, I wish I was on the end of that!'. It had great pace, it was at a great height, all you've got to do is stick your head on it because the pace is already on it. Ben saw it on Sky on Saturday night and said: 'Why doesn't he cross like that for you, Dad?!'

The afternoon is also spent watching the box, or the big screen. The Easter holidays started today so I have the perfect excuse to drag the kids along to the cinema to watch *The Cat In The Hat*. Luckily, they enjoy it almost as much as I do!

Tuesday 6th

It's going to be a big week as we're at home to Wigan on Friday and away to Reading on Easter Monday and both games are live on Sky. So we're off today for a change. Julie and I take the kids into the city as we've promised them a trampoline for Easter. We eventually find one in B+Q, but the kids are disappointed: it's been raining on and off all day so we can't put it up in the back garden yet. I must admit, I'm itching to have a go too.

It's a big lads' night in tonight, as Ben's friend Mark is coming to stay and watch the Arsenal v Chelsea game with us. Mark's a big Arsenal fan and Ben hates them, so I'm referee. Chelsea score the winner with about five minutes to go and poor old Mark suffers a barrage of micky-taking.

Wednesday 7th

Training is not quite as intense as usual, as the season's drawing to a close, so our base fitness levels should carry us through. We haven't been doing quite so much lately. Which is good this morning as I'm booked in at the Bupa hospital to have a second operation to remove tissue from my forearm as they just want to be sure they've got any last cancerous cells. It will leave me with quite an impressive scar (I'll be going round saying: 'Yeah, you should have seen the state of the other fella!'). I've had loads of 'good luck' texts from the lads. For some reason, no-one was expecting me to turn up to training this morning, not even the gaffer, but I'd rather be in, enjoying a bit of banter with the lads, than moping around the house counting down the hours until it's time to go.

After finally putting up the kids' trampoline (it's 12 feet in diameter, so I think my fitness gets more of a boost from putting that together than training!) Julie drops me off at the hospital. I'm given six jabs of a local anaesthetic, am in the operating room by 4.30pm and out again by 5.10pm. It doesn't hurt at all. I wouldn't have minded watching but Dr O'Neill advises me not to. Probably just as well. I casually glance over to the table of scalpels and other tools and see this big chunk of flesh lying on the side. It feels weird seeing a bit of me lying on the side. The nurse asks whether she's to throw the flesh away, but the doc says 'No!'

There are 13 big blue stitches in my arm. It looks like a joint trussed up for Sunday dinner.

Thursday 8th

Wake up feeling good: my arm's very swollen but it doesn't hurt. I head straight in to see Neal and he takes the dressing off. I almost faint when I see how much tissue they've taken from my arm. There's a big dent there where a bit of my arm used to be. Neal advises me not to train, but just to ice my arm to try to take the swelling down.

Later I take Jimmy B and Hucks to a tattooist I know in nearby Dereham. I want another tattoo on my back, to go with the ones of my children's names, Hucks wants one on his wrist and Jimmy B wants one, but doesn't know where. While we're looking through the tattooist's books, my arm really starts to throb. The anaesthetic's obviously wearing off. I look down and it seems even more swollen and red, angry even. It feels as if it's going to burst, so I drive straight back to Colney and see Neal. He rings the doc, who reassures us that it's a normal reaction to the size of operation I've just had, so Neal gives me some painkillers and just tells me to rest it. It's really itchy, which apparently means it is getting better, but I am going to be driven mad by it.

The painkillers do the trick nicely and I'm able to give my son a big hug later when we find out he's been named 'Player of the Year' by Thorpe Rovers. I'm very proud of him. He has had a great season at centre-half but what I have really liked about his performances is his attitude: he always tries hard and really encourages his team-mates.

Friday 9th

Nationwide League Division One
Norwich City 2   **Wigan 0**
Svensson 55
Huckerby 72
Carrow Road   Att: 23,446

My arm feels a bit better this morning. The redness has gone, but it's still swollen and still very sore to touch. I have a chat with Neal and the doc and they decide it would be better if I didn't play any part in the game tonight. I still feel fine and I am sure with a bit of strapping I'd be okay, but they know best. So I'll rest it and hope I can be involved on Monday.

I feel a bit lost this afternoon as I'm not playing. I don't really know what to do with myself. I mooch around for a while and eventually go to the ground, taking my place on the bench, even though I'm all suited and booted. I was offered a seat in the directors' box, but I gave it to Keith Webb, as he likes to see the game from a different angle and I just wanted to feel more involved.

We play extremely well and beat Wigan 2–0 with a great finish from Matty just inside the box and a typical Hucks goal. He picks up the ball from just inside Wigan's half, runs all the way up the pitch, finally slips past two defenders and then slides the ball under their goalie. Sweet as. If that had been Thierry Henry everyone would be raving about it and saying it was a goal of the season contender. But that's Hucks: he's liable to do that every game. He's a match-winner.

The crowd go wild. To be fair, they've been brilliant all game: the pressure was doubly on as we knew Sunderland had beaten Sheffield United earlier in the afternoon, but they got behind us right from the start. The New Stand really has made a difference: now they seem to be singing in every part of the ground, which does give the lads a big, big boost. The buzz around the place is incredible. I reckon we could be just two games away from achieving our dream of getting back into the Premiership.

Wigan's manager Paul Jewell is great afterwards.

'You were the better side. We couldn't cope with your tempo, the way you worked,' he says.

He's good enough to say the best team won. Not many managers have had the decency to say that about us this year. Yes, Mr Royle, you are much better than us and every other team in the division. That's why you've conceded twice as many goals as us and are 16 points behind us. Now, run along and fight for your play-off spot. And you too, Mr Pardew and Mr Warnock.

Saturday 10th

The lads are buzzing this morning. We've achieved our goal of 12 points from the last six games and now there are only six games to go, four of those away from home. We still have to go to Sunderland and Watford, which are never easy places, but overall our run-in's not too bad, with home games against Walsall and Preston to come. We just have to stay focussed.

Only 11 of us actually train this morning: the lads that played last night just do a warm-down. Neal straps up my arm as if it were the crown jewels and I'm pleased to say I come through training without any knocks.

We're chatting in training about who we think is going to get the fans' 'Player of the Year' award. Hucks will obviously be the favourite as he's had an amazing impact on the side since he came here and is probably the difference between us finishing in the play-offs or going straight up. I will be very surprised if he doesn't get it, but my choice has got to be Craig Fleming. For consistency over a 46-game season he's been outstanding. Obviously Malky and Greeno would have to be up there, as would Adam and Eddy – they've all had great seasons.

But you have to pick one and if you asked any manager – ask Bruce Rioch who still comes to watch us week in week out – he'd probably pick Flem. As would most of the team. Hucks has been amazing for us, but there was a period earlier on in the season when he didn't score for seven or eight games and it wasn't quite happening for him: he was quite quiet by his standards. Flem has been solid in every game he's played this season. I'd really like him to get it. I feel guilty that I've just pipped him to it a couple of times, but strikers, if they have a decent season, do tend to get the award.

Mind you, I missed out the year I scored 17 goals and we avoided relegation. Our goalkeeper, Andy Marshall, had a tremendous season and he beat me to the award by a few hundred votes. Bastard. It would have been my hat-trick of titles. He left at the end of the season to go to Ipswich on a free transfer. He knew he was going well before it came out, but I think he kept quiet until he got the 'Player of the Year' award. If the fans had known he was off, on a free transfer, to Portman Road of all places, it might just have tipped the balance in my favour! I felt really daft next season whenever opposition players asked me: 'So who was your player of the year then?'

'Oh, he's down the road, playing for our local rivals.'

In the afternoon we head off to Calum Edworthy's birthday party. The kids have a great time, but I must give special mention to the children's entertainer, Uncle Ted, who should be renamed Super Ted, as he kept his cool brilliantly, despite the fact that some of the kids were little horrors and running riot.

Sunday 11th

Boo! We don't have to be in training until 11.30am, but I have to meet Neal at 9.30am and go to hospital to get a special cast for my arm so I can be involved tomorrow. It's made by a lovely Geordie lady and she does a great job: it's very lightweight so I won't be classed as carrying a dangerous weapon. Well, at least, I hope not. I'll still have to run it by the ref tomorrow.

I play for the oldies in training this morning and once again we come out on top. Oh yes, there's life in this old dog yet. At 2pm, we head off for Reading. I still manage to win at Hearts, despite my throbbing arm. And no, I don't hide any aces up my cast. It's a nice easy journey and I'm delighted when we get there: we're staying in the hotel built in to the Madejski Stadium complex so getting to the game will be a doddle. I have a quiet night in watching the Masters on telly. The course looks beautiful. I bet I could lose a few balls there.

Monday 12th

Nationwide League Division One
Reading 0   **Norwich City 1**
                    Mulryne 86
Madejski Stadium   Att: 18,460

Stressful morning as we wait to see how Malky is – he picked up a slight knock on Friday – and how Flem got on at the back specialist he went down to see in London last night. Thankfully, both our defensive rocks are fine. We have a long walk, then head back for an 11.45am lunch, before hitting our rooms for a doze. We're offered soup and sarnies at 2.30pm, but I decline: I wouldn't be able to run if I had all that – I haven't even burned off last night's dinner yet! At 3.45pm we begin the long trek to the ground. It takes us a full five minutes to walk round to the players' entrance and we're all knackered by the time we get there. There's green and yellow everywhere: we've sold our full allocation of 4,000 tickets so once again, it should be a cracking atmosphere.

Neal and I are straight in to see the ref to get my cast okayed but my heart drops when I see who it is: Neale Barry, someone I haven't always seen eye-to-eye with in the past. 'I've got no chance,' I tell Neal. 'We just don't get on.' But he's brilliant and says it's no problem.

Chris Kamara, watching the game for Sky, stops me for a quick chat and asks me whether I've heard anything about a new contract. When I tell him I haven't, he's reassuring: 'Well, you've looked after yourself and kept yourself fit, so I can't see why not, Robbo, mate.'

West Brom drew earlier this afternoon and Sunderland lost, so if we win we could go clear at the top of the table. But I think we'd be happy with a point. Reading are a good side and we go in at half-time thankful the score's still 0–0. We're the better side in the second half and we're passing the ball around patiently, but it's still 0–0 when I get on with about six minutes to go. It turns the game!

Two minutes after I come on, the most bizarre thing happens. We take a long throw into their box, one of the Reading lads clears it, but only as far as the ref and the ball hits him on the back of the neck. From there, it bounces straight to Mullers, who controls it superbly and unleashes a great strike into the top corner of the net. It's right in front of our fans, who all go mental. There's no time for Reading to get back into the game, so that's it.

Neale Barry apologises to Reading and their fans straight afterwards, which is fair enough. But it's not like Mullers still didn't have a lot of work to do. It's not like it hit the ref a yard out and all he had to do was just poke it in. It was a great finish. And we've had our fair share of bad refereeing this season . . .

It's very quiet on the bus home for some reason, only livened up by a pizza fight between Crichts and Jimmy B. Jimmy B started it last night at dinner when he got the biggest slice of beef you've ever seen, walked up to Crichts and just slapped him across the face with it, leaving a trail of gravy everywhere. He didn't hurt him, just made a mess. They're always at it those two. So, there's a Pizza Hut right by Reading's ground and the Fridge has ordered tea for everybody. We're sitting there on the coach, arguing about who ordered the Meat Feast and who's got the garlic bread, and I say to Crichts that it's the perfect opportunity to get Jimmy B back. So Crichts shouts to the Fridge sitting down the front, 'D'you want your iPod?', just to have an excuse to walk down the aisle. Jimmy B looks round: he knows something's going on, but can't work out what. And then Crichts hits him with the pizza from behind, straight in his eye. Bits of tomato, mushroom, cheese and ham are flying over everyone, especially poor Briggsy, who's sat next to Jimmy B.

Apart from that, the coach is deadly silent, with everyone doing their usual routine of cards or laptops. When I got promoted with Leicester we'd blast out Oasis' first album as soon as we got back on the coach if we'd got a result. We have got to sort out some CDs, lads. We're top of the League for Chrissakes, not about to get relegated. It's like a morgue in here!

Tuesday 13th

Get a great sweat on in training this morning, which is just what the doc ordered. The problem with only getting on as a late sub is that you still prepare the same way as the other lads, still eat the meals provided by the hotel and load up with carbs, just in case you have to come on in the second minute. But if you only get on for the last six minutes, you don't burn it off and you know how scared I am of lardy boy returning. That's why I tend to have a lot of saunas.

In the afternoon Julie and I head down to a place called Freeport, near Colchester, which has all the top-name brands at discount prices. The only problem is, it's far too close to Ipswich, so I get a fair bit of good-humoured stick from a bunch of Town fans.

While we're out I get a phone call from my old mate Kenny Jackett, who I've known since my Watford days, offering me a job as player-coach at Swansea City. He's just got the manager's job there. It would be a great opportunity for me and chances like this don't come along very often. There are so many football people out there without jobs, but I tell him I need to sit down with the gaffer for a chat once we get promotion. Going back to Wales would be a big draw – it would mean I could also do my TV and radio work. I still haven't a clue whether I'm part of the manager's plans for next year: I'd hate to play poker with him: he's giving nothing away.

Wednesday 14th

Day off. Meet up with Hucks in the sauna and he fancies a bit of shopping so, with nowt better to do, I join him. Which means I end up with a pair of jeans I don't really need and a pair of trainers I don't really need either. Still, that's pretty good for me! On the way home I call in at former Norwich defender Rob Newman's new suit shop. The official opening is on Sunday, so he gives me some invites and I promise to try and get as many of the lads there as possible. Well, I could do with a cheap suit!

Embo calls me this afternoon to tell me that Andy Roberts' wife had a little girl. He's just had a text from Kevin Muscat saying she was 10lb 5oz! Blimey – Andy's wife's only little. He's coming to stay with me and Julie on Friday night because the rest of the Walsall team aren't travelling down until the morning of the game. I say to him: 'Just one thing: bring your own Lucozade.' But he's not having it: 'No way – I want an all-inclusive. And I want steak for my tea!' Cheeky git!

Thursday 15th

I know my way to the Bupa hospital pretty well now, so I'm there in plenty of time to have my stitches taken out.

Dr O'Neill says they will only remove half the stitches today as a precaution in case I'm playing on Saturday. Then he tells me that the tissue they removed last week for analysis was tested and there were no cancerous cells! Yes! So I've been given the all-clear and hopefully that's an end to it all now.

I get back to training around 10.30am and they've already started. You can tell we're doing well, because there are quite a few fans watching us train this morning and queuing for autographs after. Naturally, we're happy to oblige.

Crichts went fishing yesterday and has brought in the head of one of the trout he caught, to put in goalkeeper coach Jimmy Hollman's wash bag. I don't know what Jimmy's done to upset him. I thought Crichts was after Jimmy B or Mullers. Crichts cut the laces of Mullers's trainers about four weeks ago and ever since they've been winding each other up. Mullers got Crichts's brand new trainers and cut the tongues out in revenge. Then the other day all Crichts's clothes were found in the bin at Colney. All apart from a silver bangle, which wasn't expensive, but was bought for him by his kids. Crichts went mad, shouting at the lads, but no-one's owned up to putting his clothes in the bin or taking the bangle.

Thing is, it could be any one of the lads. We don't go as far as Wimbledon, where they used to burn your clothes, but we do make it quite clear what we think of dodgy gear. Flem's got the worst taste in shoes – they're like Hush Puppies, so his quite often end up in the fridge (the real one, not Neal). Easty's normally a sharp dresser but he's got a pair of razzle-dazzle bowling shoes. I chucked them in the fridge the other week. I must admit I have got a pair of pink trainers I got in Rome a couple of years ago, which the lads take the piss out of. We don't cut up suits – they're too expensive – just shoes, laces, socks, stuff like that. Flem kept on cutting up Crichts's socks last year, but he eventually got done. Crichts didn't have a clue who it was and was getting madder and madder. Dave Carolan hid a camcorder on top of one of the lockers, caught Flem red-handed and outed him at the 'Player of the Year' dinner last year.

But the one guy everyone wants to get is Malky, because he's such a model pro who never does anything wrong. Ever. Mullers and Squiz have been trying to get him fined or get his gear for ages, but he's too clued-up.

Friday 16th

I'm really keyed up for tomorrow's game at home to Walsall: I think if we get three points we'll be there. It will be our fifth win in a row if we do it. But it's not going to be easy: Walsall are fighting for their lives and have just sacked their manager, Colin Lee. Paul Merson and my good friend Simon Osborn have taken over as joint caretaker managers – and teams usually raise their game for a new boss.

Embo arrives late in the afternoon, ready for his steak. Sorry, mate, Molly's had it. I've really missed not having him around the place since he left us last June. But he's doing really well at Walsall: he had injury problems when he was with us, but has played over 30 games this year and stands a good chance of being voted their 'Player of the Year'. I think – and hope – that he'll get a very warm welcome from our fans tomorrow as he was well-liked down here and only injury kept him out of the side.

It's good to see him and it's also handy because he tells me their team – they're going to play with a back five: three centre-halves and two full-backs. I've never heard of anyone doing that before. (It would have been six defenders, but they decided they only needed five when Embo told them I'm not starting!)

My cousin Arfon and six of his friends from Wales are also down visiting. They come at least once a year and are all dyed-in-the-wool Canaries now as they have such a great time down here. Arfon reminds me of when I was a young pro at Watford and went back home for a couple of days. I was a bit flash, had all the Lacoste gear and a gold bracelet. Me, my brother and my cousin were in the local chippy, waiting for our food and this lad said: 'Look at him with all his gold on – what a fool!' So I turned round and said 'Listen mate, the only fool in here is you.' Of course, it all kicked off. So what did I do? I curled up into a ball. I could see my brother and cousin knocking hell out of the other lads: there was blood everywhere. One of the lads ripped my bracelet off, so I was rummaging around on the floor while the lads were getting spanked, defending me. Typical brave me, causing all the trouble then doing nothing about it!

Saturday 17th

Nationwide League Division One
Norwich City 5   Walsall 0
Francis 2
McKenzie 45
Svensson 51, 86
Huckerby 73
Carrow Road   Att: 23,558

We need to take the game by the scruff of the neck against a struggling side like Walsall. And we do. Two minutes into the game and we're ahead. Damo lifts the ball over a helpless James Walker from six yards out after a great ball in from Hucks. Then, just before half-time, Leon gets his first at Carrow Road with a fantastic 12-yard header from a Hucks cross. We are absolutely hammering them and 10–0 isn't looking out of the question.

It's 2–0 at half-time but the gaffer's still not happy. He says the defence are sitting too far back and inviting pressure. So we go straight out and score another goal. Poor old Merse: at one point in the second half I catch him having a wry smile as yet another pass goes astray and he realises it's just going to be one of those days.

Matty hasn't stopped bloody scoring since I had a pop at him a few chapters ago! He scores two more today to make that six goals in five games. And of course, Hucks gets on the scoresheet with a slick finish. There's a huge noise from the stands. As I'm warming up, I have a bit of banter with the Snakepit boys. The fans are loving this: we're in cruise control and asking everyone 'What's the score?' It's 4–0 at this point and I don't really like replying to these kinds of chants because I feel as if I'm disrespecting the opposition, taking the piss. Trouble is, if you don't signal the score you get booed, so what the hell. I stick up four fingers and get a round of applause for my counting ability.

I get on for my contracted three minutes, but I'm gutted not to get on sooner: we're ripping them apart and I'm sure I could sneak a goal in front of all my Welsh mates. I really feel for Embo. He's trying his socks off and is probably their best player, but that's scant consolation. We are irresistible this afternoon and wind up winning 5–0. We are now five points clear of West Brom and 14 clear of Sunderland in third and they have to play each other tomorrow night at the Stadium of Light.

A draw would be nice. I'm 100 per cent convinced we are up now, but I want the title – I think we deserve it. We've been the most consistent team and more attractive to watch. Even West Brom's manager, Gary Megson, says they've been poor on quite a few occasions this season. They play long ball and they've had quite a few last minute wins – in two of their last three wins they've got the winner deep into stoppage time. We might not have played great football all the time, but no-one works harder than us and when we do pass it, we pass it really well. And to all those who still think West Ham are the best side in this division: have a look. The League table doesn't lie.

A whole gang of us head out to HaHa's restaurant for dinner afterwards. My cousins are totally star-struck and amazed to discover that not only does Darren Huckerby walk on water (well, actually he races on it), he's also very generous at getting a round in. Is there no end to this bloke's talents?

Sunday 18th

Head off to the Nelson Hotel first thing to say goodbye to my mates, who are all nursing hangovers. I don't envy them the five-hour journey back to God's own country.

Then I head off to Rob Newman's shop opening. What a surprise – the chance of a free glass of champagne and the first person I bump into is Mike Milligan. It's good catching up with Gunny, Gossy and some of the other lads from years gone by. I think Rob will do very well in his new venture: well, he managed to persuade me to cough up for a new suit.

Boring afternoon watching the Sunderland v West Brom game over at ours with Hucks, Lindsey and their two little boys, Thomas and Ben. It's a typical West Brom performance: in the very last second of the game Jason Koumas has their only effort on goal and scores. It's daylight robbery: Sunderland have dominated the game and deserved at least a draw. I'm not sure whether it's a good result for us or not: we now only need two points from four games to ensure our return to the Promised Land, but on the other hand, West Brom are only two points behind us. Having been top of the League for four months now, we don't want them overtaking us in the closing stages. Especially after a performance like that. If they win the League it will be an absolute travesty.

Monday 19th

My arm's very sore and swollen again this morning and I'm worried it's infected. The nurse who takes out the rest of my stitches this morning agrees, and tells me to get some antibiotics from the club doctor.

It's sod's law: whichever part of you is injured, some-one will always catch it in training and today proves the rule. Coops is trying to win the ball and charges over, losing his balance a bit, can't stop, and catches me with his elbow right slap bang on the scar. The lads think I'm milking it, but it's agony.

Tuesday 20th

I feel a lot better this morning: the antibiotics are doing the job and scaring the hell out of the infection. We're back up to training at full tempo again this morning, although the gaffer's quite relaxed. Unlike a lot of managers who leave training to the assistant or coaches, he gets really involved. He's a stickler for the basics and is always stopping sessions to pull us up for some mistake or other. Sometimes you would think we are at the start of the season rather than near the end: despite having been top of the League for four months now he's still desperate to make sure we're using good technique and getting rid of bad habits.

I still haven't talked to the gaffer about my chances of

getting a new contract, but I know he's started talks with Holty, so I'll leave it a couple of days and have a chat with him then if I still haven't heard anything.

Robbie Savage rings this afternoon: he's delighted we're so close to promotion and says he's really looking forward to playing at Carrow Road again next season and having a night out with me and Darren Eadie afterwards. I'm really excited about the prospect of playing in the Premiership. *If* I get a contract. If not, maybe I'll head off to Real Madrid on a Bosman. Sometimes I daydream about what it would be like to play with David Beckham. People say he's over-rated, but I disagree. His crosses are the stuff strikers dream about. He's not the quickest, but he only needs to get half a yard on the defender and he crosses the ball. The thing strikers really hate is when a player shapes to cross the ball and doesn't: you've already made your run, but you have to check yourself and get back onside. As soon as Beckham's got the ball you know exactly where it's going and when. He'll put it on your head and with the pace he puts on it, you don't even need to head it – it's just a case of directing it in. I think he sets a great example on the pitch tear-arsing round, getting tackles in and covering.

And I think he sets a great example off it too. A few months ago my mate Stony was organising a charity auction to send this little kid to America for an opera-tion he needed. My shirt raised £300 and the auction raised around £3000, but they needed £10,000. Anyway, at the same time, he wrote to Victoria Beckham and asked if she could send something for the auction. He got a letter back from her mum saying they'd send a signed Real Madrid shirt and that whatever the shortfall was they'd pay the rest. Imagine how many letters they must get like that every week. They really went up in my esti-mation after that. But that sort of thing never seems to come out in the papers.

Ben and I spend a quiet evening in, rooting for Chelsea against Monaco. I'd love them to win as I think Claudio Ranieri has endured some shocking things this season and managed to maintain his dignity throughout. Not sure about his tactics tonight though, as Chelsea get dumped 3–1 by Monaco, even though the French side were down to ten men.

Wednesday 21st

I wake up with the butterflies in my stomach doing backflips. We could be promoted tonight without even kicking a ball if Sunderland fail to win at Crystal Palace. You can tell the whole county is aware of what a big game tonight might be: even when I drop Eva and Chase at school, a few of the mums stop me to talk about tonight's game. They ask if I'll be glued to the radio. The answer is a resounding 'No.' We haven't relied on other results all season so we're not going to start now. We have four games left to get the two points we need and rack up as many points as we can to go for the title. Don't get me wrong: I will be delighted if Sunderland fail to beat Palace, but it won't be the end of the world if they don't. I think most of the fans going to the Watford game on Saturday would much rather us win promotion there than be handed it tonight, although they are expecting a big gate at our reserves game down at Carrow Road this evening. It would be very odd to get promoted without actually playing, but I'd rather get promoted as soon as possible.

I spend the day pottering round and am sitting watching telly when my mobile phone starts to buzz with texts. With just 20 minutes gone, Crystal Palace are winning 1–0 and Sunderland have had their goalie sent off. Oh, okay, I'll get excited then. Forty minutes later: buzz! 2–0 to Palace. Buzz! 3–0 to Palace with ten minutes to go. After all the wondering and dreaming, after seven long years – nine for the football club – we are back in the top flight. My first thoughts are for Delia and Michael. They have done so much for this club and deserve this so much.

At 10.20pm the phone goes. It's Squiz. 'Robbo, get your arse over here. Now!'

Julie gives me a lift over to Squiz's place. All the lads are there. We break open a few cold ones and retire to the communal lounge area in a sort of conservatory, shared by all the flats. We're trying to be fairly quiet, out of consideration to the other residents, but Matty gets a few drinking games going – you know the ones where you have to waggle your hands if someone points to you, fuzzy duck, that sort of thing. Thankfully, Matty doesn't do his Borak impression. We don't go mad – although Matty and I do debate whether to steal Jimmy B's little dog on our way out – and I'm sober as a judge by the time I get home at 4am. All right then, as sober as a slightly pissed, but very happy judge.

Thursday 22nd

I drop the girls at school as Julie has gone with Becky Edworthy and Nicola Fleming to do interviews on Radio Norfolk, giving their reactions to promotion. The atmosphere at Colney is amazing. Fans have tied green and yellow balloons, letters, cards and flowers to the gates and the building is swarming with press and camera crews. The gaffer was at the reserve game last night, but he must have gone home early: he looks really well. At 9.45am he comes in to the dressing room and shakes everyone's hands.

'I'm fucking proud of you. Very fucking proud,' he says,

beaming like a lunatic. 'But the job's not done yet. I don't want it for myself, but I want every one of you lot to get a medal, because you deserve it. The three and a half years I've been here, you've all been superb and worked your bollocks off. So let's do it!'

His words get a round of applause and a cheer. We all want a medal. Especially me. If it is going to be my last season here, I'd love to finish it in style. I've seen the hard times. Three years ago we won away at Tranmere with four games to go to keep us in this division, after a miserable season in which we were pretty much always in a relegation dogfight, scrapping for points in front of 12,000 pretty miserable fans. What a turnaround.

We open a few bottles of champagne before training – just for the photographers, mind, although I'm trying to lick some of the spray off my arm! After posing for a few team shots, it's straight back down to earth – we've got a big game against Watford on Saturday. I'm hoping we'll still be able to keep our focus. Watford's not an easy place to go and the pitch is shit, all dry and bumpy, but we are taking another 4,500 or 5,000 fans so it will be like a home game for us, which should help. I think Watford are relatively safe. They don't have a lot to play for, whereas we do. And we are professionals at the end of the day.

So it's straight back down to business. 'Matty, mate, you won the yellow jersey on Tuesday, so here it is. Now put it on!'

Julie and I head for the early showing of *Monster* at the cinema later, before turning in early.

Friday 23rd
We get the coach down to Watford at about 1.30pm and are safely tucked up in our rooms by 4pm. All my old mates

at Watford are long gone, but I still always look forward to playing there. Especially this time! I really enjoyed my five years there. Their fans always give me a bit of stick – and I suppose tomorrow will be no exception.

Saturday 24th

Nationwide League Division One

Watford 1	Norwich City 2
Blizzard 78	*Francis 29*
	McKenzie 48
Vicarage Road	Att: 19,200

It's going to be very hot out on the pitch today. It's a gorgeous day – and our fans look amazing. It takes my breath away when I walk out and see the whole of the Vicarage Road end stand is a sea of yellow and green. It's like being back at the Millennium Stadium: flags, inflatable canaries and beach balls, fancy dress, wigs, silly hats . . . There look to be one or two fans dotted around the rest of the stadium too – apparently the Watford ticket office has been inundated with people from places like Sheringham, Lowestoft and King's Lynn asking to renew their Hornets' membership so they can get tickets!

The noise is incredible – and our fans just don't stop singing. It makes you feel so proud.

We start really well and go 2–0 up thanks to goals from Damo and Leon, before taking our feet off the gas a bit in the second half and conceding a silly goal. But as usual we don't panic and the result's never really in doubt. I come on for the last couple of minutes and nearly score with my first touch. I find myself unmarked in the box, but I'm in two minds. Fatal. I should have had a touch and hit the ball with my left foot, even though it's not my best, but I try to bend it round him and don't catch it at all. It sails straight into the keeper's arms. I'm disappointed, but I've only been on the pitch a minute and, as I keep saying to the lads, 'Give me at least *two* minutes to get into the pace of the game, will you, before you set me up?'

No matter. At the final whistle, someone from the Nationwide League gives us a banner saying 'Going Up Up Up' and a few bottles of champagne and we jump around in front of our travelling faithful. I spot Ben going wild in amongst ecstatic fans and point him out to Malky who waves and gives him a thumbs-up. Watford have also got a big screen down at the Vicarage Road end and I'm keeping one nervous eye on that while jumping up and down with the banner. How the fuck have West Brom got on? They had been drawing 0–0 but scored two in the second half. Damn. They don't deserve to win the title. We do!

We have now won six games in a row. I don't think I've ever done that in my career before. I said a few weeks ago that now would be a great time to put a little unbeaten run together: I meant a few draws in that as well, lads!

Only about 13 of us decide to go back on the coach. The London lads are off to see mates: even the gaffer is staying down for some reason. Club secretary Kevan Platt comes back on the coach with us so we ask him if we can stop at an offie and get a few cans for the journey. He rings the gaffer to check it's okay, but the gaffer turns us down. I suppose I can see why: we've got to pick up our cars at Colney. Oh well, we'll just have to go out afterwards then!

Darren Eadie joins me, Eddy and a few of the other lads for a meal at HaHa's. We end up in the nightclub Mercy, where I opt for my usual comfy chair and watch the others throw what I believe they call 'shapes'. I don't like sitting in the VIP areas of clubs: I think perhaps the club owners like to see footballers in their VIP areas, but you're looking down at the dancefloor, thinking all the fun's down there. Not that I dance: I've definitely got two left feet on the dancefloor, unlike on the pitch, where I haven't even got one. At least we don't get bothered in the VIP area and we can relax a bit more.

But, as you know, I don't like people thinking I'm a big-time Charlie. The one time I do take advantage is not having to queue to get in somewhere, but that's only because I sometimes get hassle from people after they've had a few drinks. After we played Millwall last year, Stevie Claridge and Andy Roberts stayed up and we all went out to Delaney's. I went to get another round in and this group of lads at the bar got chatting to me. So I talked to this bloke for about ten minutes and then said, very politely: 'Excuse me, I'd better take these drinks back to the others before they die of thirst!' And this lad starts shouting: 'Fucking typical Norwich footballer: doesn't give a shit about the fans. What a fucking attitude!' I was completely taken aback. I said 'You what, mate? Doesn't give a shit? I've just spent ten minutes talking to you! What do you want me to do – spend the night with you?' Then he said: 'Don't talk to me like that! I pay your wages!' I was so angry: I really could have lost it. But his mates were quite sensible and dragged him away, saying, ignore him, he's pissed. And I finally got back to Stevie and Andy again!

But most people are fine. Tonight I'm mobbed by people thanking me for what I've done for the club. I feel a bit of a fraud, as I haven't really been that involved and start feeling a bit sorry for myself. Hang on, no, I *am* proud. I haven't been as involved as I would have liked, but I can share in this. It feels odd though, as I don't even know if

I'll be here next season. Julie said she felt a bit out of it the other night and doing the interviews on Thursday. Obviously she's delighted we won promotion, but there's so much up in the air for us that she hasn't really felt ecstatic, like a lot of the other players' partners.

Sunday 25th

I have a bit of a sore head this morning so I take the girls swimming and head off to Greens, to sort myself out. Unfortunately it doesn't work. There's a new car valeting service in the car park so I hand over my keys, expecting my gold Volvo C70 to be as sorted as my head when I get out. But when I emerge, my car's nowhere to be seen.

I always have around £30 in pound coins for car parks sitting on the dashboard, so someone must have clocked them and thought 'Wahey, petrol money'. Mind you, it had a full tank of petrol, so they could be anywhere by now. Greens' assistant manager Nick and Mark, who owns the valeting service, can't believe this is happening. Nick rings his manager, Grant, who's off duty, but immediately offers to lend me his car.

I ring the police and a very nice policewoman comes and takes my statement. She's quite funny and tells me she'll have to put her car in for a valet as she could do with having it stolen. Aside from a few CDs, a couple of golf bags, a couple of Rolex watches oh and the, ahem, sunglasses I got in Venice last year (gold with diamond studs, worth about £3,500!), I tell her there's nothing of great value in the car.

The thing is, I'm pissed off the car's been stolen, but really upset that I had a great photo of my three kids and me on my key-ring, taken on holiday in Florida. I don't think I've got a copy of it and it's my favourite picture of us all. Damn, all my keys are on the keyring too, so I'll have to get the house locks changed.

Monday 26th

Still no sign of my car. I don't want it back now; he'll have thrashed it. I hope he's written it off. People who steal have a right nerve. People work very hard for their possessions and people like that just take them without a care in the world for who they're hurting.

It's baking today, so I slather on the sun cream for training before heading off to Greens. The people at Greens keep apologising, but it's not their fault.

Tuesday 27th

The back page of the *EDP* asks the question: Will Saturday's game against Preston be Iwan's last home game? For the first time this season, I think it might be. Holty's agreed a new contract, despite the gaffer previously saying he wouldn't open contract talks with anyone until the season's over. And the gaffer's not been the same with me in training over the last week or so. He usually comes round and has a bit of banter, but he's not really been very chatty with me of late. Nor has Kevan Platt, the club secretary. I saw him today at the club and he couldn't quite meet my eye, although he'd normally come out of his office and have a chat with me. Maybe he knows something I don't. Maybe I'm just being paranoid. I've been here seven years, we're friends. I know people have got their job to do and that, at the end of the day, the club comes first. I totally understand that, so I don't know why people haven't been able to be straight with me.

I'm babysitting tonight as Julie is out with Delia and the rest of the girls for a celebration meal. I'm nearly asleep in bed when Julie gets back at 11.30pm. She hasn't had a great night and tells me about a minor upset between the girls. As she climbs into bed she says: 'I'm sorry to say this, but I think we're going to be on our way.' I ask her what she means and she says: 'For the first time in seven years Delia couldn't really look me in the eye tonight.'

I say maybe she's being over-sensitive, maybe Delia was just tired. But we both know. Delia's always got on brilliantly with Julie and would always make a bee-line for her to give her a big hug and a kiss. If Delia knows I'm not staying, she would have found it really hard tonight. So I must be off.

Julie lets out a big sigh and we both roll over and try to get to sleep. But my mind's whirring, and I'm sure hers is.

Wednesday 28th

I drag myself out of bed after what feels like two minutes' sleep and take Eva and Chase to school, followed by anything to take my mind off things: putting the rubbish out, reading the paper, raking up the leaves in the back garden. Luckily, I have a big distraction lined up for lunchtime. I'm doing some modelling. Yes, modelling. No, not balaclavas and flipflops. Rob Newman asked me, Hucks, Flem and Greeno if we'd model some of his suits for him. Not a problem as Rob is a top bloke. Greeno, the muppet, actually turns up without any shoes, so he has to borrow Platty's.

Even more amazing than me being asked to be a model is the fact that this evening I will finally be able to sit down to watch Malky get his first cap for Scotland after someone presumably took the blinkers off Berti Vogts. Good luck mate! Holty's also starting for Scotland and Mullers is playing for Northern Ireland.

I race back from picking up a few bits from the shops and Julie tells me that the gaffer called this afternoon and asked me to go in at 8.15am tomorrow morning for a meeting. Well, that's that then.

To cap a great day, Scotland lose.

Thursday 29th

Somehow, I feel it's appropriate to dress all in black this morning: black combats, black T-shirt and black Prada shoes. I get in early, about 8am, but the gaffer and Dougie are already there in their office. 'I'm not being funny gaffer but I'm dressed like this because I think it's going to be a sad day,' I quip and the gaffer cracks a smile.

But I can see his eyes glazing over, filling up. And then he starts to speak. 'This is one of the hardest decisions I've ever had to make,' he begins. 'We've all thought long and hard about it, but I'm afraid we won't be renewing your contract at the end of the season. I'm sorry.'

I've prepared myself for this moment; I've had a hunch about it for a few weeks now. I don't show any emotion outwardly, but inside I'm gutted. This is our home. This club, this city, these friends – and we love it here. But I don't want them to give me a contract because of what I've done in the past – I want them to give me one because I deserve it. The gaffer's still talking.

'You have been a pleasure to work with and are a credit to yourself and your family. If all players were like you, managers would have no problems.'

I feel very down and very empty. A big part of my life – this club has been my life for the last seven years – has been ripped away. He doesn't mention the youth team job and, in a way, I'm glad. He knows I want to continue playing and if he'd offered it to me, I wouldn't be able to. I don't know what I'd do if he did offer it to me – and I know I'd have to make an immediate decision. I'm not going to say, 'What about the youth team job?' as if I'm desperate. I think maybe he knows I'd be tempted but he sees me training every day, knows how fit I am and knows I can still play, so maybe he's deliberately not putting that temptation in my way.

Maybe, if he'd offered me another year, I'd have spent

even more time on the bench, been training with the ressies. He knows how much I'd have hated that, to be so near and yet so far, so maybe he's also taken that into consideration. At least this way I get to go out on a high. I've achieved what I came here to do: fire the club back into the Premiership and, although, I haven't always been that involved this season, I have scored some important goals for the club, like the one at home to Sheffield United. My head's reeling. I can see that it's hard for the gaffer though, so we shake hands and go to tell the players. There's a stunned silence as the gaffer tells them the news.

'One of the hardest jobs in management is to tell a player or players that their contract won't be renewed. And I have to tell you that Robbo and Crichts won't be getting a new contract,' he says grimly.

And that's that. The lads all come up and shake mine and Crichts's hands. Steve Foley comes up to shake my hand. He's nearly in tears. I'm looking at him going, 'Don't.' He nearly sets me off. I try to lighten the mood: 'Well, at least I won't have to have all those nasty injections for our pre-season trip to Malaysia, eh lads? And I get out of the fitness test next week!'

The gaffer has delayed the morning press conference until 9.45am. Immediately afterwards, I'm deluged with requests for interviews. I think this is one day it might be all right to be late for training. Outwardly, I'm very calm. I still get on very well with everyone here and don't want this to end in recriminations. I've got so much respect for the gaffer and feel I can count him as a good friend. So I tell it like it is: 'I'm disappointed but I completely understand the club's decision. I would like to wish them all the best. Norwich will always be the first result I look for.'

And I mean it. But, inside, I'm gutted. Roy Waller is

fuming: 'I'm not happy with them treating you like this,' he storms.

All through the afternoon I get texts from mates saying 'You wanna buy the gaffer a dictionary and get him to check the meaning of the word 'Loyalty'.' Lay off, lads. He doesn't owe me a living. At the end of the day, it's a business and the gaffer has to live or die by his decisions to hopefully do the best for the club. I can understand. I've got another challenge now, another chapter in my life. My only wish is that the lads who got us into the Premier will get their chance, not some 'last pay day' guys. Of course we need four or five new players, but I hope these lads get their chance – they've earned it.

I eventually escape the clutches of Colney – God, I'm so popular, suddenly! – and go to pick the girls up from school. Unfortunately, by the time we get home, there's a very red-eyed Ben sitting there waiting for us. He was sitting on the school coach coming home when he heard the news on the radio: 'Norwich City striker Iwan Roberts will be leaving the club in the summer, having not had his contract renewed.'

He looks at me, his little eyes filling up.

'Is that true, dad?'

I tell him, yes, it is, but it's cool, because life goes on and we'll go and build a new life somewhere else. Chase doesn't want to; she likes her school. Ben says he's not upset that he'll have to go to a new school: 'No . . . I'm just upset at how my dad's been treated.' Oh mate, don't!

I finally shed a quiet tear when I read the *Evening News* later that evening, long after the kids are in bed. Rick Waghorn has written a lovely article about me and ends it with: 'Come 4.45pm on Saturday there's one thing you can guarantee: there won't be a dry eye in the house.' I'm not crying, I'm not! I know I will be on Saturday, though. At least now I know I can say goodbye and thank everyone at Carrow Road on Saturday. It's going to be a very emotional day for me, Julie and the kids.

Friday 30th

Jimmy B is a star. Just when I'm gloomily walking into the dressing room, thinking 'It's the last time I'll be doing this' he cheers me up with something I've never seen in 18 years as a pro-footballer. As he's getting changed I catch sight of something on his chest. I ask him to turn around and he reveals a very sore, red, swollen, pierced nipple. The lads burst out laughing and Jimmy covers it up quick in case the gaffer walks in. The gaffer's got very strict rules on things like that: if he sees them, he takes the piss. Big time.

There are some great photos of me in the local press today and I'd like to thank them for their support over the years, too. I've become quite good friends with most of them – something else I shall miss when I move on. The Norwich City Independent Supporters Association chairman, Roy Blower, came to training today and tells me I should take as much credit as anybody for where we are today. That's quite touching. He says NCISA want to throw a party for me. Oh, go on then!

Roy Waller wants me to go on his radio show on Monday from 9–10am. So I ask the gaffer if he minds if I come in a little bit late then. 'No problem at all,' he says. 'By the way, anything you need – references, advice, you've got my number, just give me a ring any time you need me.'

He's been very supportive. Unlike my so-called mates. Again my phone is going crackers with text messages. Adie from Delaney's: 'We're looking for a couple of glass collectors if you're looking for a job!' Actually, they're all really shocked and supportive too. My mate Joe, a local taxi driver, texts: 'Please ring me before training or after as I can't sleep. I have had so many people ringing me saying 'Please tell Iwan we wish him all the best and we want him to stay.' Love you Joe.' The Forest fan we met on holiday in the States sends his support: 'Sorry to hear you're not getting a contract. Please come and sign for us. Least you're leaving on a high note – the Championship can't be bad!'

The phone continues to ring every five minutes this afternoon: Steve Claridge can't believe they let me go, Mike Newell wants me to join him at Luton and Steve Evans wants me to go to Boston as player-coach. Hull and Barnsley are interested too. But I'm not going to be rushed into making a decision. First and foremost I want to get a champions' medal with Norwich, then enjoy the celebrations and then I will sit down and think about what's best for me and my family. Until then, I'm off to bed as I've got a big day ahead of me tomorrow. And I'm looking forward to it and dreading it, all at the same time.

Nationwide League Division One

Pos	Name	P	W	D	L	F	A	W	D	L	F	A	GD	PTS
				HOME					AWAY					
1	**Norwich City**	43	17	3	2	41	13	9	7	5	32	22	+38	88
2	West Bromwich Albion	43	14	5	3	34	14	11	6	4	29	21	+28	86
3	Sunderland	43	12	7	2	31	14	8	5	9	27	29	+15	72
4	Ipswich Town	44	12	2	8	48	35	9	6	7	34	35	+12	71
5	West Ham United	44	11	7	4	38	20	7	9	6	24	24	+18	70
6	Wigan Athletic	44	11	7	4	28	15	7	9	6	31	28	+16	70
7	Crystal Palace	44	9	8	5	33	25	11	2	9	37	34	+11	70
8	Sheffield United	44	11	5	6	36	24	9	4	9	25	28	+9	69
9	Reading	44	10	6	6	28	25	9	4	9	26	31	-2	67
10	Millwall	44	10	8	4	27	15	7	7	8	27	31	+8	66
11	Cardiff City	44	10	5	7	39	24	7	7	8	27	32	+10	63
12	Coventry City	44	8	9	5	32	21	7	5	10	28	30	+9	59
13	Stoke City	43	10	6	5	31	23	6	5	11	21	31	-2	59
14	Preston North End	44	11	6	5	40	26	4	7	11	24	39	-1	58
15	Nottingham Forest	44	7	9	6	32	25	6	6	10	26	33	0	54
16	Watford	44	8	8	6	30	28	6	4	12	23	36	-11	54
17	Burnley	44	9	6	7	36	30	4	8	10	23	42	-13	53
18	Crewe Alexandra	44	11	3	8	32	23	3	7	12	23	39	-7	52
19	Rotherham United	44	7	8	7	28	27	5	7	10	20	31	-10	51
20	Gillingham	44	10	1	11	26	29	4	7	11	20	33	-16	50
21	Derby County	44	10	5	7	37	33	2	8	12	14	33	-15	49
22	Walsall	44	7	7	8	26	29	5	5	12	16	33	-20	48
23	Bradford City	44	6	3	13	23	33	4	3	15	15	33	-28	36
24	Wimbledon	44	2	4	16	20	40	5	0	17	19	48	-49	25

MAY

Saturday 1st

Nationwide League Division One

Norwich City 3   **Preston North End 2**
McKenzie 2   *McKenna 5*
Francis 28   *Healy 48*
Huckerby 84
Carrow Road   Att: 23,673

I slept quite well last night, much to my surprise, but I'm still up early and out walking Molly by 8.30am. She must know something's going on. I don't know what to think at the moment – it's going to be a mammoth day. This club is in my blood and I've loved being here, but life moves on. The last home game of any season is always a special one, but now we're promoted it will be an amazing atmosphere. But it's also going to be very, very sad for me and my family. Terry the kit man has had a special T-shirt printed up for me to wear. It has 'Thanks for Seven Great Years' on the front. I've debated whether to dye my hair green for the occasion, but . . . nah. I might throw my shirt into the Barclay though.

  I get to the ground just after 12.30pm and manage to make the 500 yards from the car park to the burger stand outside the club shop before getting well and truly collared! At 1.15pm I'm still there signing autographs and getting fans' gifts of flowers and cards. It's magic, but eventually, Trevor – hubby of gaffer's secretary, Val – and Joe Ferrari suss out that I'm not actually in the ground and come and save me, ushering me through a little entrance I've never seen before through the back of the River End. Thank God! I'm loving standing out there signing autographs, but I don't think I'd have made it to the pitch before kick-off if they hadn't come and got me! One guy has printed off all the emails he got on a website he set up wishing me good luck. There's hundreds there and some of the things people have written – let's just say, I'm really touched.

Before the game kicks off, I'm absolutely delighted: my old mate Flem is voted the fans' 'Player of the Year'. Sorry, Hucks, mate, and sorry Greeno – who come in second and third respectively – but I do really think Flem has been one of our unsung heroes of the season and he deserves it. But then, you all do!

I get on for Matty with 11 minutes to go (and with a HUGE reception that makes my spine tingle) and we're drawing 2–2. Hucks gets the victory with a great goal, despite telling me he was going to fall over in the box every five seconds so I could get the chance of a pen!

Back in the dressing room we're preparing for the standard lap of honour, due at every last home game, when someone tells us that West Brom have lost to Reading. Now only need one point for the championship from our last two games. Yeeeeeeeeessssssssssss! I'm about to run out with the lads when the gaffer says: 'No, you stay here and come out last.' So I sit there, all alone, wait for about a minute, take one last look around my home for the last seven years and then stretch my muscles for one last time. Running out into the tunnel, I see my kids. Shit! Ben's eyes are as red as if he's been swimming underwater for three hours. It really upsets me. So I grab his hand and with my other hand, grab Eva and Chase and head out to where my fellow players have formed a guard of honour. I have to let go of the kids's hands for a minute to keep up with all the high-fives.

I feel terrible, but proud. We've just got promoted and this is the first chance home fans will have had to applaud that, but all around the ground chants of 'Iwwwwwww aaaaaaaaaaaannnnn' are ringing out. It's very touching, but I feel a bit embarrassed. We've just got promotion (look at me, I keep saying 'we') and I'm walking round the pitch with a bunch of players who have been outstanding all season but all I can hear is my name. I get to the corner between the River End and the new Jarrolds Stand (they finally decided on a sponsor) and start to well up. It's the lads' day: not mine. But it is my day, too. Calm down, mate, calm down. Oh no, I'm off again. Flem, Holty and Malky tell me they couldn't look at Ben when they came out of the dressing room as it was obvious he'd been crying his eyes out. 'I just had to turn away,' says Flem. 'He really got to me.'

I give Ben a big hug and tell him not to cry: it's all right. Dad's all right and everything's going to be fine. 'We've got to enjoy moments like this.'

Eva's a bit given to the dramatic, bless her, and is very tearful as we walk round the perimeter of the ground. Chase seems fine, but she might just be trying to be a big, brave girl for her daddy!

The noise is unbelievable, but by the time we get to the Barclay End, Ben is feeling a bit better and has a little kickabout with the other players' lads. Unbelievably, Roy Waller stops me in front of the Barclay – my spiritual home! – to do a radio interview. I want to say 'Get out of here!' but I do the interview, throw my shirt into the crowd and catch up a few steps to join the others.

I'd just like to place on record my reaction to a very special reception. It was incredible to hear my name sung by everyone in the ground and it will live with me until the day I die. Thank you all so much. You're great fans and I'm honoured to have played for you. I'm very sad, very emotional, but very proud. It's the best moment of my career. I've taken the city, the team, the club and the fans to my heart and you've all taken me to your hearts. And that will stay with me always. Always.

Being the easily embarrassed sod that I am, I'm delighted when a few of the lads, including Gary Holt and Matthias Svensson, go over towards the Barclay and the crowd starts singing their names too. I don't really know what to do. I certainly don't want to blast one into the net down there, which a photographer tries to get me to do. After 15 minutes or so we head back for the dressing room.

The match sponsors have voted me 'Man of the Match', which is a nice touch, so after a quick shower, I have to leg it to the Gunn Club for all the presentations. Roy Waller is the MC and asks me a few questions, but I'm not sure what: they're drowned out by all the chants of 'Iwaaaaaaaannnnnnnnn'. It feels good, although again I'm a bit embarrassed.

After the presentations, I head home for a quick change: it's the annual away supporters' party this evening back in the Gunn Club. All the players turn up and it's usually quite a good laugh. There are hundreds more fans than normal and people are constantly thanking me. I'll say it now: 'You don't have to thank me, I've enjoyed every minute of it. Thank *you*!' It's the first time I've seen Delia and Michael since the news. Delia puts her arms around me and tells me I should go away for a year or two, like Gunny did, and then come back in some capacity. She says I'll always be welcome back here. Etty, her mother, a fellow Welsh-speaker, starts filling up. 'I don't want you to leave,' she says. 'I'm going to lose my favourite player.' And gives me a big hug. I feel like I'm saying goodbye to old friends. Delia, her mum and Michael are fantastic and it couldn't have been easy for them to be involved in that decision. We're mates. I reassure them there's no problems and head off for dinner with Hucks and Eddy and our wives after a great night.

Sunday 2nd

Apart from being in training in preparation for a tough game against Sunderland at their place on Tuesday, normal service has been resumed. Greens, Pizza Hut for lunch with Julie and the kids; Norwich shirts everywhere and a few autographs are happily signed.

I've always said the time to start worrying is when they don't ask for your autograph. I think the older you get you appreciate it more. When you're 17, 18, you just want to play football and that's it. When you're a family man, you can appreciate how excited people get at meeting you, especially kids and you don't mind doing it. But it's hard for my kids to take sometimes. I often get that 'Can I have a kiss, can I have a photo?' Eva doesn't half get jealous! 'I thought you loved Mummy!' She thinks I'm going to run away with the girl!

No chance. I might still get the eye off one or two, but it's usually glass. I don't think I've ever been asked to sign a bra – it's always been thongs, ha ha! There will always be girls interested in you because of what you do, but I've been about a bit too long and I always make a point of introducing my wife before ten seconds have passed. Hucks is quite popular but he keeps himself to himself. Jimmy B's a good-looking lad, as is Malky. And of course, there's the new Furby: little Squiz, the cuddly little thing. He's what every girl of a certain age wants for Christmas.

Anyway, I might have helped this club win promotion,

but I'm still not going to change my routine. Sunday nights are for *Dream Team* and basketball. Besides, I've got to be up early for Roy Waller's show tomorrow. Life does go on, you know . . .

Monday 3rd

A great start to the week as I join Roy Waller for an hour on his morning show, dedicated to people telling me how much they're going to miss me! Loads of people call in, text and email to wish me and Julie all the best – it's unbelievable.

After dashing back for the rest of training, we head for Norwich airport for our 1.30pm flight to Newcastle. When we get there, Terry the kit man does his bit for the boys' drinking fund by leaving his mobile on the plane, so we have to sit on the coach in sweltering sunshine for 45 minutes while he goes back to retrieve it. See you in court, Terry!

My mate Wayne Jones, who's now assistant manager at Gillingham, rings me to offer me a job as player/coach. Notts County's Gary Mills, who I played with at Leicester, rings to offer me a job. I've also had an offer from Hull City, which is attractive as they're quite ambitious with a new stadium and good support, and Paul Hart rang the gaffer last Friday asking me to go to Barnsley.

Swansea want me to go and see them on Wednesday, but that might be the day after we win the title. I don't want to rush things. I really want to get the season over and done with first before I think about my future. It is reassuring, though. Anyway, nobody's put an offer on the table yet. They won't want to pay my wages from the end of May; they'll want to save themselves some money and sign me up in July.

Tuesday 4th

Nationwide League Division One
Sunderland 1   **Norwich City 0**
Robinson 44
Stadium of Light   Att: 35,174

The gaffer wants everyone down for breakfast by 9.15am
– he doesn't want anyone lounging in bed, all lethargic,
at 11am. It's not a problem for me, as I'm up about 8am
and raring to go – a full 12 hours before kick-off. After
an orange juice and a hot chocolate, the gaffer calls us
together for a chat. He names the same team that has
won the last seven games (what a surprise – it's the club's
best record for 18 years) and then talks us through what
could happen tonight. Sunderland need one more point
to guarantee a play-off place and we need a point for the
championship, so it's all to play for.

After the meeting we head off for a walk along Sunderland
seafront. I'm sure it's very nice in the summer, but right
now it's horrible. It's very windy and freezing, not exactly
shorts and T-shirts weather, but a few of the lads are wearing exactly that – so much for southern softies.

Back to the hotel for lunch at 12pm and disaster strikes
– there's no chicken. The Fridge is responsible for the
food and making sure we're looked after, so he gets
hammered for it and will probably hammer me for
saying so when this book comes out. Utterly disappointed, totally miserable and completely de-motivated
by this lack of interest in our welfare, we head up to
bed for a couple of hours, before leaving for the Stadium
of Light at 6.15pm. I'm excited at the thought that we
might be champions by 9.45pm this evening, but I still
manage to do the professional thing and get a bit of
shut-eye.

There's no radio on the bench. The gaffer is insistent, as ever, that we live or die by our own results. He doesn't want anyone getting distracted by the West Brom score – they are playing Stoke City and kick off at 7.45pm, 15 minutes before us. However, he's not completely daft: he has got someone relaying him the latest scores from the Britannia Stadium.

We start the game brightly and could be a couple up after just ten minutes. But Sunderland are determined to get at least the point they need to be sure of the play-offs and they force their way back into the game and take the lead on 44 minutes through Carl Robinson. But we're not too fussed: we've been playing well and news has filtered through that ex-Canary Daryl Russell has remembered his roots and scored for Stoke. Given that we have a far superior goal difference, if the scores stay like this, we'll still be champions.

Not too fussed? What the fuck was I thinking? The gaffer goes completely mad at half-time. We get in to the dressing room and Leon and Malky start having a pop at each other. Leon's upset because he feels Malky's talking to him like he's six years old. So the gaffer loses it.

'I wish you'd fucking save all your anger and energy for out there!' he shouts. 'Some of you are going through the motions. And that's not good enough!' Then Hucks wades in: 'Fucking hell gaffer, you're telling *them* to calm down, but *you* need to calm down!'

The gaffer turns on him: 'You just do your job, all right?'

'Yeah, I'll fucking do my job like I've been doing it all season.'

The gaffer turns and boots the kit skip and makes a right dent in it – he must have broken his toe – and Hucks and he are at it like hammer and tongs. What the fuck's going on? Me, Malky, Flem and Eddy step in to try and calm things down.

'Come on, we've not argued all season, we're not going to start now.'

Dougie Livermore, the gaffer's assistant, smoothes things over: he's always brilliant with things like that, just calms everyone down.

It might have something to do with the fact that, while we're in the dressing room the skanky sods West Brom equalise. Shit. Calculators out. We don't want to have to go to Crewe for our last game on Sunday needing a result.

So it's fingers crossed for the second half. West Brom are already 15 minutes into theirs. Sitting on the bench on the halfway line, looking across at the stand to my right, I suddenly spot my co-author in the crowd, going completely mental, jumping around and shouting with about five others, including a bloke in a ridiculous jester's hat. What's going on? We're losing here and West Brom are drawing. Has she finally lost it? (Well, there have been many times this season where I've thought she's come close.) A couple of minutes later all becomes clear(ish). For a second I think our fans are singing 'The Scum are losing 2–1' so I ask one of the lads on the bench whether Ipswich are playing tonight. But no, it's 'West Brom are losing 2–1.' Ah, that explains it. Well, some of it, at least . . .

The gaffer never once asks what the score is at the Britannia Stadium. Quite right: we should concentrate on our game. He does, however, wave a hand of acknowledgement to our exuberant fans, so maybe he's not completely deaf . . .

The fans keep us up to speed about developments elsewhere, with chants ten minutes later of 'West Brom are losing 3–1' and 13 minutes later, simply, 'Championes, championes, olé olé olé!' Final score, four minutes later: 4–1 to Stoke. The fans are going mental by the time I get on with five minutes to go. Amazingly, a few of the lads still ask me what the score is. 'Er, they got battered 4–1.'

Hucks doesn't ask. He just waits until the ball goes out for a throw near the halfway line and makes a point of going up to the gaffer and shaking his hand. On the bench, we're thinking he's apologising for the row at half-time, but he tells me later that he went up and said: 'Congratulations on winning the title, gaffer!'

The final whistle blows and it gives me great pleasure to say, 'WE ARE THE CHAMPIONS!!!!!'

Yes! That feels so good, I'll say it again.

'WE ARE THE CHAMPIONS!'

The feeling is amazing. I really can't describe it. I'm going to get that little medal at the end of the season! There are 2,500 of our fans packing one end and we just run straight over to them. To their great credit, the Sunderland fans, who have been joining in Mexican waves all evening (I think that's what put us off, watching the carnival) stay behind to applaud us. I shake hands with Mick McCarthy and tell him I really hope they can join us through the play-offs. They are a decent side and he's a great manager. All their lads are shaking hands with us and being equally sporting: 'You've been the best team all season,' says Carl Robinson. 'Now go on and do us proud.' 'I'm so glad you won it and not West Brom,' says Gary Breen. 'Congratulations, you deserve it.'

Norwich and Sunderland fans have a special relationship because of the 'Friendly Final' of the Milk Cup back in 1985. But tonight takes the biscuit. I feel really emotional. We don't get the bloody trophy though. Apparently, it's all right for Premiership sides to get the trophy on the opposition's ground, but not Nationwide League sides. I'm not too fussed. We already had a big civic reception planned next Monday to celebrate promotion and I'd rather get the trophy there, in front of

30–40,000 fans, than here, where only 2,500 fans can see it.

Some bloke from the Nationwide League gives us another banner to play with: 'Division One Champions'. It's kinda fun, until Leon spots a bloke down the front with a big trophy: a real Blue Peter job, although it's more silver tin foil than sticky-back plastic and he grabs that off him to celebrate with. It must be really hard for people like Rivvo, Zema, Shacks and Briggsy who weren't even on the bench. I drag them into the centre of the lads, because they're as much a part of it as anyone else.

Our fans don't look like they're going anywhere. Hell, even the Sunderland fans seem reluctant to leave. Eventually, we're shepherded off the pitch and back into the dressing room, where complete pandemonium breaks out. The place becomes a swimming pool. It starts off with us opening a few bottles of champagne and spraying them around (can't drink 'em: none of us really like the stuff and we've all got our cars waiting at Colney). Then everyone grabs the nearest thing to hand: bottles of water, cans of lemonade . . . It's mayhem. Everyone who foolishly pops their head around the door gets drenched. We always have one of those big tubs of blackcurrant squash: the gaffer's first in line for that. He takes it well. Webby and Jim Hollman get covered in water. Greeno refills the blackcurrant tub with water and stands by the door, waiting for his next victim. Ah, here comes Roy Waller! He gets battered. Director Michael Foulger comes in and gets sloshed. Fellow director Barry Skipper sticks his neck round the door and sensibly buggers off. The only people we wouldn't soak are Delia and Michael, but they're quite cute: they know not to take the gamble of coming in. I wouldn't be surprised if the club get a bill for it: by the end, we're all paddling around in a good few inches of water. I take advantage of the mayhem to grab myself a little souvenir: one of the champagne bottles with Division One Champions on them is just sitting there on a bench, so I grab it and stuff it quickly in my locker.

And finally, we have music! On the coach back to Newcastle airport, someone has had the foresight to bring a Queen CD. I like Queen: they're catchy songs. And what do we listen to? Over and over and over again? *We Are The Champions*. We don't need to ask the Fridge to put it on again. And again. And again. Ah, go on, one more time then.

We finally land at Norwich airport at 1.45am. Three flights full of fans have arrived just before us, so we're greeted by a sea of cheering yellow and green. I'm absolutely shattered, but Squiz rings up the manager of Mercy and asks if it's all right if a few of the boys come down in their tracksuits. He says he'll keep the club open for us. Not for me, boys. We've got a big day tomorrow and I want to enjoy it (the gaffer's buying us lunch!) so I head off for bed before I collapse.

Wednesday 5th

Obviously I'm not a complete lightweight: I was just saving myself to get absolutely bollocksed today (although I make sure I have a sauna first). After we won promotion two weeks ago, the gaffer told us he wanted to take us all out for lunch to celebrate. So the gaffer, all the coaching staff and all the lads meet at Zizzi's pizza place at 12.30pm. The gaffer warns us to be on our best behaviour, so we have to sing *We Are The Champions* under our breath. We have a great afternoon, loads of banter and the gaffer picks up the tab. Cheers, gaffer. Very much appreciated.

Unfortunately, at 3.30pm, he goes home. We'd have

loved him to have stayed and have a few beers with the boys. The Fridge, his assistant Pete, Jimmy Hollman and Dave Carolan are up for it though, although Holty has to go and pick up his wee lad. We're outside and this photographer from the *EDP* has been waiting for ages to get a photo of us. He intends following us around all afternoon, so we tell him he can have one posed pic if he leaves us alone for the rest of the day. Then we walk up the road to Delaney's. As we're getting the first round in, I turn to ask Damo, Zema and Leon what they're drinking, but they've gone. One of the lads says they've gone down to London for a night out at Chinawhite. Most of the lads are cheesed off with that; we feel we should all be together. It's not every day you win a championship, after all!

Anyway, we're having a great afternoon, so I'm not going to let my disappointment get in the way of having fun. Jimmy B and the Fridge have a bit of a tussle: the Fridge throws something at Jimmy, it hits his bottle and beer goes all over him. So Jimmy pours his three-quarters of a pint all over the Fridge's head and down his nice white shirt and jeans. Adie lends the Fridge another shirt and the Fridge bides his time. About 8.30pm he gets a pint of Guinness and pours it all over Jim's head. We hold Jimmy B back: if you dish it out mate, you've got to take it!

I guess the alcohol's taking effect now. We head upstairs, gate-crashing some kind of school reunion party, but no-one minds. The DJ sees us and sticks *We Are The Champions* on every second song. We're all standing on bar stools, arms round each other, singing. Well, all except for Squiz, who's on the bar, to make sure people can see him (he is Hobbit-size, after all, and we don't want to lose him). We end up in Chicagos, a nightclub cum bar. We're surrounded by people congratulating us. About 11.30pm,

I've had enough. Well, I don't drink shorts, do I, and 11 hours drinking lager is enough to make anyone even more bloated than blotto. Taxi for Roberts!

Thursday 6th

Jimmy B tells us the water running off him was black when he got in the shower this morning. Quite a few of the lads stayed until the bitter end – around 1.30am. I'm glad I didn't. I don't feel too bad this morning, especially considering the amount of alcohol that passed my lips yesterday!

Not that good, mind – Julie and I go for lunch at the Rushcutters with Darren Eadie and his wife Kelly – and I wimp out and have a pint of lemonade and lime. Kelly tells Julie she should be very proud as Darren never got a send-off like I did on Saturday. Jockey himself says to me: 'Great send-off, mate. I wish I'd got something like that.' And looks a bit sad. It's a crying shame because he was a great legend for Norwich, and the fans adored him, but he just sort of left and never came back.

Friday 7th

I'm doing an interview with Miranda for the club's website and the first question she asks me is: 'How do you feel about being captain and starting the game on Sunday?'

'Er, to be honest I didn't know. I think you've put your foot right in it!' I tease. She's mortified, poor girl.

I finally find out officially when the gaffer calls a team meeting at 10am. He doesn't name the team, just says: 'As it's his last game Robbo's going to be starting and he'll be captain.' The lads burst into applause and I go beetroot. The gaffer comes up to shake my hand, leans over and whispers in my ear: 'D'you want me to tell the lads it was all down to Julie asking if you could play Sunday?' I go from beetroot to pillar box. 'Nah, nah, gaffer, you're all right, cheers.'

He gives me a little wink. Julie had gone up to the gaffer at the away fans' party last Saturday night. 'If it's all over by then, is it all right if Iwan starts on Sunday? His mum and dad and all his family will be there and Ben's going too.' I think he would have started me, anyway – really I do – although I suppose the fact she was holding a gun to his head at the time might have had a bearing on his decision.

I'm well pleased. It's a really nice gesture on Adam's part to give up the captaincy for the day. Sunday will be another emotional day. I'll know then it will be the last time I pull the yellow shirt on. It won't hit me until the final whistle. I think I'll be fine until then. Then I'll be like, 'Fucking hell! I'm never going to play for the club ever again.' And that will be hard.

I'm going to be taking everything on Sunday: free-kicks, corners, I'm going to take them, then run round and try and get on the end of them. I've told Hucks to go down every time he's in the box. I want six penalties! If I could just get one goal I'd be happy. I don't know why but 95 sounds better than 94. I don't think I've got any mates at Crewe . . . but the good thing is they've got nothing to play for. Whether I'll last the 90 minutes I don't know. I'll bust a gut to try and do it – well, I'll bust something anyway. I'll probably give myself a hernia.

Terry gets a £25 fine this morning for leaving his phone on the plane. Then the gaffer's phone went off in the team meeting, which should see him hit with a £50 fine, but we decide that if he shaves all the acres of hair off his chest we'll let him off the fine. So he's agreed to do that before the season finishes.

Then Steve Foley steps up: 'I'd just like to say, you all saw the gaffer boot the skip on Tuesday. Well, I've got his X-ray here . . .' and he brings out this X-ray of a foot with a big crack right down the middle of it. The gaffer creases up laughing, then it's outside for a decent training session. We want to finish the season in style. Once again, we will have brilliant support at Crewe – a lot of people have paid a lot of money to see us – so there's no chance of us taking our feet off the pedal.

My mum phones this afternoon: Dad's been struggling with a very bad back for the last six months and won't be able to make it on Sunday. They're devastated when I tell them I'm starting and will be captain for the day.

Saturday 8th

My last ever away trip as a Norwich City player. The whole of the past week or so has all been about lasts (apart from that bit where we came first!). We get to our hotel in Crewe about 4.30pm and head for dinner – my Last Supper. I had my very last training session with the boys this morning and I'm feeling quite sad. It's really starting to hit home now. I cheered up a bit this morning when we had what will now be my last ever young v olds game – I'm delighted to say that, although the young lads won to level the series, us oldies are a bit more experienced at shoot-outs and took the title on penalties. Of course we didn't rub it in . . .

I'm gutted to be away from home this afternoon as Chase is dancing at Ben's school, Thorpe High. Julie can't make it either as she's doing the Run For Life at the Norfolk Showground. The lads have all sponsored her and she phones me to tell me she did the 5km course in 35 minutes. I'm dead proud of her.

Wandering down the hotel corridor to get a glass of

squash, I bump into Paul Taylor, tomorrow's referee and one of the few you can actually have a chat with. He asks me whether I'm looking forward to the game tomorrow, as he's heard it's my last for the club. 'Yeah, I am,' I say. 'But in a funny way I'm dreading it too. It's going to be so emotional. You couldn't give us six pens so I can get my 100 goals, could you?' And we both laugh.

Sunday 9th

Nationwide League Division One
Crewe Alexandra 1   **Norwich City 3**
Ashton 82   *Fleming 28*
                         Roberts 31, 88 (pen)

Gresty Road   Att: 9,833

Leap out of bed at 8.30am for my last ever breakfast with the lads. I still can't get it into my head that I won't be here next season. Looking round the breakfast table, it really sinks in just how much I'm going to miss the boys. Me, Flem, Malky – we've kind of grown up together – and I'd count most of them among my very best mates.

I'm desperate to sign off with a goal. Apart from anything else, I've never ever scored in the first or last game of a season – and you know what I was doing on the opening day of this season. It seems the lads are all desperate for me to score too – almost as soon as we kick off Hucks is trying to lay the ball off to me and Eddy's trying to pick me out with a cross.

Our fans have taken over two stands in Crewe's neat little ground. We could have filled it several times over, I think, but Crewe have given us the maximum 2,200 tickets they have available and there's a real party atmosphere. We're playing some really good stuff and

I'm feeling very sharp and thoroughly enjoying myself. With 28 minutes gone Flem heads us in front. He runs over to our fans and does a belly flop right in front of them and we all pile in. Three minutes later my dream comes true. Hucks knocks the ball down to me, just about on the penalty spot and I blast it with my left foot – MY LEFT FOOT! – into the top corner of the net. I don't think I've ever struck a ball that sweetly with my right, let alone my left. Our fans go wild. I run over to the same spot where Flem celebrated and attempt to do the same routine. Except I'm so creaky I kind of go down in three stages – back, knees, belly – thinking, 'What the hell are you doing?' All the lads jump on top of me. I can hear voices, but I don't know what they're saying. I'm in dreamland. As they all get up off me, I suddenly realise I'm a bit winded from having 100 stone of bloke on my back.

As I turn to run back to the centre circle, I have to put my left arm up in front of my face for a minute. To shield my eyes from the sun. Honest.

A while later, I nearly get a second, but my header flies straight into Crewe keeper Ben Williams' arms. Damn. No matter. We're totally in control. At one stage in the second half, Malky and Flem are enjoying themselves so much they're in the opposition box laying the ball off to each other. I look round and right-back Eddy's taken up the role of Hucks out on the left wing. This is weird. Not to be outdone, Adam picks up the ball from inside our half and runs the length of the pitch before unleashing a shot which . . . well, let's just say it stayed inside the stadium. Just. The fans start chanting 'That's why you're left-back' and Adam laughs and gives them a round of applause before they launch into 'There's only one Adam Drury'.

Yet another Mexican wave passes round the ground. I

don't know if we're too busy watching it, but Crewe somehow pull a goal back on 82 minutes when Greeno misses the ball and in his desperation to claw it back, just helps it over the line with an outstretched leg. No matter. He's still a fucking star.

Five minutes later, we win a penalty. It's at the end in front of our fans who have propped a giant cut-out painting of my head up against the ad hoardings behind the net. I'd like to say it's my head that puts me off, but I try to place the ball for ages – the grass is quite long and the penalty spot is actually slightly below the level of the grass so it makes it hard to get underneath the ball. Anyway, I scuff it. Badly. The keeper saves. But the ref blows his whistle. One of their players was apparently encroaching. I've got a second chance! A fan shouts out: 'And we'll bloody well keep retaking it until he scores, all right?!' I scuff the second one too, but, to my enormous relief, it goes in. 3–1! 96! I can hear our fans singing: 'Four more! He only needs four more!' Yeah and I've got about four minutes to get them in.

I do nearly get my hat-trick a couple of minutes later when we get a free-kick just outside their box, deep into injury-time. I'm not sure whether to take it, then I think 'What the hell' and step up and blast it. Williams does really well to get a hand to it: it's low to his left but he manages to claw the ball away just when it looks like it might trickle over the line. Bastard!

It's all over. The ref blows for time and we head off to applaud our fans before getting off the pitch so the Crewe players can enjoy their lap of honour. The stewards say we can go back on afterwards, but back in the dressing room, the gaffer's saying 'No, that's it lads. No more.' I think he doesn't want to be seen to be milking it, but we're all flabbergasted: if we'd known we weren't going out again, we'd have said goodbye properly. Luckily, a steward comes in to tell us we can go back out onto the pitch. As we go out the Crewe players are lined up to form a guard of honour to applaud us onto the pitch, which is very sporting of them.

What a moment. All our fans are chanting my name and fans are desperately trying to hand me cards, scarves and presents. Someone gives me a green and yellow curly wig, which, for some reason (perhaps too much sun?) I decide to put on. I also get an inflatable champagne bottle, another cardboard trophy, a metal trophy, cuddly toy . . . Webby's first to pick up the inflatable doll some spark chucks on the pitch: God knows where she'll find a home tonight! The atmosphere is amazing: the Crewe players have scarpered, leaving us to milk the applause on their pitch. Most of the Crewe fans have stayed behind to cheer us too. It feels very surreal. I don't know what I feel: a complete mix of every emotion I've ever felt, I think. As we make our way back to the tunnel, I stop, turn around and have one last look. I want to remember this moment forever.

Back in the dressing room we can still hear the fans singing. Someone comes in and tells us there's been a pitch invasion – the Crewe fans all encouraging the Norwich fans to join them on the pitch. Delia has obviously come out to join them too now – we can hear a massive cheer and chants of 'Delia's barmy army!'

Someone tells us West Brom lost, which means we finished the season a massive eight points clear of them and 15 points ahead of Sunderland in third. Our final goal difference was +40, West Brom's +22. Makes it look easy, really! Fabian Wilnis, Joe Royle, Colin Warnock, Alan Pardew – your boys took one helluva beating!

The gaffer uses the fact that we're all on such a high to forget about his promise to shave his jacket, sorry, chest. Which is a shame for his wife, Sandra, as she's desperate for him to do it.

The club doctor bags my shirt for me in case it goes astray and I get all the lads to sign the big cut-out of me, which now has a Norwich scarf round its neck. It will be a great reminder, although I'm not sure Julie will let me keep it on display in the lounge!

We fly back to Norwich and head straight for the club, where there's a private party for all the staff. It's a fantastic night, the first chance we've all had to celebrate together – you sometimes forget how many people there are in the same boat as you, all working behind the scenes to make this dream come true. I can't remember what time I get home. I can, however, remember that I scored the last two goals of our championship-winning season!

Monday 10th

Around 11am Julie and I head into the city to get my three gorgeous ladies new outfits. Thankfully Ben's quite happy with what he's got in his wardrobe. Every stall in the market in front of City Hall, where we will have the civic reception later today, has green and yellow bunting and balloons on. Most of the shops are decked out in green and yellow, there's a giant inflatable canary above City Hall and already a couple of hundred fans are queuing for a prime spot.

I head up to Colney to meet the rest of the lads around 2.30pm. The lads are all having their injections for the pre-season trip to Malaysia. Jimmy B saunters by and says casually: 'All right, Robbo? Had your jabs yet?' He stops suddenly. 'Shit. Er, sorry mate.'

If I didn't know him better I'd think he was doing it deliberately. An hour later the gaffer calls us together for the final team meeting of the season and hands out some papers to Greeno, detailing what we, sorry *they*, have got to do in the summer to keep fit. Greeno takes one and passes them round. They get as far as Jimmy B, sitting next to me and he tries to pass me one, thinks better of it and then passes them over my head to Flem with an apologetic look. Okay, now it *is* starting to sink in. I'm not going to be part of this any more.

After the meeting – basically the gaffer just telling the lads what he expects of them over the summer and congratulating us on a job well done – me, Jimmy B, Mullers, Briggsy and Coops escape to the nearest pub. It's decked out with green and yellow balloons and the landlady buys the first round, which sets us up nicely.

We dash back to Colney for the obligatory big team photo – complete with a beaming Delia and Michael in a ridiculous white Del Monte man suit. Leon is hammering him for wearing blue moccasins. Finally, everyone piles onto the open-top buses and we set off down the Earlham Road with a police escort, surrounded by tooting cars.

The civic reception is . . . well, civil, I suppose. Someone hands me a glass of champagne and offers me a plate of nick-nacks. I'd thought there might be a proper buffet so I haven't eaten and now I'm starving, but too nervous to eat. Fifteen minutes later we get our mitts on the oldest football trophy in the world. The noise outside is incredible. We step out onto the balcony and I'm well and truly gobsmacked. It's an ocean of yellow and green. The organisers were expecting 30,000, but apparently there are at least 50,000 out there, people crammed into every corner to get a view. I can see people on the castle hill half a mile away, people hanging out of office windows, up the top of the church, up lamp-posts . . . I've been promoted twice with Leicester, but I've never, ever experienced anything close to this. Adam lifts the trophy to deafening cheers and we all take our turn with it. A shiver runs down my spine as I touch the trophy and then lift it, to enormous cheers. This is incredible. Unbelievable. I'd never have thought at the start of the season that I'd be standing here, doing this. In my last season for the club. It's all too much to take in. I feel happy, sad, proud, elated, a bit tearful . . .

I'm a bit disappointed our wives and families aren't allowed on the balcony straightaway. There's a limit of 50 people allowed on at any one time, so at the greatest moment of our careers, our families are on the steps underneath, looking up at us. But there are loads of people on the balcony who I've never seen before in my life; I don't think they should have been there. I'm a bit upset as our wives have been a massive support to us players and deserve to have their role in all this acknowledged.

We're live on both local TV news programmes and do a variety of interviews for them and the radio boys, where we say things like: 'Whoooahhh' and 'Yeah!!!' I say something about the fans being fantastic, I think. After about an hour, just before our buses start the tour of the city, Gunny takes the microphone and announces to the crowd that I will be leading them in a last rendition of the fans' anthem *On The Ball City*, as he's been teaching me the words. There's a huge roar as the crowd takes up the song. Thank God. I don't know anything past the first three lines: I'm so relieved they didn't listen to me, it would have been dead embarrassing.

Then we all pile onto the buses, but Eva's so excited she gets on the first bus she sees, before realising we're all on a different one. Thankfully, we manage to get her onto ours before setting off. We're the second one in line, with a third being for sponsors and competition winners. The bus is mad. We're all bouncing around on the seats and it's so crammed I can't really see my kids to keep an eye on them as the bus lurches unsteadily down the road.

Every time I catch sight of them though, they're loving it. The route lasts about an hour and all the way round people are chanting my name. I'm really starting to lose it now, but compose myself. Then, as we hit Tombland, the crowds let out a huge chant of 'Iwwwwwwwwaaaaa aaaaaannnnnnnn!' and I start filling up again. I nearly properly lose it, but just about manage to hold myself together. It's incredible and the scenes – every side street is full, people are standing on the top of public toilets, phone boxes, everywhere – will stay with me for the rest of my life.

On the way back, we're heading up the Earlham Road to applause, tooting, cheering – and one bloke in a house who stands at his window with his middle finger up. There's always one.

Quite a few of the lads are heading out for the night but, to me, today's a family affair, so we head home. Besides, I'm still starving. Unfortunately, the local chippy is chocca with Norwich fans and I just don't fancy being the centre of attention for another three hours, so we head for the Chinese on the A47. I get some chips and, when I get home, bung three frozen quarter-pounders under the grill, before collapsing into bed. It's been a great day – an amazing day – but I'm knackered now.

Tuesday 11th

My final day as a Norwich player. It's the 'Player of the Year' awards dinner tonight and I'm really looking forward to it, although that will be it then.

Most of the players meet up this morning at the Lotus racing car headquarters at Mulbarton where we're given some instruction and then allowed to drive a couple of laps in a Lotus at 120mph. Me and Eddy are the next James Hunt and Nigel Mansell, but Hucks is very disappointing given his pace on the pitch and Flem actually crashes! Then we're each taken out by one of the pros. I said to my guy, 'I want you to frighten me' and, my God, did he take me at my word. It must have been more frightening for Greeno though: he's too tall for their cars and his head sticks out over the top of the convertible roll-bar.

The lads at Lotus look after us fantastically well and would-be F1 mechanic Ben's made up as they give us all a bag of branded goodies to take away.

All the players host a different table at the awards dinner and there are around 300 guests. It's great to catch up with Delia and Michael, Roger Munby and his wife Judy, Michael Foulger – people I regard as friends, rather than people who pay (paid!) my wages. My table is luckily behind one of the big pillars, so I can hide relatively unseen. We have a fabulous three-course dinner and then there's a video of the season's highlights. Actually, there are some great pre-season highlights: all the redcoats in action when they were young lads. I'm just laughing my socks off at some really bad mullets when the screen changes. 'Goodbye legend'. I'm a bit shocked: I didn't know this was coming up. Dave Carolan has apparently put together a tribute to me. Oh, I'm off again. Ah, at least Julie's well ahead of me. Everyone in the room gives me a standing ovation after that, one of four or five this evening. I'm really touched – it makes me feel appreciated.

Right at the end Gunny asks me to say a few words. I'm really reluctant to – shyness again – but Julie urges me to, saying I haven't thanked the lads or the gaffer yet. I go up to the mic and am halfway through my little speech when I see Nicola Fleming sitting at the table in front of me, crying her eyes out. Oh no, Nic, don't! I manage to tell the lads I think they're the best in the world, thank the gaffer, Dougie, Steve and Webby for being such good mates and pay tribute to my gorgeous wife and leg it before the waterworks start. The gaffer comes straight over to give me a hug. As I sit down, I'm gutted. I meant to mention Crichts – poor sod's been a bit overlooked.

Julie and I eventually leave, a bit worse for wear, around midnight. I'm knackered, but elated. It's been one hell of a year. I think I'll leave it until tomorrow morning before I see what the next year will bring. Whatever it is, it can never be this good.

Nationwide League Division One

Pos	Name	P	W	D	L	F	A	W	D	L	F	A	GD	PTS
			HOME					AWAY						
1	**Norwich City**	46	18	3	2	44	15	10	7	6	35	24	+40	94
2	West Bromwich Albion	46	14	5	4	34	16	11	6	6	30	26	+22	86
3	Sunderland	46	13	8	2	33	15	9	5	9	29	30	+17	79
4	West Ham United	46	12	7	4	42	20	7	10	6	25	25	+22	74
5	Ipswich Town	46	12	3	8	49	36	9	7	7	35	36	+12	73
6	Crystal Palace	46	10	8	5	34	25	11	2	10	38	36	+11	73
7	Wigan Athletic	46	11	8	4	29	16	7	9	7	31	29	+15	71
8	Sheffield United	46	11	6	6	37	25	9	5	9	28	31	+9	71
9	Reading	46	11	6	6	29	25	9	4	10	26	32	-2	70
10	Millwall	46	11	8	4	28	15	7	7	9	27	33	+7	69
11	Stoke City	46	11	7	5	35	24	7	5	11	23	31	+3	66
12	Conventry City	46	9	9	5	34	22	8	5	10	33	32	+13	65
13	Cardiff City	46	10	6	7	40	25	7	8	8	28	33	+10	65
14	Nottingham Forest	46	8	9	6	33	25	7	6	10	28	33	+3	60
15	Preston North End	46	11	7	5	43	29	4	7	12	26	42	-2	59
16	Watford	46	9	8	6	31	28	6	4	13	23	40	-14	57
17	Rotherham United	46	8	8	7	31	27	5	7	11	22	34	-8	54
18	Crewe Alexandra	46	11	3	9	33	26	3	8	12	24	40	-9	53
19	Burnley	46	9	6	8	37	32	4	8	11	23	45	-17	53
20	Derby County	46	11	5	7	39	33	2	8	13	14	34	-14	52
21	Gillingham	46	10	1	12	28	34	4	8	11	20	33	-19	51
22	Walsall	46	8	7	8	29	31	5	5	13	16	34	-20	51
23	Bradford City	46	6	3	14	23	35	4	3	16	15	34	-31	36
24	Wimbledon	46	3	4	16	21	40	5	1	17	20	49	-48	29

EXTRA TIME

March 1st 2005

And what an understatement that last line was. Well, I thought it was the last line of the book, but then they bloody phoned me up and said something about 'due to popular demand, blah, blah, blah . . .' For a minute I thought the gaffer had had second thoughts and my publisher was phoning to negotiate a new contract. But no, he just wanted to know what's been happening with me since May 2004. Doesn't he read the papers?

Well, having just finally moved my family to Gillingham, the club I joined last summer, I'm about to go on loan to Cambridge United – a bright new beginning after months of misery. It just hasn't worked out for me here, basically because I hate the boss, Stan Ternent.

It all started so well: I got three goals in my first five games and got booked within four seconds of my debut on the opening day against Ipswich (for fouling Kevin Horlock – you wouldn't have been able to get odds on that). I didn't score but the Norwich fans dotted around Portman Road loved it. And then I got injured, tendonitis. Luckily, it also coincided with the FA banning me for three games for my 'revelation' that I deliberately fouled Kevin Muscat a million years ago. I was a bit pissed off about the £2,500 fine though – especially as David Beckham gets away scot-free with saying that he deliberately got himself booked so he'd miss the next game for England. Harry Redknapp and I were in the Sky studio watching Man City play Norwich when Ian Payne mentioned the book and said I was banned. When I told Harry why, he said, live on Sky, "That's ridiculous. You should have got a medal for that!" Anyway, my Gillingham chairman Paul Scally was furious with the FA and we were going to dispute it but when I realised it could potentially cost my new club a lot of money, I decided to pay the fine.

Up until then I'd been having a great time at Gillingham. I got on really well with the manager, Andy Hessenthaler. The fans were good with me, I was feeling good, sharp, and then Big Man [Mamady] Sidibe, who replaced me when I got injured, started playing really well. He wasn't scoring, but he was doing everything but, so I couldn't get my place back in the team, even though we weren't doing very well in the League. He was doing everything right, and I know if that had been me I'd have been gutted to be dropped.

Then my mate, assistant manager Wayne Jones, left. I think he was made a scapegoat for the team's lack of success. Johnny Gorman came in, full of enthusiasm. Then Andy stepped down as manager. That was a massive shock. Andy is a great bloke, he'd done so well, been manager for four-and-a-half years and only spent £250,000, but still managed to keep the club in the First Division (I still can't handle that Championship crap). Gillingham fans may not like me for saying it, but we've been punching above our weight. With average gates of around 7,000 we're really a Second Division club and we're definitely never going to be a top six First Division side – and I think Andy had done really well.

Johnny G then went off to become the manager of

Wycombe and Paul Scally asked me and club captain Paul Smith to be in charge of the team for the next game against Cardiff. Well, he asked us to be in charge, but I think really he desperately wanted to pick the team – he kept coming in and asking me what I thought of 4–5–1 over 4–4–2! Actually, he's been fine with me. He did recently ask us to pay £3 a day for our lunches though – I think the expense was getting to him!

Anyway, he got Stan Ternent in as manager, and ever since then I've had a nightmare. I really like the club, the fans, the other lads, Scally himself, but Ternent and I just don't get on. He's old school, big on discipline, but I'm just too old to be bullied. Fair enough, Graham Taylor and Bruce Rioch were old school, but they had also achieved something in their careers. What's on Ternent's CV? Burnley? Bury? And both Graham and Bruce knew how to talk to people – Ternent just shouts and talks down to you. He's offhand and dismissive. Yet, when he first came in back in early December, he said he'd tried to sign me a couple of times in his career but I was too expensive. Funny that, I was once his top target and he's now mine . . .

To be fair, he knows his stuff (although maybe not that much, given the club's current position in the relegation spots) and when he arrived we had a chat and he was quite happy for me to carry on as a coach. But then we played Portsmouth in the Cup, a game we just narrowly lost, and he had a right go at me in the dressing room, saying that I didn't track back enough. He was ranting and raving and I lost it and shouted back that I thought we had been playing well and did he not want to win the game?

Shortly after that we had a staff meeting and I got

demoted to reserves coach. And even then I didn't get to do any coaching. I wasn't playing either, although I was fit to and I was getting more and more frustrated. I've got another year's contract, so I could just sit here and do nothing and pick up my pay cheque for the next year but that's not me. The worst bit is it's killed my enthusiasm for the game – I just feel so miserable all the time – and I always said that when that happened I'd pack it in and go and do something else.

The crunch came ten days ago, a Thursday. Steve Thompson, the Cambridge manager, had been ringing Ternent constantly asking if I could go there on loan. He was really bothering him, so Ternent told me to go upstairs and see the chairman and get it sorted out. Scally said to me, 'Listen big man, I'm sorry, but for one reason or another it hasn't worked out. You're not really in his plans, so maybe you should think about the Cambridge move.' Not in his plans? First I'd heard of it.

So I went away for the weekend to think about it and a reporter from the EDP in Norwich rang me up to ask how it was going and why I wasn't playing. I told him that I wasn't coaching or playing and I didn't seem to be part of Ternent's plans so I doubted very much if I'd still be here next year. I'd come down with flu so I didn't see Ternent until a few days later. When I did he went mad at me.

'Frozen out?' he shouted.

'Is there a quote from me actually saying that I've been frozen out? No! I didn't use those exact words, but that's how I feel.'

'No coaching duties?' he screamed.

'Name me one coaching session I've done since you've been here.'

'Well, you're not qualified,' he said.

'Pardon? Pardon? I've got my Uefa B coaching licence, which qualifies me to coach anywhere in the world and I've played either in the First Division or the Premiership for nearly 20 years. I think that bloody well qualifies me, don't you?'

It was then that I wished I did carry around my Champions medal. He went quiet. For a moment.

'So you're not going to be here next season? Where d'you think you're going to be then?'

'No disrespect, gaffer, but it's got sod all to do with you. I'm not part of your plans. Apparently.'

'I never said that.'

'No, the chairman told me when I went to see him.'

'Well, you shouldn't have gone over my head, you should have come and seen me first.'

'Um, you told me to go and see the chairman. We were in this office, you sat there, Ronnie sat there, Steve Thompson kept phoning you up and pissing you off and you told me to go and sort it with the chairman.'

'That's it. From now on you're just a player. I'm relinquishing your coaching duties.'

I smiled.

'Well, I'm hardly going to notice that, am I?'

So, the next day I got changed with the lads, leaving my black coaching staff kit stamped with IR in the staff locker. After training I spoke to my old mate Rob Newman, the guy I modelled suits for, now assistant manager at Cambridge. 'Looks like I might be seeing you sooner than I thought, mate.'

Julie's been brilliant about it all. It's hard on her – not just all the uncertainty, hardly seeing me all season and me being a grumpy bastard when we do meet up, but she hasn't been able to plan. She's wanted to do a couple of courses for years, for example. The family finally moved down to Gillingham on December 17th. We knew my future at the club was still up in the air but we had to complete on our new-build house the week before in order to secure a discount – if we'd waited another week it would have cost us tens of thousands more – and I really wanted us to be all together as a family for Christmas. It was hectic though; friends didn't know where to send cards, Julie had to get all the shopping done early and sent off. She was very organised, but it's a lot to ask.

She's settled in well down here, she's good mates with quite a lot of the players partners, although obviously she doesn't have as many friends yet as she acquired over seven years in Norfolk. I think we both miss our friends. And there's no Delaney's down here or even a KFC! I would walk back to Norwich tomorrow. I'm not sure whether she feels the same. I'm sure we'd have no problems getting the kids back into their old schools, but they've only just got settled in their new ones and it would be a big upheaval for them. So I think I'll have to grit my teeth and commute to Cambridge. They're a good bunch of people and Steve Thompson has told me that he's happy for me to take the strikers for a coaching session or three, so I'm going to sign for the rest of the season on loan tomorrow.

I'm not looking forward to the M25, I must admit. On the plus side, I can make it from my house to the ground in about an hour and a half and I'm desperate to get away and play some football. The situation here has really dragged me down. I don't feel my normal bubbly self. I think that's why I've had the flu for the last couple of weeks – everything just got on top of me. I was worried it was something to do with the cancer coming back – 'Oh my God, my immune system's not working' – especially as the arm still itches sometimes and aches in certain positions. But I've had my latest three-month check-up and everything's fine. Still got to go for the next four years, but hey, at least it gives me an excuse to go back to Norwich. And I'm clear, touch wood . . .

Wish I could do that with my career. It's reassuring in a funny kind of way that when you're in the shit people rally round. Most of the Norwich lads have rung me. Colin Todd rang me to get me to go to Bradford and Barry Fry actually rang me when I was having a shit! He couldn't believe the way I was being treated.

It's sad, because I've made a lot of friends here in a short space of time. Once again me and the kit man, Bob, have become good mates. And Gwen, the secretary, is really nice. I get on with most of the other lads, although I did find it hard making the transition from player to coach: I wanted to be in the dressing-room, swapping stories, taking the piss out of each other's gear and haircuts, enjoying the banter – instead I was in the office wondering whether it was appropriate to go to the Christmas party. As a player-coach you have a foot in both camps. Or, in my case, neither camp.

The Christmas party turned out to be the final straw for Tommy Johnson, a big mate of Malky's and one of my best mates at the club. He asked Ternent if they could go to Dublin the Tuesday before we played Rotherham, he said yes and so Tommy organised it all, booked and paid for it with the intention of getting the money off the lads later. Then about two days before, Ternent said, 'I've thought about it and you can't go. You can go on Sunday after the game.'

So Tommy was out of pocket, but he reorganised it, paid again for all the flights and accommodation, I think he laid out about £2,500, and then Ternent said, 'Injured players can't go.' There were five or six players out injured at the time. Well, injured players have had permission at every club Tommy and I have been at. Tommy was furious. 'What about your favourite saying, gaffer: 'We all piss in the same pot'. Surely, we all stick together?' Tommy had a contract until the summer, but he negotiated an early settlement with the club soon after.

Nigel Worthington would never have done something like that. I do hope Norwich stay up. I think they'll be fine – I've been glued to the telly every time they've been on this season and they've been playing some good stuff, just not getting the breaks. Damo's been unbelievable this season. I'm so pleased for him because he's such a nice lad. He was on *Soccer AM* recently and a friend asked me if he was arrogant, as that's how he came across. I just about pissed myself laughing. Damo, arrogant? Big-time Charlie? He's about as far away from that as it's possible to get – very shy and retiring. I still keep in touch with most of the lads. Delia and Michael want to take me and Malky out for a meal in London soon, I speak to Eddy about twice a week and regularly hear from Malky, Flem, Jimmy B, Hucks, Mullers, Hendo, Jarve, Steve Foley. I think most of them have read the book and enjoyed it. The only one I know of who wasn't very happy was Leon. When he scored against Everton I texted him 'Great finish mate, I'm well pleased for you.' Five minutes later I got a text back: 'Er, cheers . . . who is this?' 'It's Robbo mate. You probably deleted my number after you read the book!' And he texted back 'Yeah! I did!' He was upset about the penalty incident at Derby, but we had a good chat about it and we're mates again now.

A few of the Gillingham lads have asked about the book – I'll have to send them a few copies, probably my new Cambridge team-mates as well. I haven't shown them my Championship medal (I'm not one for showing off, although I had to laugh when one of the young lads at Gillingham actually asked me 'Did you win the League last year?'). I have been tempted to take it in to show Ternent a few times though! 'And THAT also gives me the fucking right to coach!'

Actually, winning the title didn't really sink in until September when I went back to Norwich to collect my Football League champions medal (the ones we got at the time were from the sponsors Nationwide). Club Secretary Kevan Platt had kept it for me, which was nice as I was a bit worried I wouldn't get one – out of sight, out of mind – you know me and my paranoia! I sleep with it under my pillow now, although I have worn it in bed on the odd occasion my wife has requested me to! I look back now and feel enormously proud of what we achieved, but, more than that, just a bit sad. I'm slightly envious of where they are now, as I do think I'd have had something to offer coming off the bench for the last 20 minutes, but it wasn't to be and you have to move on. I really miss those days, those people, but you can't turn the clock back. At least I'm going to be playing football again. Bring it on!

Sunday 8th May 2005

Oh God. You couldn't have had two more different seasons. I've just been relegated with two clubs – a couple of weeks ago with Cambridge and now, today, Gillingham have gone down to League One.

I'm so sorry for Cambridge – they are relegated out of the Football League and will have to play in the Conference next year. And this week they called the administrators in. I don't know much about it, there's a lot in the financial set-up I haven't got to grips with, like the fans trying to buy back the ground – but they have got a good young squad and if they manage to keep that together they will bounce straight back up. If Steve Thompson had had another five or six games I think we would have escaped relegation.

Getting relegated was awful. I'd come off with about ten minutes to go and as soon as the final whistle went there was this horrible deathly silence all over the stadium. I sat in the dugout for a couple of minutes to collect my thoughts and then went in the dressing room. Everyone sat with their heads in their hands, utterly dejected. It was horrible. And there's nothing you can say in that situation. Julie and the kids were at the game, so we just got in the car and went straight back home.

So my future's all up in the air again – both Steve and Ternent's contracts were only until the end of the season – and you can't sign players without a manager! I would love to go to Cambridge and help them back into the League but I don't know if that's a possibility yet. I know my future's definitely not at Gillingham, much though I liked the fans, players and staff. I've done nothing wrong, but I'll have to go and see Paul Scally.

Thing is, I've never fallen out with a manager before in 18 years as a player – and I've worked with some 'strong' characters – Bruce Rioch and Graham Taylor, for example. I actually saw Graham a few weeks ago when we played at Scunthorpe. I was signing autographs after the game and somebody thrust a programme in my hands and said, 'Can you sign this please?' I said, 'Sure mate', and started signing and this voice laughs and goes, 'You don't even know it's me, do you?!' I looked up and it was Graham. His father worked for Scunthorpe for years and the club had had a minute's silence for him before the game as he'd died that week. It's a measure of the man that, despite all that was going on that day, he waited around after the game to have a chat with me, check how I'm doing. Bloody hell, I must have done something right for someone of that stature to be hanging around to talk to me!

After being shut out by Ternent, Cambridge has given me back my enthusiasm, although I hope that doesn't sound odd when you consider that their world has just ended. I scored on my debut away to Bury, my 200th League goal, only six months after my 199th League goal! It was a bit odd as I was up at 7.30am to travel up for the game on the day – something I've not done since I was at Watford all those years ago – but Cambridge just can't afford to stay overnight in a hotel.

I've been playing regularly, scored three goals in my first five games (although not since) and I've taken four or five training sessions – mostly working with the strikers, although last Tuesday I took training proper for the first time. And that's another reason why I think they'll bounce back. We'd just been relegated, and you couldn't have blamed the lads if they had just gone through the motions, but they worked their socks off and I was so proud of them. They definitely enjoyed the session – they didn't have to say, they said it all in the manner they trained.

Cambridge have been really good to me – they gave me Mondays off so I only had to go into training Tuesdays, Thursdays and Fridays. They couldn't have done more for me – they even lent me a Suzuki jeep to travel up in so I didn't have to put the extra mileage on my car. But the journey's been killing me. It's alright most of the time but three weeks ago it took me five hours to get back to Kent after an accident on the M11 and then the M25 was closed about 100 yards from the turn-off to where I live in Rochester. I was dying to get back to see my kids and I was just sitting there tearing my hair out.

But aside from that I've loved everything about Cambridge. The staff are brilliant – and they're operating out of a Portakabin. And the fans have been really good to me. There's been loads of Norwich fans too – a couple of hundred came down for the Fans United day recently and on Saturday there were quite a few I was chatting to during the warm-up who said they couldn't stand the pressure of being at Carrow Road to watch their must-win game against Birmingham!

It just hit me the other day: tomorrow is the anniversary of the civic reception for winning the title. I'll never forget that day. It just goes to prove that you've got to enjoy the good times while they're there. And this year I've had to take the rough with the smooth. I really hope Norwich stay up. It was Jimmy B's birthday yesterday – the day of that potentially all-important victory over Birmingham and the start of the most important week of their lives. I really feel for Eddy though – he's played 32 games this season, but hasn't been able to get a look-in since Thomas Helveg started a few weeks ago – and you can't argue with the form they've shown over the last six games.

I'll be seeing them all a week tomorrow, the day after their final game against Fulham, when I turn out for a Norwich XI for my old buddy Alex Notman's benefit game, and I'm just keeping my fingers crossed it's going to be a big celebration.

I'd love to go to the Fulham game but at least someone I know has had a successful season – Ben's team, the Blue Eagles, have got a cup final at 3pm that day so I'll be cheering him on – although I'll have the radio on too!

EPILOGUE

By Karen Buchanan

You know you've made it when you're a one-word name. Madonna, Kylie, Iwan . . .

The first two are in illustrious company, in my humble opinion. It is 12.25pm, Saturday 3rd July 2004, and I've just arrived at Jarrolds, an institution of a department store in the centre of Norwich, the venue chosen for the launch of *All I Want For Christmas...*, and I'm amazed to discover that the thousands of people outside are not in fact queuing for a bus, but for Iwan. Of course I know the man is a legend in Norwich, but to see devotion on this scale is gob-smacking, slightly alarming even. Men in black buzz round with walkie-talkies, debating whether to stop people joining the queue, which now stretches around three sides of the store and right up London Street. The man himself arrives, all smart-casual-like, and grins sheepishly. 'God, are they all for me?'

He is knackered, having been at a pre-launch event with members of the Northern Canaries in Huddersfield last night and a similar event with the Capital Canaries in London earlier in the week. He squirms embarrassedly into a chair, but then – ever the pro – flashes the trade-mark toothy smile and starts signing. It's a measure of the man that nothing sums him up better than the fact that he seems to know every third person (and has probably been out for a drink with every fifth) and, as he signs, he asks after children, brothers, parents and mates. He happily poses for pics with 18-month old Iwans, 75-year-old groupies and blokes who feign embarrassment before throwing their arms round him and happily gurning for the camera. For the next three-and-a-half hours he signs books, yes, but also postcards, shirts, bags, pencil cases and all manner of unofficial things that cause consternation among the Men In Black due to the ever-growing queue. The only time that famous grin falters is when a young woman produces a pair of pink, fluffy handcuffs and tries to drag him away with her. 'I've been queuing since 7am,' she tells him. One of the Men In Black leans over, conspiratorially. 'We never had this much bother with Harry Potter,' he whispers.

That evening, the football club throws a £40 a head dinner to celebrate the official launch of the book. More than 350 fans have crammed into the Norfolk Lounge to catch a glimpse of their hero and say a final farewell. After nearly a year in his company, I know that he's bricking this. It's not that he's shy exactly, but, oddly, he's very uncomfortable being the centre of attention. A night out with the lads, fine, but he's strangely unconfident when asked to be in the spotlight rather than the floodlight. Part of his charm is that he's genuinely surprised that someone who's third in Norwich's all-time goalscoring charts, who's been Mr Norwich for the last seven years and who is such a bubbly character, could cause all this fuss.

As soon as he arrives, to the tune of *Simply The Best*, naturally (last time he did one of these Q+A sessions at the club the entry anthem was *Sex Bomb* and he actually swaggered with mortification) he is deluged. Swamped. After dinner we manage to grab a quick half in the quieter neighbouring bar. 'God that was mindblowing today,' he says, ever the master of the understatement. 'Really, really mental. But, yeah,' he concedes, a tad coyly, as if I might suddenly think he thinks he's all that, 'I *did* enjoy it.'

Aside from another book signing in Lowestoft a few weeks later (queues as far as Woolworths etc) I don't see him again until early December when there is a special signing at the club's store in the Castle Shopping Mall. Different audience this time – mums and grans caught shopping and realising that a book signed by that bloke their son/daughter/partner was always going on about is the perfect Christmas present. I can hear them in the queue, 'Ooh, he's quite handsome actually, isn't he?' One 30-something makes me laugh. He tells me he hasn't read a book since *James and the Giant Peach*, 'but y'know, it's Iwan, so I had to. In fact, I enjoyed it so much I read it twice.'

Iwan is obviously a bit down given the way things have gone at Gillingham, but he's still bubbly as ever for the public. I ask him if he's got the DVD of last season on constant play at home. To my amazement, he says he's never watched it. 'I don't know if we've got it,' he says. 'Actually, I'm sure Ben must have it somewhere.'

He also leaves it until now to tell me he's had dozens of letters about the book from fans from all over the country, even Ipswich supporters. 'They said 'I Always thought you were a bit of a sod on the pitch, but I read your book and just had to say what a nice, family man you seem. Good luck to you',' he grins, his face a mixture of surprise and pride.

And that's Iwan all over – 'A really nice family man'. He doesn't need the praise and the plaudits, he doesn't feel the need to wallow in success by watching his finest hour on DVD, he doesn't court or assume the love of the fans, he's self-aware enough to know when he's done a good job and when he's messed up without needing to be told. Sure, he cares deeply what other people think of him, but a large part of his charm, his charisma, is that he's not so self-aware that he knows how much we, as football fans, love him.

Although he might do now . . . if he reads this far.